THE PARCHMENT PEACE

The United States Senate and
the Washington Conference
1921 · 1922

A PORTION OF THE DELEGATION TO THE WASHINGTON CONFERENCE

Seated at the table, left to right, TOKUGAWA, JUSSERAND, SARRAULT, VIVIANI, BRIAND, UNDERWOOD, ROOT, LODGE, HUGHES, BALFOUR, LEE, GEDDES, BORDEN, PEARSE, SALMOND, SASTRI.

JOHN CHALMERS VINSON

THE PARCHMENT PEACE

The United States Senate and
the Washington Conference
1921 · 1922

THE UNIVERSITY OF GEORGIA PRESS

Athens

Printed in the United States of America

BY FOOTE & DAVIES, INC., ATLANTA

6002009414

TO

ALMIRA JOHNSON VINSON

CONTENTS

PREFACE

✦ ✦ ✦ THE years following the close of the First World War saw a swing in governmental authority from the president toward Congress. In foreign affairs this movement was signalized by the bitter debate on the League of Nations. After the final defeat of the League and the passing of Wilson from power, the responsibility for a new approach to foreign policy devolved upon the Senate. The solons seized the initiative and proceeded to formulate a policy in keeping with their interpretation of American traditions. The Senate had long advocated the principle of world peace and championed disarmament as the most American means to this end. World peace and disarmament had wide appeal to the public mind. However, the executive branch of the government recognized that international affairs were more complicated than the Senate or the public realized, and Charles Evans Hughes, Secretary of State under Harding, sought to utilize the enthusiasm of the Senate without challenging its basic approach to foreign policy. While broadening policy enough to meet the issues concerned, he sought to achieve strictly limited objectives.

Thus the development of policy by the Senate was influenced and molded by the public and the Executive. Yet, the outlines of the policy itself were established by the Senate. These included the belief that the United States must keep its sovereignty unimpaired; international problems should be met by conferences; international law could be upheld by moral law; world order could be maintained by public opinion; and peace could best be preserved by disarmament. This pattern of policy was adhered to throughout the twenties. A closer study of the important role of the Senate in shaping American policy in this critical period is the aim of this work.

In making this study, I have had recourse to the official publications of the government relative to the Washington Conference, and the complete files of the State Department. These files had been closed to scholars until 1948, the year I began my study. These sources along with the *Congressional Record*, newspapers, and magazines disclosed the outward pattern of the Senate's role during the Conference. Desiring to learn the inward motives and purposes of the Senate as well, I studied the papers of Charles Evans Hughes, Elihu Root, and Senator Henry Cabot Lodge, delegates to the Conference. Unfortunately, the voluminous files of these collections show evidence of editing and contain almost no information of a personal or confidential nature relative to the Washington Conference. The papers of the other delegate, Oscar Underwood, are unlocated. The papers of William E. Borah were invaluable, and those of John Sharpe Williams, Woodrow Wilson, Chandler P. Anderson, Robert Lansing, Albert Beveridge, Thomas J. Walsh, Philander C. Knox, Charles P. McNary, and Josephus Daniels contributed much toward expanding the record of the Senate's work. Even so, as is ever the case, there are questions unanswered, and motives unexplained.

In the preparation and completion of this work, I am indebted to Dr. Paul H. Clyde of Duke University for his aid, encouragement, and criticism. I am also grateful to Dr. S. Walter Martin, professor of history and Dean of the College of Arts and Sciences at the University of Georgia, who first interested me in history as a profession. Completion of the work would have been impossible without financial assistance for research and publication. For the former I am indebted to Dr. Henry King Stanford, former Director of the University Center in Georgia, for funds made available jointly by the Carnegie Foundation and the University of Georgia. For the latter I am most grateful to Dr. George H. Boyd, Director of Research and Dean of the Graduate School at the University of Georgia, for a grant from the research funds of the University. My thanks are likewise due to Dr. Boyd and to Dr. E. Merton Coulter, head of the History Department, University of Georgia, for making available to me the time needed for the work on this book.

I would like to acknowledge my appreciation to the many members of the staff of the Library of Congress and of the National Archives who extended to me every courtesy and aid in my research. Special thanks are due C. Percy Powell of the Division of Manuscripts, Library of Congress, and Almon R. Wright, Archivist in charge of Foreign Affairs Section of the National Archives. Also of great help were Paul S. Barry, Jr., and Richard S. Barry, who assisted in the research on the Lodge Papers.

Finally, I wish to thank my wife, Almira Johnson Vinson, for her patience and inspiration during the writing of this work, and for her valuable suggestions for its improvement. Special mention should also be accorded my young sons, John Chalmers Vinson, Jr., and Douglas Cloud Vinson, for their unexpected cooperation, which was a vital factor in the early completion of this work.

J. CHAL VINSON
Associate Professor of History
University of Georgia

Problems, Precedents, and Policy in Foreign Affairs, 1921

. . . THE United States Senate played a vital role in shaping the foreign policy adopted by the United States at the Washington Conference. Victorious in its struggle with President Wilson in the debate on the League of Nations, the irreconcilable bloc in the Senate, with many influential members of the Republican party within its ranks, made a concerted attempt in the Harding administration to establish its supremacy in the long struggle with the Executive for control of foreign affairs. President Harding, with the able assistance of Charles Evans Hughes, preserved the traditional powers of the Executive in the first contest of his administration—the initiation of a conference to settle the outstanding problems of naval armament and Far Eastern policy. However, in the actual policy adopted at the Washington Conference, the Senate seemed the victor over the administration, for every treaty was carefully tailored to meet the Senate's predilections in foreign policy.

Before the Senate's work in the period of the Washington Conference can be fully understood, it is necessary to examine briefly the background of the principal problems in foreign affairs which confronted the Harding administration and to trace the growth of the traditions which influenced the policy adopted at the Conference.

When William E. Borah proposed to his senatorial colleagues, December 14, 1920, a resolution calling for the limitation of naval armament by the United States, Great Britain, and Japan, the Senate took its first constructive step toward bringing order out of the chaos which had engulfed the government in its efforts to formulate a post-war foreign policy. Borah's resolution and the Washington Conference, which to a degree was a product of the resolution, were the channels for formulating an important part of this policy. It was high time that action be taken. The Armistice had been signed two years before, and the United States had not even settled the problem of peace with Germany. Little progress had been made toward the solution of numerous and complicated international enigmas which were the aftermath of the war. The most immediate of these problems concerned the chaos in China, the increasing American-Japanese tension, the alleged menace of the Anglo-Japanese Alliance, the rapidly mounting cost of naval preparedness, the relations with the League of Nations, and the possibility of establishing Harding's promised "Association of Nations."

Added to the inherent difficulties in each of these questions was the problem of securing cooperation between the Senate and the Executive in formulating policy. The relations between the two had become so strained in the debates on the League of Nations as to make agreement on the adoption of any policy virtually impossible. The Senate in 1921 was in no mood to allow policy to take a form which would infringe upon its prerogatives or fail to fit its prejudices. These prejudices of the Senate were based on the traditional policies of the United States in foreign affairs and built on the belief that these policies needed no modification to render them the only safe guide to charting a course in twentieth century diplomacy.

Among the basic ideals upon which the Senate was insistent were sovereignty and independence in the management of foreign affairs. This policy was based on the tradition originating in the days of the Revolution that America should maintain unimpaired sovereignty and freedom of choice in all questions of foreign policy. Thomas Paine, in 1776, admonished his fellows: "It is the true interest of America to steer clear of European contentions, which she can never do while, by her dependence on Britain, she is the makeweight in the scale of British politics."[1] Through the years this independence had been zealously protected, and the determination to maintain it was as strong in 1921 as it had been in 1776. In the former year Senator Thomas Watson, in a speech filled with allusions to the bravery of Patrick Henry, Nathan Hale, and George Washington, declared that Americans wanted a foreign policy that would "hold in perpetuity the absolute independence which their forefathers had won with the musket and the sword." The entry of the United States into international agreements of any sort, according to Watson, would "cage the American eagle. He will not have

2

the freedom to look into the eyes of the sun and beat the heavens with perfectly free wings."[2] In the Senate in 1921 were many men who believed in this tradition of absolute independence in foreign affairs. They believed that devotion to this ideal had inspired the birth of the nation and was absolutely necessary for its continued well-being. In the composition of the Republican foreign policy, 1921 and 1922, the complete protection of absolute sovereignty and absolute independence was a paramount principle inspiring an emphatic zeal in the Senate.

Another ideal, also nurtured in the American past, was a desire for peace. One aim of the independence movement was to free Americans from the necessity of fighting the wars of Europe. Benjamin Franklin argued that independence was the only means of preventing England from dragging the United States into "all the plundering wars which their desperate circumstances, injustice and rapacity may prompt them to undertake." Thomas Paine seconded this idea urging his fellow men to fight for liberty as the only road to perpetual peace.[3] ". . . Any submission to, or dependence on, Great Britain, tends directly to involve this Continent in European wars and quarrels . . .," wrote Paine in *Common Sense.*

Evidence that this desire for peace was undiminished in Harding's day was reflected in the opinions of many leaders. Secretary of State Charles Evans Hughes declared that the State Department was primarily "the Department of Peace."[4] Another authority in the field of international relations asserted in 1924: "The ultimate aim of the foreign policy of the United States is the preservation of world peace."[5]

A tradition in American policy closely related to peace was an abhorrence of military establishments. In part this ideal sprang from the fixed belief, traceable to Colonial times, that a free government could not coexist with large standing armies. It was recognized that strife and crisis, vital foods of autocratic governments, were the deadly poison of democratic institutions. Thomas Jefferson, in 1801, told the young nation to preserve its republican ideals by guarding "the supremacy of the civil over the military authority." [6] More than a century later the same ideal was reaffirmed in terms equally strong by Woodrow Wilson. "You know how impossible it is, in short, to have a free nation, if it is a military nation and under military order."[7]

3

The Harding administration and the Senate were steeped in and loyal to these century-old American fundamentals in foreign policy: sovereignty and independence in foreign affairs, peace, and non-militarism. Agreement existed that these values must be preserved, but controversy arose as to the safest course to take in accomplishing these purposes. Should the country continue in the traditional course of isolation from Europe, or was safety to be found only in the new path of international cooperation? Again the reactions of 1922 were conditioned by the past. Actually, the United States had been called on many times to choose between isolation or cooperation; and, while the official policy of the government was the former, a minority of its citizens had always advocated the latter.

It is unnecessary to trace either tradition in its entirety, but examples may be cited of the origins and persistence of the ideals of isolation and internationalism. Washington had crystallized the policy of isolation, as old as the first colony, in his famous Farewell Address.[8] "Why, by interweaving our destiny with that of part of Europe, entangle our peace and prosperity in the toils of European ambition, rivalship, interest, humor, or caprice?"[9] This view had been seconded by succeeding presidents and codified by James Monroe. During the nineteenth century the "detached and distant situation" of the United States, its westward expansion, and the preoccupation of European countries with their own domestic and foreign affairs had done much to transmute these ideas into the conviction that isolation was a positive policy which alone had solved the problems of American foreign affairs.[10] In 1920, when Harding became President, this sort of isolationism was very strong, and there were many adherents to the ideals of Washington as interpreted by the Senate.

An example of this tendency was reflected in the work of Henry Watterson, a well-known editor, who was, in 1919, president of an organization known as the "League for the Preservation of American Independence." This organization reprinted for distribution a full page of quotations including extracts from the Declaration of Independence, Washington's Farewell Address, and the Monroe Doctrine. It advised that the United States should never be party to any international organization that did not recognize these principles.[11] In the United States Senate a solon typical of many declared his

4

loyalty to the principles of Washington and to the "solemn injunction laid upon us by the great inspired Father of his Country . . . ."[12] Senator Borah represented this same opinion when he told the Senate in 1922:

My idea is the same policy we have pursued for 150 years, and that is to remain aloof from political associations and political connections and political arrangements with other Governments and take care of ourselves as best we can as an independent, self-governing people. So far it has been successful. Political pacts foment war, they do not augment peace.[13]

In Harding's day those who favored the alternate plan of international cooperation could point to a long line of precedents also. Complete isolation was never practical. Moreover, this theory had always been balanced, to some degree, by the belief that international problems could not be avoided. Consequently, the United States should cooperate with other countries in their solution. Thomas Paine, although a champion of independence in foreign affairs, also advocated the establishment of an alliance of nations in which all disputes were to be referred to arbitration and all aggressors were to be punished. The American government, although reluctant to obligate itself to a permanent policy of arbitration, had on several occasions settled outstanding disputes with foreign nations by this method and looked upon itself as a world leader in this field.

Throughout the nineteenth century, peace societies in the United States tried to direct the government toward an international peace policy. These societies regarded war as the greatest menace to America's future and condemned it on idealistic, moral, and economic grounds. Although never large and generally ignored by the government, these organizations worked zealously to bring about international congresses for peace, the establishment of international arbitration, and the limitation of armament by international agreement. To these ends they attempted to win individual converts and stir the public at large. However, they did not neglect official channels, for they constantly interviewed presidents, secretaries of state, and individual congressmen in their attempts to gain official sanction for their programs. Their labors, unrewarded at first, resulted by the latter part of the nineteenth century in American participation in international organizations for peace and the government's willingness to attend the Hague Conference of 1899.

5

In the twentieth century the movement reached its flower. Philanthropists Edward Ginn, Andrew Carnegie, and others contributed huge endowments, and the number and membership of peace organizations grew rapidly. Just as the movement appeared to be at its zenith, World War I interrupted the hopes of these idealists. However, there were many who redoubled their efforts and contributed to the movement for a League of Nations and the Washington Conference. Although small and unofficial the American movement for internationalism was deeply rooted and strong. Its vitality was attested by the calling of the Washington Conference which fulfilled many of its long cherished dreams.

Thus, the threads of foreign policy which the Harding administration picked up were long and tangled, and the process of weaving them into a new fabric strong enough to endure in twentieth-century America was by no means simple.

2 . . .

The Disarmament Movement
and Congress to 1916

◇ ◇ ◇ THE ideals which highlighted the Washington Conference, peace and the limitation of armament, emerged from the American peace movement of the nineteenth century. The advocates of these policies during this century, while constantly emphasizing the waste and burden of armament, argued that their plans for permanent peace would release huge sums of money for more productive use. In regard to the practicality of armament limitation they cited the example of disarmament on the Great Lakes by Britain and the United States, which was first suggested in 1794 and achieved in the Rush-Bagot Agreement of 1817.[1]

An outstanding leader of the movement for peace through disarmament was William Ladd, the author, in 1840, of a proposal for a Congress of Nations for the settlement of international disputes without resort to arms. He pointed out that the adoption of his plan would eventually make armaments obsolete because nations would not resort to war to settle their differences. The powers, who were then spending seven-eighths of their incomes on preparation for war, could turn this sum to "increase the comforts and education of the poor."[2] The Ladd plan was presented by another American, Elihu Burritt, at the peace congresses held in Brussels in 1848, at Paris in 1849, and at Frankfort in 1850. Each of these conferences endorsed resolutions demanding simultaneous reduction of armaments by all nations. This ideal was later espoused by the Universal Peace Union, organized in 1866, which adopted a plank calling for "immediate disarmament" of all nations, and by the First American International Congress for Peace, 1893, which emphasized the cost and waste of armament. With the way thus prepared much interest was stirred over the nation in the Hague Conference, 1899, and considerable demand was mustered for representation by a strong delegation which would work effectively for disarmament.

7

After 1880 a growing tendency toward navalism and militarism in the United States caused the peacemakers and disarmament advocates to concentrate their attention on Congress. In this way the limiting of American expenditures for armament and a world policy of disarmament could be directly promoted. The earliest of these efforts sought to get the United States to commit itself to permanent treaties of arbitration which would gradually eliminate the need for armament. By the 1880's the peace organization had a well-established lobby in Washington which interviewed every President and Secretary of State during the last two decades of the century. Congress also was solicited by this lobby. In the year 1886, for example, twelve resolutions sponsoring peace and arbitration were introduced by the legislators at the behest of the peacemakers. Petitions for peace sent by the public to Congress had become so common by the middle eighties that one lobbyist declared them to be useless unless they came in an avalanche. Peace seekers were advised, by this lobbyist, to get candidates for Congress to commit themselves to a program of peace before their election, rather than to try to win them by petition after their election.

Congress responded to the pleas of the peacemakers on several occasions during the latter years of the nineteenth century. In 1874 a resolution was adopted commending arbitration as a practical method for the settlement of international difficulties. In 1882, and again in 1890, resolutions urging the Executive to negotiate permanent treaties of arbitration for the settlement of disputes which could not be solved by diplomacy were introduced in the Senate. The latter resolution was adopted, and in recognition of his efforts to this end Senator John Sherman was made vice-president of the American Peace Society and of the Universal Peace Union. Part of the success of this measure was also due to the active encouragement and support of the British House of Commons. During these same years the anti-armament crusaders likewise were overwhelming Congress with suggestions that the United States take the initiative in calling an international congress to establish a world court, draw up a code of international law, and limit armaments.[3]

The identification of Congress with plans for disarmament and world peace became much more marked after 1899, largely through the work of Richard Bartholdt, a member of Congress and an ardent crusader for peace. In 1899 he became interested in the Interparliamentary Union, a quasi-official organization composed of members of parliaments and congresses in various countries. Eventually, he was able to influence more than two hundred members of the United States Congress to join the Union, thus enlisting them directly in the work for arbitration and peace. Bartholdt, a tireless worker, was able to arrange in 1904 for a meeting of the Interparliamentary Union in the United States. At this meeting in St. Louis, he and his fellow congressmen drafted a resolution urging President Theodore Roosevelt to call a second world conference to meet at the Hague.[4] Following this success, Bartholdt introduced a resolution in Congress urging the administration to take a strong stand for compulsory arbitration, a more effective world court, periodic meetings at the Hague, and the limitation of armament.[5] Although Roosevelt did not issue the call, the second Hague Conference did meet in 1907 and once again considered the question of limitation of armament.[6] One result of this consideration was the formation in Congress of a bipartisan anti-navy bloc. This group defeated some appropriation bills, notably in 1906. However, its members soon realized that the limitation of armament was an international problem, and the real importance of the bloc lay in the sponsorship of international agreements on the limitation of armament.

In these years a major battle developed for the control of Congress between the new peace societies, which emphasized preparedness and arbitration first and the limitation of armament eventually, and the older societies, which favored immediate disarmament. This struggle reached a climax in 1910, for by this time interest in international peace societies, arbitration, and the limitation of armament had become widespread in the United States. Congress was made aware of this new surge of interest by petitions from various state legislatures calling for international congresses to consider the problems of peace.[7]

Peace societies were numerous by 1910, and one of the most active, the North Carolina Peace Society, took steps to organize a nation-wide group known as the American Peace and Arbitration League. This group differed from the older societies in its aim. It favored the establishment of a commission to formulate plans "to meet needs of national security and of international peace and justice." This implied that the United States would maintain a strong navy for present emergencies, but at the same time would work toward eventual adoption of the principle of arbitration. When this was accomplished, navies would become obsolete. President Roosevelt approved the work of this organization, and in Congress Richmond P. Hobson, naval hero of the Spanish-American War, worked for its cause.[8] Hobson introduced in 1908 and 1909 resolutions to appoint a committee to consider the problems of armament and arbitration but failed to get a hearing on them.[9] However, at the next meeting of Congress, in 1910, a veritable rash of resolutions on naval armament and arbitration broke out. For the first time in the history of Congress one of these resolutions on disarmament was adopted.[10]

Congressman Hobson opened this debate by presenting a resolution to set aside one per cent of the cost of each vessel of war "for the purpose of promoting the cause of peace and arbitration between nations. . . ."[11] Although he denied that the American Peace and Arbitration League sponsored his proposal, the proposal definitely represented the ideals of the League. There was a heated debate on the resolution during which Hobson advocated an American navy strong enough to establish "an equilibrium in the two oceans." At the same time, he advocated arbitration. Armaments and peace were, he maintained, linked in "an intimate and inseparable relation . . . as correlative means for justice." Armament was a grim but temporary necessity; arbitration was the great hope of the future.[12]

The fact that the Hobson Resolution originated with the Committee on Naval Affairs and Hobson himself favored the building of six new dreadnaughts somewhat tarnished his reputation as a champion of peace. Representative Bartholdt, long a congressional leader in peace movements, declared that peace and war were like the ends of a seesaw. If one end went up, the other went down; it was impossible for both to be in the ascendancy.

Representative William S. Bennet, who agreed with Bartholdt, offered a substitute for the Hobson Resolution, requesting the President to consider the expediency of calling immediately an international conference for the limiting of armaments by mutual agreement.[13] Subsequently, the Hobson Resolution was defeated and Congressman Bennet offered his substitute measure on April 11,

10

and again on June 1. Still another resolution was presented by Congressman Bartholdt providing for a commission to study the problem of international federation and related problems.[14]

Eventually, the outstanding provisions of the Hobson, Bennet, and Bartholdt proposals were combined into a compromise resolution, providing for the appointment by the President of a five-man commission

to consider the expediency of utilizing existing international agencies for the purpose of limiting the armaments of the nations of the world by international agreement and of constituting the combined navies of the world into an international force for the preservation of universal peace, and to consider and report upon any other means to diminish the expenditures of government for military purposes and to lessen the probabilities of war.[15]

By the passage of this resolution Congress revealed its opinions on international organization. Although the advocates of the final resolution hoped for an immediate reduction of armament, they believed that the security of the nation must first be guaranteed before effective limitation of armaments could be effected. However, they hoped to provide security by an international organization to keep the peace rather than by American naval supremacy. In the course of this debate, many Congressmen showed their willingness to join a world federation and to establish an international police force.[16] They did not advocate unilateral or complete disarmament under any circumstances, but approved international adoption of a drastically reduced relative scale of armament. This plan, felt the Congressmen, would provide security, peace, and economy. The importance of the latter was not overlooked for it was widely recognized that the ever increasing cost of preparedness was unpopular with taxpayers.

This resolution, signed by President Taft on June 25, 1910, was reported in Congress to have won the approval of the British Cabinet and unofficial sanction in the other countries of Europe.[17] In spite of these propitious omens the measure was never implemented, and the committee for which it provided was never selected. In view of President Taft's interest in international peace it is difficult to understand his inaction. Representative Bartholdt, the author of the joint resolution, declared some years later that Taft's desire to continue negotiations on his arbitration treaties with England and France without the added complication of the proposed conference had

11

caused him to ignore the resolution.[18] However, Representative Frederick C. Stevens maintained that Taft had sound reason to believe that the other nations would not respond to such a resolution. Therefore, rather than be humiliated by rebuff, the President had let the matter drop.[19]

Despite these evidences of interest in the cause of peace it would be a mistake to picture Congress as wholeheartedly endorsing any and all plans to promote international amity. The next year, 1911, saw the Senate frustrate the attempt of President Taft to negotiate treaties of arbitration with Britain and France which would serve as models for a general system. The Senate demonstrated indifference to an almost universal demand on the part of the public and to the most strenuous efforts of the President, who made a speaking tour across the country in an effort to stir enough popular feeling to override Congress. To the Senate the paramount question seemed to be the safeguarding of senatorial prerogative and the safeguarding of American sovereignty and independence in foreign affairs. To guarantee these objectives the Senate modified the Taft treaties until there was exempted from arbitration almost every question which any other nation might wish to arbitrate.[20] This incident made it evident that in 1911 the Senate's devotion to peace was strictly limited to proposals which fitted into the framework of ideals espoused by it.

Despite this prevailing senatorial attitude, leaders in the peace movement were not downhearted. Nicholas Murray Butler stated this same year:

Never before has the mind of the world been so occupied with the problems of substituting law for war, peace with righteousness for triumph after slaughter, the victories of right and reasonableness for those of might and brute force. . . . The long years of patient argument and exhortation and of painstaking instruction of public opinion in this and other countries are bearing fruit in full measure.[21]

Government officials outside of the Senate continued to work for the attainment of peace. President Taft continued to recommend an international court. In 1912 he advocated also a proposal for the universal reduction of armaments. Josephus Daniels, Secretary of the Navy from 1913 to 1921, recommended in each of his annual reports a conference to formulate plans to reduce the cost of preparation for war.[22] Another cabinet member under President Wilson,

12

Secretary of State Bryan, succeeded in negotiating during 1913 and 1914 thirty treaties of conciliation, twenty-two of which became effective.

In Congress interest in disarmament was rekindled in 1913 by the efforts of the British government to come to an understanding with Germany on naval building. At this time it was proposed by Winston Churchill, First Lord of the Admiralty, that Britain and Germany agree to a one year naval holiday. Although Churchill did not specifically invite the United States to take part in his plan, Congress became interested in the proposal. Congressman Walter Hensley of Missouri introduced a resolution "authorizing the President to cooperate with the United Kingdom of Great Britain to the end that naval construction may be suspended for one year."[23]

This measure, while not introduced in the Senate, revealed the attitude of the House toward disarmament in 1913. Representative Bartholdt, speaking in behalf of the resolution, declared that America had broken the traditions of the Old World by advocating the liberty of man, and should break tradition, once again, to speak for "justice, humanity, and peace, in the matters of settling differences between nations."[24] Representative Hensley dwelt on more practical matters in his defense of the measure emphasizing, as did several other members of the House, the tremendous and ever increasing cost of maintaining an adequate navy. Pointing out that the cost of the navy had risen from $33,003,234.19 in 1898 to $136,935,199.05 in 1910, Hensley placed the blame on the greed of the munitions makers. The theory that security was dependent on an ever larger navy was, he felt, an argument "forged in hell" and utilized by the industrialist who sold materials of war. "The God of War is now a man of business with vested interest," he declared.[25] Another advocate of the Hensley Resolution and of economy protested that there is "nothing more cruel than war unless it is the burdens borne by the taxpayer in preparation for war in time of peace.[26]

The opposition to the Hensley Resolution was led by the redoubtable Richmond Pearson Hobson, who reiterated: "An adequate navy for America . . . is the only way for peace and security at home. . . ."[27] He maintained that military strength and foreign policy were closely linked, and held up to scorn the notion, expressed earlier in the debate, that the Monroe Doctrine had been maintained

13

for ninety years solely by "the simple expression of the President of the United States."[28] Hobson admitted that the achievement of "universal peace by signing a parchment" was most desirable. He did not feel, however, that peace could be attained so simply. The obligations of the United States in foreign affairs—the Monroe Doctrine, the Open Door, and the Panama Canal—could only be discharged by the maintenance of an adequate fleet.[29] Therefore, disarmament would be safe when the United States had a fleet equal to or superior to any other fleet in the world. Then if the nations agreed to a proportionate reduction of armament, this country would still hold a position of predominance through which American security might be maintained.[30]

Hobson's lesson in international politics, that obligations can be maintained only by military power, was not received with favor in the House. The defenders of the resolution inundated the fearless hero of Santiago Bay with a flood of oratory. Although many tried, few exceeded the heights of eloquence reached by Representative Finly H. Gray, who declaimed, "I want this Nation to herald the coming of this new day. I want this great constellation of states to give the signal to the world for the march to victory over war and the triumph of universal peace."[31] Representative Thomas Heflin of Alabama exhausted his own eloquence and turned to poetry, as was his custom, to phrase his thought:

> Sow Thou the seed of happy peace;
> All evil drive from us afar;
> And bid the rage and tumult cease
> Of hateful war.[32]

Some sort of record for borrowed eloquence was set by Representative Claude Weaver who in a single speech on the folly of war cited Shakespeare, Milton, Byron, Tiberius Gracchus, Homer, Tennyson, Gibbon, President Wilson, and others.[33] Representative Perl D. Decker, adding to the fervor of the moment, asserted that Hensley, through the introduction of this resolution, had made a contribution which would make him known throughout the United States and "loved at every fireside in Missouri."[34] A fitting climax to these eloquent expressions was the statement on the resolution by Representative Clement Brumbaugh: ". . . it has been said of old that it is braver and better to dry a tear than to make a wound, and that is

14

what this resolution will attempt to do."[35] With something akin to camp meeting ardor the House passed the Hensley Resolution December 8, 1913, by a vote of 317 to 11.[36]

This resolution was not the only evidence of interest in the limitation of armament. In the course of the debate Representative Gray had offered an amendment to empower the President to call a conference of all nations in Washington in the fall of 1914. This conference was to consider the matter of immediate suspension of naval building programs and the reduction of all military establishments.[37] Although this provision was not incorporated in the Hensley Resolution, the President was urged from other quarters to call a conference for the limitation of armament. Edwin D. Mead of the World Peace Foundation wrote President Wilson in October that ". . . the most auspicious occasion which has recently been presented for a combined effort on the part of the Great Powers for the limitation of naval armament and expenditures is at hand." Mead felt that the Democratic majority in the Congress was determined to attack the problem of armament, and that the United States could and should assume world leadership in the movement for disarmament.[38] Following the passage of his resolution, Hensley read in Congress a clipping from a Berlin newspaper stating that Germany was willing to join in the plan for a naval holiday, pointing out that: "Practically every power in the world has admitted that naval armaments have been excessive and that it is absolutely necessary to call a halt."[39] President Wilson, after receiving the Hensley Resolution, wrote Secretary of State Bryan ". . . that it might be well to consult with the representatives of the leading naval powers as to the feasibility of agreeing on such a policy as Mr. Churchill suggested."[40] Despite these encouraging signs no action was taken by the United States government to carry out the provisions of the Hensley Resolution.[41]

President Wilson did make an effort in the spring of 1914 to stop naval competition between the United States, Germany, and England, although no connection is apparent between this action and the Hensley resolution. He sent Colonel House to Germany in May, 1914, as his personal representative on a mission to get a joint agreement on the limitation of armament. Colonel House, who originated this plan, first mentioned it in January, 1913, and discussed

15

it with Wilson on December 12, 1913. House's scheme called for the use of the armies of Germany, England, Japan, and the United States in a manner designed to encourage cooperative effort, bring about a reduction of armaments, and ease the friction in Europe. In May, 1914, the Colonel discussed the proposal with Kaiser William II. The latter wished to exclude Japan and include France in a formal alliance. The United States, on the other hand, would not approve any agreement which might be construed an alliance. These disagreements added to the rampant militarism of Europe, doomed the House mission to failure, and the Colonel returned to the United States just before the declaration of the war.[42]

The outbreak of the First World War redoubled rather than ended the American effort to bring about an international order to secure peace. In January, 1915, a group of American statesmen and students of public affairs began a series of meetings to work out a definite program for achieving peace in the future. This movement resulted in the organization later in 1915 of the League to Enforce Peace with a membership that was small but distinguished. William H. Taft, former President, headed this organization which adopted a platform advocating a world court to settle justiciable questions, a conciliation commission for hearing all disputes not submissible to the court, and international coercion of members who went to war without first using these legal agencies.

Late in 1915, the year that the League to Enforce Peace was organized, Congress began, largely under the inspiration of this organization, consideration of a number of resolutions suggesting the procedure to be followed by this country in achieving world peace. These included a resolution providing for the establishment of an international court with power to enforce its decrees, a proposal for an international conference at The Hague at the close of the war, a plan for a world organization to establish and secure peace, and a proposal to authorize the President to invite all nations to a conference. Also submitted was a resolution that the President invite all nations to a convention which would provide for disarmament, for an international legislature, an international court, and an international army and navy for police purposes.[43] None of these suggestions was acted upon by Congress, but the peacemakers were undaunted, and the session of 1916 saw them reintroduce the same

16

proposals.[44] The resolutions fared no better the second time, but Congress did approve an international organization for peace and the limitation of armament in an amendment to the naval appropriation bill passed August, 1916.

The proposal for disarmament had two champions, Representative Bennet and Representative Hensley. The former reintroduced, in the form of an amendment, the text of a resolution which had been approved by both the Sixty-first and Sixty-second Congresses. The original resolution authorizing the President to appoint a nineman commission to utilize existing international agencies for the purpose of limiting armament by international agreement was augmented by a clause calling for the establishment of an international military force for the preservation of peace.[45] Bennet's resolution was tabled in favor of an amendment presented by Walter L. Hensley of Missouri, although drafted by James L. Hayden, former president of the American Peace Society.[46] Hensley's proposal, the culmination of congressional efforts to establish an international organization for the purpose of securing peace and the limitation of armament prior to the Washington Conference, read:

Upon the conclusion of the war in Europe, or as soon thereafter as it may be done, the President of the United States is authorized to invite all great Governments of the world to send representatives to a conference, which shall be charged with the duty of suggesting an organization, court of arbitration, or other body, to which disputed questions between nations shall be referred for adjudication and peaceful settlement, and to consider the question of disarmament and submit their recommendations to their respective Governments for approval; that the President is hereby authorized to appoint nine citizens of the United States, who shall be qualified for the mission by eminence in the law and by devotion to the cause of peace, to be representatives of the United States, in such a conference; that the President shall fix the compensation of the said representatives and such secretaries and other employees as may be needed, two hundred-thousand dollars, or so much thereof as may be needed, is hereby appropriated and set aside and placed at the disposal of the President to carry into effect the provisions of this paragraph.[47]

In its final form after being amended in the Senate the Hensley Resolution read:

It is hereby declared to be the policy of the United States to adjust and settle its international disputes through mediation or arbitration, to the end

17

that war may be honorably avoided. It looks with apprehension and dis-favor upon a general increase of armament throughout the world, but it realizes that no single nation can disarm, and that without a common agree-ment upon the subject every considerable power must maintain a relative standing in military strength.

In view of the premises, the President is authorized and requested to invite, at an appropriate time, not later than the close of the war in Europe, all the great governments of the world to send representatives to a confer-ence which shall be charged with the duty of formulating a plan for a court of arbitration or other tribunal, to which disputed questions between nations shall be referred for adjudication and peaceful settlement, and their recom-mendation to their respective governments for approval. The President is hereby authorized to appoint nine citizens of the United States, who, in his judgment, shall be qualified for the mission by eminence in the law and devotion to the causes of peace, to be representatives of the United States in such a conference.

If at any time before the construction authorized by this Act shall have been contracted for there shall have been established, with the cooperation of the United States of America, an international tribunal or tribunals com-petent to secure peaceful determinations of all international disputes, and which shall render unnecessary the maintenance of competitive armaments, then and in that case such naval expenditures as may be inconsistent with the engagements made in the establishment of such tribunal or tribunals may be suspended, when so ordered by the President of the United States.[48]

The Congress in this resolution reversed the policy of immediate armament limitation, expressed in the resolutions of 1910 and 1913, in favor of the policy, advocated by the American Peace and Arbi-tration League between 1907 and 1910, of eventual disarmament after the establishment of a successful world organization. Further-more, this resolution did little to promote disarmament, since it stipulated that this strong world organization must be established before "the construction authorized by this Act shall have been con-tracted for." Thus disarmament had been by-passed with a graceful but meaningless gesture. However, the measure was a significant milestone in the disarmament movement.

The debate on this resolution revealed the attitude of Congress in 1916 toward world organization. Representative Augustus P. Gard-ner, who objected to the Hensley proposal, warned that if the United States were to keep out of Europe's troubles, it "had better stop med-dling with European affairs." Foreshadowing an argument used in the Senate debate on Article X of the League Covenant, Gardner maintained that he wanted no part in an organization which could drag the United States into wars in which it had no vital concern. He attacked arbitration because it was more inviting in theory than in fact. Would the United States arbitrate the Monroe Doctrine? Would this country be willing to arbitrate the question of Chinese exclusion? America, Gardner asserted, would not and ought not to submit to arbitration on these matters, but joining an international organization would make such arbitration mandatory.[49]

Equally revealing was the argument advanced by one of the adherents of the resolution, Representative Champ Clark of Missouri. He was certain that the United States would "never arbitrate the Monroe Doctrine while the earth spins on its axis and slides down the ecliptic," nor would it submit the issue of Chinese immigration to the judgment of a tribunal. He also agreed with the opposition on the advisability of staying out of Europe's affairs. The United States would never be engaged in war if "we attend strictly to our own business." However, Clark favored the resolution because it provided for disarmament. Unless a plan enabling all countries to disarm down to the "irreducible residuum" were found in the immediate future, bankruptcy could not be avoided.[50] Still another view was represented by Representative Hensley, who, believing in the practicability and necessity of arbitration, felt that the United States must give its wholehearted support to an international organization.[51]

The next successful congressional resolution for disarmament was not approved until after the close of the war in 1921. Thus, the 1916 Hensley Resolution was the final precedent for the action of Congress in authorizing a conference for the limitation of armament in 1921.

Congress had now on three occasions in six years shown its interest in the limitation of armament and in international organizations for the keeping of the peace. The appeal of this program was genuine and deep, for it stemmed from a traditional desire for peace, abetted by the possibility of economic gain. In the years after 1910 the public demand for peace had grown too strong for any prudent Congressman to ignore openly. However, in this compliance certain reservations were plainly noticeable. In the resolutions adopted by Congress ultimate aims had been very clear; specific means for their accomplishment were not well defined. A close reading of the debate in 1916 reveals the ominous fact that as plans for securing peace became more precise, Congressmen became increasingly cautious and fractious lest the new benefit be purchased at the cost of old ideals and prerogatives. As time was to prove, the religion of peace was prone to subdivide itself into many warring sects.

3 . . .

Complications in Disarmament and Far Eastern Policy During World War I

. . . THE movement in the United States for the establishment of a world organization which would maintain peace and accomplish universal limitation of armament has been examined largely in the abstract terms of aims and aspirations. However, as Secretary of State Charles Evans Hughes observed, "Foreign policies are not built upon abstractions. They are the results of practical conceptions of national interest arising from some immediate exigency or standing out vividly in historical perspective. . . ."[1] The election of 1916 saw both American political parties dedicated by platform to the abstract ideal of peace by international cooperation. When the Wilson administration attempted, however, to translate this ideal into reality through the medium of practical politics, complications resulted. A policy had to be worked out with foreign nations and approved at home by the Senate.

Of major concern to Wilson in his dealings with foreign nations were Japanese expansion, naval rivalry with Britain, and the Anglo-Japanese Alliance.

Relations with Japan had been strained since the signing of the Treaty of Portsmouth in 1905 and the rise of Japan to the status of a major power. America's chief interest in the Orient was exploitation of the opportunities for trade in China, and its Far Eastern policy was therefore primarily commercial. This policy ran into direct conflict with the rising power of Japan as it sought to expand into China. A bitter commercial rivalry was the result. This ill feeling was abetted by the frequent outbreaks of controversy over the immigration of Japanese into California and the legal status of those Japanese who were in this country. Agitation in the United States led finally to the Gentlemen's Agreement of 1908 in which Japan voluntarily limited the number and class of her nationals entering the United States. This did not quiet those in the United States who favored complete exclusion and, in 1913, the Webb-Henry Act made it impossible for aliens ineligible for citizenship (Japanese for the most part) to own land. The presence of the Japanese in California, together with the passage of these acts, did much to embitter relations between Japan and the United States. By 1913 talk of war filled the air.

With the outbreak of the First World War, the European powers withdrew from the Far East, leaving the United States as the only interested power which could oppose Japan's evident intention to seize this opportunity for expansion. To America it appeared that Japan was attempting to establish control of the far Pacific with a view to the ultimate exclusion of Western nations.[2]

To meet this threat, the United States intervened with the traditional tools of the Far Eastern policy, diplomatic notes, capital, and bluff. The equivocal position of the American government was well illustrated by President Wilson's statement that his policy would be "to protect China out of sympathy, and American rights out of interest, but to move cautiously lest Japan be antagonized against the United States and be more severe with China."[3] Although in instances like this it appeared to falter, the American policy was one of constant opposition to Japanese expansion. The first step by the United States in this direction was an attempt in August, 1914, to gain the consent of the powers to observe the neutrality of the Pacific Ocean and the entire Far East.[4] This plan failed because of the opposition of the Japanese who soon moved into Germany's possessions in the Far East. England, the ally of Japan, vainly attempted to specify the area in which Japan was to operate. This British scheme was soon shattered by the unyielding opposition of the Japanese and the demands which the war in Europe soon placed on England.

Consequently Japan began its attempt to expand in China by driving the Germans from Shantung and presenting the Chinese government with the famous Twenty-one Demands. The United States, now standing completely alone, reacted by recognizing "that territorial contiguity creates special relations between Japan and these districts."[5] This apparent retreat was counterbalanced a few months later by the second effort to check Japan. This was Secretary

22

of State Bryan's non-recognition note which restated the traditional Far Eastern policy of the United States and reserved the right of the United States to withhold recognition of any agreement that violated those rights.[6]

Japan was not halted by this measure. Expansion continued, unopposed by the hard pressed nations of Europe.[7]

Again Japan sought to complete its conquest by getting America to recognize her gains. The outcome of this strategy was the adoption of the Lansing-Ishii Agreement of 1917, notable, even in diplomatic circles, for its ambiguities. Most of this confusion arose because of the exchange of an explanatory preamble which was kept secret by the two governments. This stated that in the negotiations it had been agreed that they would ". . . not take advantage of the present conditions to seek special rights or privileges in China which would abridge the rights of the subjects or citizens of other friendly states." In the interest of clarity, the preamble continued, it was decided to eliminate the above statement from the text of the agreement, although it was ". . . well understood that the principle enunciated in the clause which was thus suppressed was in perfect accord with the declared policy of the two governments in regard to China."[8] Hence, the preamble in effect cancelled the meaning of the note, and it was possible for Secretary of State Robert Lansing to assert that he did not renounce America's traditional policy of the Open Door. Viscount Kikujiro Ishii recognized the Open Door, but maintained his country's right to "special interest" in China.[9] Nevertheless, in their practical effect, the notes were interpreted in the United States as restraining Japan, while both China and Japan felt that they signified American acquiescence to the demands of the Japanese.[10]

America's Far Eastern policy was crumbling, and early in 1917 Wilson turned his attention to rebuilding it. He sought a means of codifying in treaty form the principles of the Open Door policy, collective security, and nonaggression.[11] It was not until the Paris Peace Conference was convened that the United States and Japan came to grips in this diplomatic struggle.

A crisis was quickly reached when the Japanese demand for the North Pacific Islands was only partially met and their suggestion for a declaration of race equality was rejected. Wilson feared that if

23

Japan's third demand—the German economic rights in Shantung—was not granted, she would withdraw, wrecking the conference, killing the League, and seeking alliances with Russia or Germany. Japan's claims in Shantung were bolstered also by the legal sanction of two treaties with China and were recognized by European powers, especially France and England. The refusal of the last named powers to follow Japan's suggestion that all three withdraw their claims in China further strengthened Japan.

The settlement of the Shantung issue was vital. Although Japan laid claim only to the economic rights and holdings in the former German leasehold at the bay of Kiaochow, an important principle was involved. By settling the question herself Japan hoped to win final recognition as the dominant power in the Far East.[12]

Japan won recognition for this claim, and thereby dealt a serious blow to Wilson's policy of reasserting American influence in the Far East. The loss was compounded by an unsuccessful participation in the joint allied intervention in Siberia. American plans called for the joint armies to be limited to 7,000 men each, but Japanese troops in Siberia eventually numbered 72,000. These troops remained when the other allies withdrew in 1920, thus strengthening the Japanese bid for supremacy in the Far East.

Japan's position in Shantung, North Manchuria, and Siberia had not been shaken by the Wilson offensive; the American President continued the struggle. Seeking to frustrate Japan's attempts to gain a financial monopoly in China proper, the United States revived the idea of a four power consortium after the pattern of the Knox neutralization scheme of 1909. The United States, Britain, and France would join Japan in extending financial aid to China, thus bolstering their own positions while maintaining a close check on Japan's politico-financial conquest of Peking. The American public accepted this proposal as a bulwark to the Open Door and as an act of friendship toward China. However, the plan was weakened at the outset by Japan's reservation of her "special position" in South Manchuria, and was nullified subsequently by the refusal of the Chinese government to be "saved." The proposal was rejected because it would have prevented China from entering a free world market where she could borrow on the best terms available.[13]

As the Wilson administration neared its close, American Far

24

Eastern policy had reached the nadir. Japan was entrenched legally, diplomatically, and by military force in Shantung, Manchuria, and Eastern Siberia. Equality of commercial opportunity existed only in theory, while the territorial integrity and political sovereignty of China stood in grave danger of total eclipse. Furthermore, the American government, although opposing all of these developments, had been unable effectively to check Japan's steady march to dominance in the Orient. The policy of paper protection of China had failed; the only alternative, war, was unthinkable. President Wilson's design to codify, in treaty form, the principles of the Far Eastern policy of the United States appeared to be outside the realm of possibility. The President turned to the League of Nations as the best hope to maintain American policy.

Another problem which vexed the Wilson administration was the naval rivalry with Great Britain which emerged from the wartime debate over neutral rights. Irritation in the United States over British interpretations of international law reached an acute point late in 1916—so intense that Secretary of State Lansing feared that Wilson would retaliate.[14] The President did not take direct action. However, The Naval Appropriation Act of 1916, providing for a large increase in the United States Navy over a three year period, was in response to a request made by Wilson. Another adviser, Colonel House, feared that this act, coming at a moment when British-American tension was at a peak, would incite a naval race between the United States and England. The President, undismayed by this possibility, told House, "Let us build a navy bigger than hers and do what we please."[15] House was, nevertheless, reasonably accurate in his prediction, for the British reaction to the American naval increases was one of acute concern lest British naval supremacy be threatened.

This naval problem was complicated still further when the United States entered the First World War. The combined navies of the Allies were adequately supplied with capital ships, but needed destroyers with which to fight submarines. Accordingly, the British proposed that the United States modify its building program to meet this immediate need. Colonel House objected to this plan on the ground that it would leave the United States at the close of the war with an unbalanced fleet. Arthur Balfour then suggested a six power defensive naval alliance designed to protect the interests of all the

Allies. These initial efforts at rapprochement failed when President Wilson rejected both plans. While the United States was ready to take its place as a world power, said the President, it intended to play a lone hand and certainly would not become a party to any sort of alliance.[16]

The British-American naval controversy flared again at Paris. When Wilson arrived in Europe for the peace conference, he found the allies approved in principle the policy on disarmament stated in the Fourteen Points. However, they disagreed as to practical application. Wilson's aim of reducing national armaments to the lowest point consistent with "domestic safety" was soon altered, at the suggestion of Japan, to the lowest point consistent with "national safety."[17] At one stroke the armament necessary to national security was immeasurably increased.

Nothing had been done toward settling the fundamental disagreement between Great Britain and the United States on naval policy. In addition, further trouble arose. Britain was unwilling to recognize America's demand for "freedom of the seas" and maintained that her national interest as an island empire required naval supremacy. The United States, on the other hand, would not assent to British supremacy unchecked by recognition of the "freedom of the seas."[18] This stalemate was most serious for it invited naval competition. The nation with the superior fleet could enforce its view in international law.

In this dispute, the two powers made an issue of the League of Nations. Britain threatened to withdraw its support of the League if its demands for naval supremacy were not met. The United States countered by threatening to use its vastly superior resources to surpass the English navy if that nation did not support the League. This "naval battle of Paris," one of the most critical controversies at the peace conference, raged between England and America, unknown to the public, throughout the month of March, 1919. Finally Colonel House and Robert Cecil reached an agreement in which Britain supported the League and Wilson's amendment, excluding the Monroe Doctrine from the jurisdiction of the League, in exchange for America's pledge not to seek parity with the British navy.[19] This was only a truce. Wilson had abandoned efforts at immediate final settlement with England. He now hoped, as he repeatedly told the British, that a naval policy could be worked out after the League was firmly established.[20]

This solution was jeopardized when Senate opposition to the League became apparent. The British sent Lord Grey to the United States to encourage American acceptance of the League and to negotiate a more definite naval agreement. Grey's visit coincided with Wilson's collapse in September, 1919. Consequently, the President did not see Grey, and the latter returned to England without accomplishing his mission.[21] What had appeared to be a promising solution for Anglo-American naval rivalry was dealt a final and killing blow with the rejection of the League by the United States in the fall of 1919.

This inability to reach an agreement with Britain, with the deterioration of friendly relations, was a factor of far reaching importance in American diplomacy.

The American quest for the ideals of world organization and universal limitation of armament was in jeopardy. This danger was increased by another menace—the Anglo-Japanese Alliance. There could be no limitation of armament by the United States until this agreement was abrogated.

As interpreted in the United States this Alliance was an anathema. It neutralized England as a counter to Japanese expansion; it bound England to support Japan in war, even if the enemy were America.[22] These facts, according to American naval experts, made it imperative that the United States maintain a fleet equal to the combined fleets of Japan and England. Otherwise, American security at home and the Open Door abroad could not be maintained.[23]

Japan and Britain had long been aware of these suspicions. With the renewal of the alliance in 1911, they had attempted to exclude the United States from joint military attack under the Alliance. The British even suggested at this time that the United States protect its interests by joining an informal alliance with Great Britain and Japan.[24] When this was vetoed by the United States the renewed Alliance specified that it was not directed at any power having a general treaty of arbitration with one of the signatories. In addition, it had reaffirmed a policy toward China which was satisfactory to the United States. By uniting Japan to England it had eliminated the menace of a German-Japanese alliance.[25]

27

Contrary to expectation, the Senate defeated the pending general arbitration treaty with England proposed by President Taft, thus canceling the immunity provided in the renewed Alliance. America's distrust of the Alliance was not quieted. Suspicion of Japan was increased by its wartime policy in China.

The United States, it was clear, must disrupt the British alliance with Japan. As early as 1917, the American government suggested confidentially to the British a naval entente which would exclude the Japanese. This arrangement would have had the effect of neutralizing the Anglo-Japanese Alliance insofar as American interest was concerned. The ostensible purpose of the proposed pact was greater protection against Germany rather than restraint of the Japanese in the Far East.[26]

After this plan failed, the United States awaited indications of the British attitude toward renewal of the Anglo-Japanese Alliance, due in 1921. In July, 1918, it was rumored that Japan and England had entered a new agreement defining their respective interests in the Far East and China.[27] The State Department immediately began an investigation. The British government denied negotiations were underway, but the rumor was not squelched until Arthur Balfour, as spokesman for the English government, officially dismissed the report as completely false.[28]

Hardly had this rumor been disproved before a new one gained circulation. It was reported that Britain, Japan, and France had formed an Asiatic *entente* which would exclude the United States. This rumor, it developed, was an outgrowth of the disclosure of the secret treaties whereby the European powers had guaranteed Japan's acquisitions in China.[29] While most of these reports were not substantiated and had only a faint tinge of reality about them, the Anglo-Japanese Alliance did exist in fact and was a very real problem.

The State Department constantly checked reports that the British were planning an immediate renewal of the Alliance. Every effort was made to discover whether the British intended, in the event of renewal, to broaden or restrict recognition of Japan's "special interest" in Eastern Asia.[30] While much was said indicating that the American government feared the Alliance because of its possible effect in the event of war, the chief concern of the government appeared to be the relation of the Alliance to America's policy in the Far East.

In May of 1920, it was reported by the American ambassador in England that the Alliance with Japan would probably be renewed when the date of expiration, July, 1921, was reached.[31] The State Department realized that since the United States was not a member of the League of Nations or a party to the Alliance, it would not be expedient to register any open objection to the renewal of the Alliance. Even so, the American ambassador was instructed to utilize all unofficial channels to acquaint the British with his country's objections to its renewal.[32] The Department also suggested that in order to promote Anglo-American cooperation in the Far East and placate public opinion in the United States, the renewed Alliance include a pledge to oppose "special rights or privileges which would affect the independence or territorial integrity of China or that would deny to any subjects or citizens of any country the full enjoyment of equal opportunity in the commerce and industry of China." Further, it was recommended that the Bryan Treaties of 1914 be recognized as treaties of general arbitration; thus would the United States be freed, under the terms of the renewal of the Alliance in 1911, from the menace of joint military action by Japan and Britain.[33]

By 1920, Britain, despite its disagreements with the United States, realized that a community of interest existed. Friendship with the United States would solve many problems, whereas enmity would greatly complicate all matters of policy. Consequently, the British government, wishing to cultivate the good will of the United States, agreed to take the American proposals under consideration in formulating policy on the Alliance.[34] England and Japan, in notes to the League of Nations, July 8, 1920, stated that the Alliance, if renewed, would be made to conform with the principles of the League. Since the League Covenant embodied the principles which the United States wished to foster in the Far East and also banned exclusive treaties involving military obligations, this British-Japanese note appeared to be an effort to meet the objections raised by the United States. Later in the year, statesmen in Britain and Japan vied with each other in an effort to reassure the United States that joint British-Japanese military action in pursuance of the terms of the Alliance would never be directed against the United States. Lord

Grey, Baron Royehei Uchida, and the Japanese ambassadors in London and Washington all made statements to this effect. The London *Times,* quasi-official mouthpiece of the British government, reported that Great Britain had informed Japan that the Bryan Treaty of 1914 should be interpreted as a treaty of general arbitration which, under Article IV of the Alliance, would exempt the United States from the application of the Alliance. Uchida and Grey publicly supported this interpretation.[35]

By these moves Britain showed itself willing to modify the pact to meet the United States' objections. Even these concessions did not satisfy the American government. The General Board of the Navy expressed the opinion that no revision could make the Alliance acceptable to the United States. Only outright abrogation would satisfy this country and free it from the necessity of outbuilding the combined naval strength of the British and the Japanese.[36]

While America could build a navy equal or superior to the combined British-Japanese fleets, such a step would not necessarily bring security. It might drive the British and Japanese together in a united effort to balance this increased power. If the United States did not attempt to outbuild the combined naval strength of Japan and Britain, it would stand in an inferior position in the event of a crisis. A blunt denunciation of the Alliance by Britain would probably force the offended Japanese into an agreement with Russia or Germany, a possibility which had been frequently reported. Hence the Anglo-Japanese Alliance was not only the key to any satisfactory Far Eastern policy for the United States, but also the key to American naval policy.[37]

If the Alliance seemed to pose an insoluble problem to American diplomats, it presented an equally complicated problem to English policy makers. While the American government realized some of the dangers lurking in an undiplomatic abrogation of the Anglo-Japanese Alliance, the British government was acutely aware of the disadvantages in such a policy. Japan was recognized as a potential threat to the British in India. This menace could be met most easily by retaining friendship and allowing Japan a free hand in China where British interests were not so extensive. This British attempt to contain Japan in the area where its expansion would damage least British interests could be fostered if the United States, already hostile to Japan, could be persuaded to deploy its fleet in the Pacific.

On the other hand, the British had to consider the fact that the American government was directly opposed to Japanese expansion in China, and the friendship of the United States was vital to any stable and successful British post-war policy. The Foreign Office had to formulate a policy which would protect British interests in the Far East and in Europe. With this objective, it could not afford to incur the ill will of Japan or of the United States, but found it necessary to cultivate friendly relations with these two expanding, unfriendly young powers.

By mid-summer of 1920, it was apparent to the foreign offices of the two English-speaking nations that a satisfactory settlement of Far Eastern and naval problems was largely dependent on the discovery of a graceful and diplomatic method to nullify the Anglo-Japanese Alliance. Further negotiation between the United States and Britain in regard to the Alliance and Far Eastern policy was all but halted with the announcement by Lloyd George in December, 1920, that the Alliance would not be altered in any way until after the meeting of the Imperial Conference in June, 1921.[38]

President Wilson in attempting to clear the way for world organization and the limitation of armament had learned that Japanese expansion, British naval supremacy, and the Anglo-Japanese Alliance were stubborn realities blocking his path.

31

4 . . .

The Wilson Administration's Failure
to Meet Post-War Problems
in Foreign Affairs

. . . As President Wilson struggled with the problems of Far Eastern and naval policy, he came to believe that they could be met most effectively through the League of Nations—"the only clue to a labyrinth in which, without it, dangers of every kind would lurk and develop."[1] Unfortunately this solution was nullified by the bitter dispute between the President and the Senate resulting failure to adopt the League Covenant. This struggle was a vital factor in the development of a policy in regard to the navy and the Far East.

In 1915 and 1916 it had appeared that there would be little opposition to the adoption of a world organization. Senate resolutions had pointed that course, the League to Enforce Peace had been organized, leading statesmen—Taft, Lodge, Hughes, Roosevelt, Harding, Wilson—had endorsed international cooperation, and both political parties underwrote plans for world organization in their national conventions of 1916.[2] As the plans were translated into action, hostility developed.

When Wilson in a peace note to the warring powers, December 1916, recommended a league of nations, there was an immediate and violent reaction on the part of the Senate. All mention of a league had to be dropped from the final note to gain Senate approval. Even thus modified, the note was opposed by seventeen senators led by Lodge and Borah; thirty-one members of the chamber refused to vote.[3]

A few weeks later Wilson specified the essential terms of peace in an address to the Senate. Opposition appeared when he declared that "the people and Government of the United States will join the other civilized nations of the world in guaranteeing the permanence

32

of peace." Such a policy would bring about "no breach in either our traditions or our policy as a nation, but fulfillment, rather, of all that we have professed or striven for. I am proposing," he continued, "as it were, that the nations should with one accord adopt the doctrine of President Monroe as the doctrine of the world; that no nation should seek to extend its polity over any other nation or people, but that every people should be left free to determine its own polity, its own way of development. . . ." Touching on another traditional policy he asserted: "There is no entangling alliance in a concert of powers. When all unite to act in the same sense and with the same purpose all act in the common interest and are free to live their own lives under a common protection."[4] Senate leaders disagreed with the President, charging that the new policy of internationalism would contravene traditional policy and would invade the prerogatives of the Senate.[5]

The disarmament movement was gravely affected by this rapidly widening breach between the President and the Senate. In the President's mind the problem of peace and the problem of armament were inseparable. A just and lasting peace, Wilson told the Senate in 1917, was

a problem closely connected with the limitation of naval armaments and the cooperation of the navies of the world in keeping the seas at once free and safe. . . . There can be no sense of safety and equality among the nations if great preponderating armaments are henceforth to continue here and there to be built up and maintained.[6]

A year later when Wilson presented Congress with the Fourteen Points as a general framework for peace, he stressed the interdependence of a league to secure peace and a policy of arms limitation. The fourth point required the nations to reduce armaments to the lowest point consistent with domestic safety; the fourteenth point recommended the establishment of "a general association of nations . . . for the purpose of affording mutual guarantees of political independence and territorial integrity to great and small states alike."[7] Wilson's philosophy was based on a belief that in international affairs the first objective, national security, could be guaranteed only by an international force sufficient to thwart any threat against a nation. A world federation of states thus could meet America's need for security while making disarmament practical. Otherwise, the United States standing alone must strive to gain security only by building the largest military force in the world—a course leading to militarism and the destruction of all the ideals which Americans had cherished.[8] As soon as he crystallized this policy, he insisted that disarmament be preceded by the establishment of a successful international organization.

Here again the Senate objected to the presidential leadership. Many congressmen denied Wilson's logic, believing that successful limitation of armament could be effected without an international peace-keeping organization.[9] How this was to be done was not explained, but by the end of the Sixty-fifth Congress there was strong opposition in that body to the continuation of a policy of building a large navy. Lending strength to this opposition was the traditional repugnance for large military establishments and the popular disapproval of the ever increasing taxes which military preparedness necessitated.

Wilson, in pursuance of his established policy, seized upon this threat of navalism, unpopular with the Senate and the public, and sought to use it to further the cause of the League of Nations in the United States. In one of his best expositions of this policy, he told the Senate Foreign Relations Committee in 1919 that it was imperative to take immediate and favorable action on the Treaty of Versailles. Such action would establish a firm basis on which to plan for foreign policy and national defense. Naval policy awaited the decision of the Senate on the League. "We cannot intelligently or wisely decide how large a naval or military force we shall maintain or what our policy with regard to military training is to be. . . ," declared the President, while the League issue was still in doubt. He then described the policy that the United States would be forced to adopt if the League of Nations was defeated. "If we must stand apart and be the hostile rivals of the rest of the world . . . we must be physically ready for anything that comes. . . . We must see to it that every man in America is trained in arms." Such a policy, the President asserted, would place American democracy in jeopardy of its life since democracy and militarism could not live conjointly.[10]

During the debate on the League the opposition to the Treaty—motivated to a degree by political considerations and personal hatred for Wilson—based its public attack on two apparent defects in the covenant. The senators, reiterating their earlier charges, declared that the prerogatives of the Senate in the management of foreign affairs were being invaded by the Executive, and that "entrance of the United States into the League of Nations" and adherence to Article X of the covenant—providing cooperative military action to keep peace—would constitute "a betrayal of American independence and American sovereignty."[11] These views carried weight with the public which was in favor of a league, but, like the Senate, was anxious to ascertain that no desirable "right" was sacrificed in establishing the new foreign policy.

Wilson's opponents not only disapproved of the League in general, but also condemned its provisions for dealing with naval and Far Eastern problems. The attitude of the Senate on the first of these problems was demonstrated in the debate on the tenth reservation. As first introduced, this reservation declared that the United States, in the event that it became party to a League plan for limitation of armament, "reserved the right to increase such armaments without the consent of the council whenever the United States is threatened with invasion or engaged in war." Senator Harry S. New added as an amendment to the reservation the provision that no plan adopted by the League council would become operative until approved by the Congress.[12] The independence of the United States and the prerogatives of the Senate were not to be infringed upon by the authority of the League council.

Senator James Reed defined the mood of the Senate when he asserted that he wanted to be sure the United States could increase its armed forces in the event of invasion, without first having to get "the unanimous consent of eight foreign gentlemen in Geneva."[13] The Senate appeared determined to preserve the independence and sovereignty of the United States—an aim approved by the general public.[14]

The settlement of Far Eastern problems through the League was sharply attacked also. Congress had taken an interest in Shantung from the time of the first Japanese moves toward China in 1914.[15] This interest increased as the peace conference negotiated a settlement. The completed plan was savagely condemned in the press. "Japan the Possessor of Stolen Goods," "The Crime of Shantung," "inexcusable injustice," "conspiracy to rob," "a damnable enterprise,"

35

"the rape of Shantung," were some of the references made to it. The Senate took its cue from these press notices and made the Shantung issue a most potent cause for defeat of the League. Senator Hiram Johnson, mindful of his numerous anti-Japanese constituents, called the settlement "the blackest page in all our history" and observed:

To the Japanese Empire, with only 60,000,000 of people, we turned over shamefully and cruelly 40,000,000 Chinese. To the autocracy of the Orient we delivered 40,000,000 republicans of China. We made the Orient "safe for democracy" by dismembering its only democracy and handing the parts to the strongest autocracy on earth.[16]

Johnson and other senators possibly were more interested in defeating Wilson's league than in helping China. Regardless of motive the net effect of the debate was to weaken and complicate the American position in the Far East. Although the Senate seemed devoted to the traditional policy of Chinese-American friendship, its noisy reaffirmation of this policy was damaging. Especially was this so in view of the fact that the Senate would not sanction Japanese claims which Wilson had previously recognized. As a result of this contradictory American policy China was encouraged to oppose Japan, and Japan was irritated by America's lack of good faith.[17]

The Senate cast its first vote against the League of Nations in the fall of 1919. The naval problem immediately came to the fore as the Navy Department, apparently verifying the President's predictions, proposed in December, 1919, an interim building program designed to provide within a year a navy "large enough to protect our national interests in both oceans."[18] This action was followed by Assistant Secretary of the Navy Franklin D. Roosevelt's grim warning that if international relations reverted to what they were before the war, the Navy would cost the American people a billion dollars a year. Secretary of the Navy Daniels reiterated this view in testimony before the House Naval Affairs Committee in March, 1920, while the second debate on the League was in progress. He stated that the administration's future policy in regard to the Navy would depend entirely on the decision which the Senate reached on the Versailles treaty. Defeat of the Treaty would necessitate building an American Navy which would be the strongest in the world.[19] Such a program of naval expansion met with little public enthusiasm. The administration hoped as a consequence to win support for the League and to place the blame for navalism on the Senate.

Congress refused to accept responsibility for navalism. The President, it said, was wholly insincere in his motives. He advocated disarmament and peace, but at the same time he was sponsoring the largest naval establishment in the history of the United States. America, claimed these congressmen, had spent its blood and treasure to stamp out the menace of militarism abroad, and now the dread monster was being nurtured at home. German militarism had been suppressed by America; now the United States seemed destined to become a swaggering, heel clicking, and sword rattling aggressor.[20]

Another charge leveled at the President was that his proposal for American naval supremacy was causing uneasiness in the governments of our late allies—Japan, Britain, and France. With Russia defeated and Germany subdued, against what country could this American fleet be employed if not one of the allies? Advocates of this precept maintained that the policy of naval supremacy was unnecessary and dangerous. America was secure from attack since there were no enemies against which such protection was needed. Furthermore, supremacy would force England, France, and Japan for reasons of security to try to keep pace with the United States. This competitive building would mean that the United States would gain nothing in relative strength regardless of how much was spent on the Navy.[21]

Wilson's naval program found support in Congress from the anti-Japanese and anti-British elements. Japan was assailed on the floor of Congress as the true successor to German militarism—a nation bent on a mad course of ruthless imperialism and expansion. Japan was a sinister enemy who would publicly play the friend for a time, but secretly would wait for a favorable opportunity to strike a blow at the United States.[22] England, in her turn, was pictured as the only serious commercial rival of the United States. The British, freed of the burden of German commercial competition, would turn their efforts toward overcoming the challenge of the United States in this field. If American economic interests were to be made secure, a navy must be built which would guarantee dominance on the high seas.[23] Added to this argument was the traditional Irish-American Anglophobia, heightened at this time by the issue of Irish independence.

The numerous American Friends of Irish Freedom, united in clubs, were not disposed to belittle England's threat to America, and incited certain congressmen to attack the English—possibly for the sake of the Irish vote in the United States.

By March, 1920, with the second defeat of the League, the Wilson program was frustrated, with no positive foreign policy emerging from the wreckage. Meanwhile problems multiplied.

To the outside world it appeared that the American government had broken faith on the League issue, refused to cooperate with foreign powers, was hurling accusations at its allies, and was madly building toward naval supremacy. The din of these war-like preparations was occasionally modified by the voice of an American spokesman declaring that his nation, although apparently a swaggering giant armed to the teeth, was at heart the world's greatest exponent of peace and good will. In any event, world politics could not become settled until the United States, one of the most important powers, decided on and carried out a clear-cut foreign policy.

With the convening in 1920 of the national conventions to nominate candidates for the presidency, the major political parties were forced to make a start toward formulating a definite and positive foreign policy. On the vital issue of the League, President Wilson, in response to a challenge by Senator Lodge, had agreed to let the election serve as a "solemn referendum."

The Republican convention, which met at Chicago, had more senators in attendance than sometimes could be found in the halls of Congress. Among the Republican delegates were twenty-two senators as official delegates; many other senators were present in an unofficial capacity.[24] William Allen White, the noted editor and a Republican delegate, wrote that the convention was "controlled by a national committee representing plutocracy and the United States Senate. . . ."[25] The *New York Times* seconded this opinion when it stated that it was "government of the Senate, by the Senate, and for the Senate." Another observer declared, "The Old Guard senatorial oligarchy was everywhere in evidence, and firmly in the saddle."[26] Nine senators were candidates for the presidency. The permanent chairman, the chairman of the committee on resolution, and the head of nearly every other important committee came from the Senate.

THE WILSON ADMINISTRATION

Republican leaders could not forget that the National Committee had wrecked the party in 1912 by nominating Taft, nor fail to realize that the great problem of the 1920 convention would be unity.[27] On the one hand, party leaders like Taft, Hughes, and Root advocated a modified League; on the other hand, the National Committee included irreconcilable senators like Hiram Johnson, William Borah, Medill McCormick, and Frank Brandegee. The latter group threatened to repeat the bolt of 1912 if the convention did not draft a platform and chose a candidate opposed to the League of Nations.[28]

Senator Lodge, who commanded great influence as permanent chairman of the convention, abandoned his former position as an advocate of the League with reservations. Elihu Root, shortly before the convention, urged Lodge to stand by such a program as the soundest political position for the party.[29] Lodge refused flatly, declaring that such a course would tend to discredit the Republican irreconcilables and tie the hand of the new administration. "I am much more interested," he asserted, "in getting the whole party to fight together against Wilson and the League as he brought it home than I am in myself or anything else. . . ."[30]

Lodge carried this conviction into his opening speech at the convention. He struck the real keynote of the meeting with a veritable "hymn of hate" in which he denounced "Mr. Wilson and his dynasty, his heirs and assigns, or anybody that is his, anybody who with bent knee has served his purpose. . . . All such persons must be driven from all control of the government and influence in it." This theme was the cohesive force in the party both at the convention and during the campaign. "Make an end of Wilson" became the slogan of the convention.[31]

The first evidence of this "keynote" was reflected in the work of the sub-committee on the platform. For two days and nights Senator Crane and William Allen White attempted to get recognition of a modified League. Each time they were frustrated by the watchful and adamant Senator Borah.[32] Senator Brandegee protested, with tears in his eyes, that he would bolt the party rather than sanction the League. Borah was tearless but equally determined.[33] Senator Lodge joined with these irreconcilables, declaring that he would fight from the floor of the convention any effort to include the League in the platform even though it included the Lodge reservations.[34]

The foreign policy plank of the platform as finally adopted was definitely unfavorable to the League of Nations but somewhat less definite in what it did favor. One of the committee members in after years declared that this plank "meant nothing except that it frankly did mean nothing. . . ."[35] This was perhaps too harsh a judgment, for the platform proved to be a fairly accurate statement of the actual policy which came to be adopted by the Harding administration and by the United States for nearly a score of years thereafter. It stated: "The Republican Party stands for agreement among nations to preserve the peace of the world." This great end was to be achieved through an international association based on international justice which should be able to summon instant and general international conferences whenever peace was threatened. Then the senators showed their skill in making reservations by a statement which was the real key to future policy:

We believe that all this can be done without the compromise of national independence, without depriving the people of the United States in advance of the right to determine for themselves what is just and fair, when the occasion arises, and without involving them as participants and not as peacemakers in a multitude of quarrels, the merits of which they are unable to judge.[36]

After the senatorial clique had succeeded in putting the convention on record as being opposed to Wilson and to the League, it turned its attention to the selection of a president who would aid in carrying out this policy. The clique was already on record as to the qualities they expected in the man who filled the job: "Our fellows are going to put in a man who will listen."[37] Nevertheless, the convention ran into some difficulty in selecting a candidate. On Friday evening, with the parliamentary aid of Chairman Lodge, adjournment was called with the two leading candidates, Leonard Wood and Frank Lowden, deadlocked.[38]

The next day in accordance with the decision of the bosses, reached late the night before in smoke-filled rooms, the obedient convention chose Senator Warren G. Harding. "He was nominated because there was nothing against him, and because the delegates wanted to go home."[39] In addition, he shared the opinions of the Senate, and would listen to its leaders. Harding in his acceptance speech pledged himself to the restoration of "party government as

40

distinguished from personal government, individual, dictatorial, autocratic, or what not." The "Party is bigger than the man," said the newly nominated candidate.[40] The senators left Chicago satisfied that they had accomplished their objective.

In San Francisco, where the Democratic Convention was staged, Wilson was not present, but his influence was in evidence. He was ably represented by his selected emissary, Senator Carter Glass, chairman of the committee on resolutions. However, the recommendation of this committee on foreign affairs was somewhat modified from the President's ideal of a League with no reservations. As finally agreed upon, the platform stated:

The Democratic Party favors the League as the surest, if not the only, practicable means of maintaining the permanent peace of the world and terminating the insufferable burden of great military and naval establishments. It was for this that America broke away from her traditional isolation and spent her blood and treasure to crush a colossal scheme of conquest.[41]

While the campaign for the presidency developed, the public showed little interest despite the vital issue to be judged. One politician observed: "I haven't heard of anybody getting mad and punching somebody else on the nose over a political argument this year yet." The greatest excitement during the campaign was raised in "jeering at Wilson," who was pictured as "at once innocent-minded and stubborn, vain and shut-minded, fatuous and gullible, and altogether a victim of foreign statesmen shrewder than he."[42]

As to the League, James M. Cox, the Democratic nominee, declared himself to be unreservedly in favor of it. Harding, on the other hand, attempted to solve the problem by appealing to violently anti-League and violently pro-League members in his party simultaneously. The Republicans, in spite of their vacillation during the campaign, declared the League repudiated once Harding was elected. He expressed this idea to a group of his townsmen: "You didn't want a surrender of the U. S. A.; you wanted America to go on under American ideals. That's why you didn't care for the League which is now deceased."[43]

The election was actually a trial of Wilson and of all his works, including the League. Even Democrats, who surveyed the wreckage, felt that it was not the defeat of Cox but rather a defeat of Wilson.[44] Ex-Secretary Lansing, in a letter to John W. Davis, emphasized this

41

aspect of the election and declared that the voters had repudiated Wilson, but had in no sense repudiated the idea of a league. The former Secretary of State thought that the United States would join some sort of league or association of nations soon after the Republicans took office.[45]

All signs indicated that the country was willing to be a party to a league, but the election had shown that if the bridge between isolationism and internationalism by way of the League of Nations had not been definitely closed, it had been relegated to the status of a very faint possibility.

The election of 1920 was not, as Wilson had hoped, a solemn referendum of the League issue, for many other factors had affected the decision of the voter. Nevertheless, it was significant as a turning point in a restatement of American foreign policy. President-elect Harding promised an international organization born of the quintessence of the wisdom of the Republican party's "best minds." The Senate was for peace, yet it specified that it be a ". . . step toward peace with American power unimpaired and rights guaranteed."[46] In this, and the other outstanding problems of foreign affairs unsettled by the Wilson administration, it thus appeared that the Harding administration might be able to formulate a policy and take action. The President and the majority of the Senate were of the same political faith. Because of the flaccid character of the new President it appeared that "willful men" in the Senate would direct foreign affairs as they saw fit.

The Borah Resolution

♦ ♦ ♦ THE entry of the United States into the First World War halted for the time the advance of the movement for peace by disarmament. The problems of peace and of policy were greatly complicated; the first effort to solve them by a League of Nations was frustrated by partisan bitterness and bias. The pressure of circumstances late in 1920 made evident the fact that decisions could not be evaded much longer. Procrastination had rendered more acute the problems of international organization, naval policy, and Far Eastern policy. America's equivocal course had embittered relations with and aroused the suspicion of the two nations most vital to the successful solution of these problems, Great Britain and Japan.

Britain was inclined to be friendly, but the naval problem was still unsettled. The United States Navy Department recommended in December, 1920, a three-year building program which included the construction of eighty-eight additional naval vessels. Accordingly, the British Admiralty announced in March, 1921, a building program designed to keep step with American expansion. The ill will engendered by this naval competition was fanned by English irritation at the pro-Irish sentiment in the United States. In addition, the Anglo-Japanese Alliance caused much suspicion of British motives in the United States, while the fulminations of Irish-Americans against Britain's Irish policy caused England to suspect American motives.

In the Far East the situation was rapidly growing worse. The Chinese government, split into warring camps, had reached the lowest ebb in its authority since the Boxer days and was approaching open financial bankruptcy.[1] America's problem was further complicated by a growing spirit of nationalism that made China increasingly resentful of aggressions by Japan, England, and Russia.[2] As for Japan, Wilson's unsuccessful efforts to halt the course of empire

43

had greatly embittered relations without checking the Nipponese. Shantung was a constant source of dissension from the time of the Peace Conference. This ill will was fanned by other controversies.

Japan's actions in Siberia had caused one American officer to write:

Is Japan preparing for a war with America, and was her Siberian expedition the first important step toward the realization of a Pan-Oriental plan calculated to make such a struggle possible and profitable? I am not a jingoist, but twenty months' intimate contact with the problem, as a staff officer of the American expedition, convinces me that such is the case.[3]

An open quarrel had developed between the United States and Japan over the cable rights on the tiny Pacific Island of Yap. The argument, dating back to the Paris conference, had not been settled by the summer of 1921. Despite numerous notes between the two governments, the problem remained unsolved and resulted in much hard feeling.[4] The *Nichi Nichi Shimbun,* one of Tokyo's largest dailies, called the controversy over Yap another indication of the "dark cloud lowering over relations between Japan and America, already evidenced by the strengthening of their defenses in the Pacific."[5] Moreover, Japan had not looked with favor on the resurrection of the consortium by Wilson in 1917, and had agreed to join the group in 1920 only on condition that her special position in Manchuria was not to be disturbed.

An additional cause for ill will was agitation over the immigration problem. California was momentarily restrained from passing further land acts in 1919 by Secretary Lansing's telegraphed plea from Paris, but the anti-Japanese excitement became stronger in 1920. This agitation, which was fanned by the Hearst press, eventually resulted in the Japanese government's decision to restrict further the immigration allowed under the "Gentlemen's Agreement." Negotiations between the two governments for a permanent settlement resulted in a general program drawn in January, 1921. This proposal was attacked so strongly by Senator Hiram Johnson that it was never submitted to the Senate.[6]

On both sides of the Pacific the jingoists were at work. One article, typical of many, was G. M. Walker's "Can We Escape War With Japan?" The Japanese statesman, Baron Shigenobu Okuma, had confided to the author that war with the United States could not be

avoided. Japan was already preparing for it. The inescapable conclusion was that the United States should meet the issue by going to
war immediately.[7]

These tensions produced a vicious upward spiral in naval competition. It was imperative for each nation continually to increase its
fleet in order to keep pace with its rivals. The Parisian journal,
L'Oeuvre, seemed justified in its conclusion that "the conflagration
appears as fatally certain as lightning which leaps from two clouds
charged with opposing currents."[8]

In the United States, the public, while only dimly aware of the
real international issues involved, was acutely conscious of their concrete manifestations in terms of increased naval building and the
continuation of wartime taxes. By 1920, the public appeared restive
and suspicious of the government's promises of peace which were
always balanced by recommendations for a larger navy. Adding to
this dissatisfaction was the growing conviction that armament competition among the nations had been the basic factor in bringing on
the First World War. Characteristic of this idea was the opinion
given in a letter from a citizen to Senator Borah: "An armed world
is a fighting world." Conversely, the first step toward peace was to
disarm.[9] Senator Johnson, an irreconcilable of the irreconcilables,
endorsed this theory when he declared:

War may be banished from the earth more nearly by disarmament than by
any other agency or in any other manner. If there is any real desire among
the nations of the earth to prevent war, they can prevent it by substantial
disarmament . . . the one great step that could be taken toward the
promotion of peace and the prevention of all future wars.[10]

The popular attitude toward the relation of armament and wars
was well expressed in an epigram: "Big warships meant big wars.
Smaller warships meant smaller wars. No warships might eventually
mean no wars."[11] According to this scheme of logic, armies and
navies were the real roots of war. If complete disarmament could be
achieved, wars would cease. Were that impossible, whatever degree
of reduction that could be effected would, in direct ratio, reduce the
probability and severity of war.

The limitation of armament had still another strong source of
appeal. Even if peace were not the final production of such a policy,
a reduction in taxes was a certain and immediate result of this limi-

45

tation. This was a vital issue to a country suffering from a post-war depression and yearning for normalcy. In addition, there was a growing belief that war was not worth its cost. One organization distributed thousands of postcards in 1920 showing the cost of American participation in all wars from 1793. Below these figures were the words: "What is it after all the people get? Why taxes, widows, wooden legs and debts."[12] Finally, military establishments were condemned because of their rapidly mounting cost. Battleships, which could be built for $5,000,000 in 1900, cost $40,000,000 in 1920, and statisticians estimated that 93 per cent of the governmental income was spent for the unproductive cause of past, present, and future wars.[13]

This general dissatisfaction with huge allotments for armament was heightened in early December, 1920, by a report from the Senate on the nation's finances. Senator Fordney McCumber, chairman of the finance committee, warned the public that if the current rate of government spending were maintained, the deficit for the year would reach $1,200,000,000, possibly going as high as $2,000,000,000 by July of 1921. He felt that unless a drastic reversal of this trend was soon effected, disaster awaited the nation.[14]

The public seemed to feel that there was nothing to lose in a policy of disarmament, and, at best, the plan might usher in Utopia. On the other hand, unless a satisfactory method for reducing the navy could be devised, an isolated United States would be drawn into a ruinous naval race with Britain and Japan. As a result of all of these factors, there was a growing public demand for the United States to substantiate its words in favor of peace and normalcy with action, and return its military establishments and tax structure to a peacetime basis.

The anti-League Republican Senators were embarrassed by this clamour. President Wilson had warned the public repeatedly that rejection of the League would necessitate unlimited expenditure for military services in the United States. The irreconcilables in the Senate had laughed at this prophecy in 1919; the laughter had grown hollow by 1920. War with Japan was a distinct possibility; and England, although not a menace, was scarcely a friend. Under these conditions, unilateral disarmament would be suicidal; the alternative, disarmament within the League, had been rejected. Senators and the

46

public began to look for some solution which would make feasible a reduction of the navy, even though the United States remained outside of the League of Nations.

The American press, in 1920, made various suggestions for meeting the problem. The *Nation,* as early as April 10, 1920, criticized the Wilson policy on the navy and declared that:

The possibility that there might be another way out—simply by inviting Japan and England to agree to stop building—never enters the minds of these two statesmen [Wilson and Daniels], nor the minds of Congress. France, England, Japan and America can disarm on the seas by mutual agreement without waiting for the league to act, and the glory of leading the way should belong to the United States.[15]

The English press, more interested in Far Eastern aspects of the problem than in disarmament, began suggestions for a conference to settle the question of American, British, and Japanese interests in the Far East and to modify the Anglo-Japanese Alliance into a form acceptable to America. One of the first periodicals to propose such a plan was the *Round Table,* in December, 1920.[16] Congressmen could not ignore this growing popular demand for disarmament with its twin promises of peace and tax reduction. Indeed, disarmament had become a part of the politician's standard campaign equipment, along with devotion to mother, the home, and American ideals.

Meanwhile, the League of Nations, in its fall meeting, 1920, began consideration of the problem of the limitation of armament. Wellington Koo, of China, in a speech before the Assembly declared that this was the major problem facing the organization. Its practical solution was blocked by the failure of the United States to join the League. He felt that the nations within the League could not disarm, while the country most powerful in potential armament, the United States, was not bound to do likewise.[17]

The Japanese, who had recently authorized an increased naval building program, made the same accusation. America's failure to join the League, according to Japan, had produced an uncertainty, which made increased armament the only path to security, in spite of the desirability of disarmament and the possibility that naval competition would eventually lead to war. This charge was reiterated by the Japanese in successive meetings and was given as their justification for opposing a proposal for the limitation of armament. This

resolution called on the League powers to spend no more on armament in 1922-23 than they had spent in 1921.[18]

This activity on the part of the League was most disconcerting
to the Senate irreconcilables who, while opposing the League in
debate, had confidently predicted that it would never become an
effective organization. Nevertheless, the situation became even more
uncomfortable for this Senate bloc. The League, not confining its
efforts on disarmament to its members, invited the United States to
take part in the consultations relative to the limitation of armament.

With these developments the American public became more suspicious of the Senate's wisdom in rejecting the League. The *New
York Times* surveyed the isolated position of the United States with
its huge naval building program and observed that "conditions
would be very different if the Treaty of Versailles had been ratified
by the Senate and the United States were included in the League
of Nations."[19]

For the Senate irreconcilables the time for oratory was over. The
time for action was at hand. Some of the fruits of the great victory
of 1920 were in danger of turning sour. More and more the country
was clamoring for armament limitation, tax reduction, and peace.
The Senate was being condemned because all three aims seemed beyond the reach of the United States, yet within the grasp of the
nations belonging to the League. The gage had been thrown down.

This invitation, carefully worded, called on the United States to
sit in a "consultative capacity" on the League's permanent military,
naval, and air commission. The commission was to make recommendations for a solution of the armament problem, but its conclusions
were not to be binding on any nation. The invitation further stressed
that "the presence of the representatives of the United States would
in no way commit the American government to whatever opinions
may be finally put forward in the report of the commission." Consequently, the League expressed the hope that the American government would not refuse to associate itself with the governments and
members of the League. It would lend to the present effort "an
assistance which can in no way encroach upon its own perfect liberty
of action." The importance of cooperation for the satisfactory settlement of competition in armament, continued the invitation, was
"one to which public opinion in all countries attaches the highest

importance." Indeed, the future of the world and escape from economic chaos were dependent on the successful management of the armament problem.[20]

This plea, sterilized of any taint that could offend senatorial prejudice, was sent to President Wilson. The President declined, giving his reasons as follows:

> The Government of the United States is most sympathetic with any sincere effort to evolve a constructive plan for disarmament. . . . The President of the United States is deeply interested in this question and is most desirous of cooperation to this end, but as the Government of the United States is not a member of the league he does not feel justified in appointing a commission to take even a *de facto* participation in the deliberations of the council or of the commission on behalf of the council in the execution of provisions in the covenant of the League of Nations.[21]

This answer stressed the responsibility of Congress for America's failure to join the League. It drew a distinction between the attitude of the President and the government of the United States. The President was "deeply interested" in disarmament, but the "government" was not a member of the League, and until such a time as the government did become a member, disarmament was impossible for the United States. Secretary of the Navy Josephus Daniels, a few days after the rejection of the League invitation, endorsed this view by declaring that the United States must be a member of a world organization of all nations before limitation of armament could safely be undertaken.[22] The next move was up to the Senate.

Judging by subsequent events, this invitation by the League served as the final catalyst which transferred the disarmament problem from the realm of discussion to that of action. Men prominent in public life began to lend their influence to the demand for disarmament in the United States. Major General Tasker H. Bliss, a professional soldier, aroused the nation when he suggested to the Peace Conference Forum in Philadelphia that the United States should take the lead in a world movement for disarmament.[23]

Petitions demanding action began to deluge the Senate. A typical plea, presented by LaFollette for the Women's Peace Society of Milwaukee, asked "the members from Wisconsin of the United States Congress to use their utmost influence to have our country take the lead among the nations in achieving joint disarmament."[24]

49

Public insistence for action was mounting. The members of the Senate could not completely ignore it. On December 11, Senator Thomas J. Walsh of Montana called attention to the charges made by Japan and China at the League Assembly. He agreed that "no plan for a reduction of armaments could receive the approval of the other great powers of the earth unless the United States joined in the plan. . . ." The United States, said Walsh, was most anxious to bring about disarmament. The real attitude of the American people "which they have long maintained" was "that there ought to be a general plan arrived at by all the great powers for a reduction of armaments." The Senator read the amendment to the 1916 naval appropriation act which empowered the President to call, at the close of the war, an international conference to consider world organization and armament limitation. To America's traditional support of armament limitation had been added an official resolution favoring an international conference to consider the problem. But, Walsh continued, the country's rejection of the League and its isolated position had caused other powers to become suspicious of America's sincerity. Judging simply by action, the United States seemed bent on a career of isolation, militarism, and imperialism. The suspicions of foreign countries were being confirmed by President Wilson's refusal to join with the League commission on armament limitation, the only agency that had at that time advanced such a plan. Senator Walsh felt it imperative that the United States take immediate steps to bring its policy on armaments into harmony with its traditions by cooperating in plans for disarmament. He rejected, as inadequate, President Wilson's reasons for refusing the invitation from the League, and introduced a resolution requesting the President to appoint, with the confirmation of the Senate, an American delegate to the League commission on armament limitation.

This seeming invasion of Executive authority by the Senate, Walsh justified on the ground that the Senate was an "integral part of the treaty-making power" and had a duty, no less compelling than the President's, to pass judgment on so important a policy as disarmament. The resolution, however, was interred immediately by Senator Lodge, who moved that it be sent to the Senate Committee on Foreign Relations.[25] Subsequently, Walsh reintroduced this proposal in the next two sessions of Congress with no success.

The Wilson administration had steadfastly proclaimed League membership as the only safe method to achieve disarmament. The Walsh Resolution recognized that the League was the only agency which offered any hope for reduction of armament. If the anti-League and pro-disarmament senators were ever to justify their position, the time was at hand. Thus, it was perhaps more than mere coincidence that the next proposal in the Senate for limitation of armament came from one of the most irreconcilable foes of the League, Senator Borah. His resolution, introduced December 14, did not recognize the efforts of the League toward disarmament and proposed for America an independent course of action. The resolution, which was destined to be the nucleus of the popular movement for the limitation of armament, had the virtue of simplicity. The fundamental problem, Borah felt, was not armament in general, but competition in naval building. A large naval establishment in the United States would in turn demand large fleets for Britain and Japan. He quoted the Japanese government's statement that it "could not consent even to consider a program of disarmament on account of the naval building program of the United States." The problem of naval competition was of importance only to the three nations which could afford to expand their navies—the United States, Japan, and England. Furthermore, the latter two countries were united by alliance. The solution of the problem lay in obtaining a mutual agreement among those nations on future naval policy. Borah proposed that this common policy be one of limitation of naval armament on the basis of a 50 per cent reduction in naval building for the next five years. The Resolution also provided that Congress would curtail its appropriations for military purposes should the conference agree to limit naval armament.[26]

An additional purpose of the Borah Resolution, widely acclaimed by the press, was to emphasize the United States' desire to cooperate for the attainment of peace, rather than to persist in a solitary and war-like course in foreign affairs. Borah declared that his resolution would "develop whether Great Britain and Japan are sincere in their talk of reducing armaments."[27]

It was not surprising that the proposal awakened an instant and enthusiastic response from the American public. In a formula that all could comprehend, was the simple and complete solution to the

51

problem of war and high taxes. In utility and practicability, the Borah Resolution was welcomed by the public as a sort of diplomatic Model "T" Ford. It was not as complete and splendid as the League "limousine," but it appeared to be much less expensive and would serve the same purpose. Here, too, was the irreconcilables' answer to the dilemma of League membership or naval supremacy presented by the Wilson administration. It was also an answer to the problem raised by Senator Walsh's proposal of cooperation with the League of Nations in a general program of disarmament by all nations. The Borah Resolution was in accord with the prejudice of the Senate and the public in that it was limited in scope, it was an American plan, and it would not infringe on American sovereignty. Furthermore, there were no commitments to action in unforeseen contingencies; it promised an immediate remedy for the problem of naval armament, without reference to or involvement in the complexities of international relations.

Borah wrote one of his constituents on December 15, 1920, the day after the resolution was presented, that he had already received many letters and telegrams approving it. One was from a student group in Japan.[28] A few days later Borah reported that enthusiasm for his resolution was rapidly increasing, with growing support in England and Japan as well as in the United States. The Senator by this time was confident that something definite would be accomplished, although he expected strong opposition from the "armament trust."[29]

This early and spontaneous response was soon augmented by organized forces which were determined to keep the disarmament issue before the public. Leader among the press was the *New York World*.[30] Its editor, Herbert Bayard Swope, telegraphed his Washington correspondent on December 29 to assure Borah of its support and to agree on a definite and simple statement of Borah's plan.[31] This aid was willingly accepted by Borah who kept in close touch with the editors throughout the campaign.[32] Although the *New York World* was perhaps the most prominent supporter of the Borah Resolution, the press in general supported the plan with varying degrees of enthusiasm. The most important exception to this chorus of approbation was the Hearst chain which, being anti-Japanese, anti-English, and pro-navy, could hardly have favored the Borah Resolution.

The *New York World* conducted a campaign well calculated to gain the attention of the public and stir the popular imagination as to the possibilities of the arms movement. A spectacular feature of this drive was an interchange of views between Secretary Daniels and Northcliffe of the British Admiralty. Discussion of the possibility of naval reduction by two such prominent officials stimulated wide public interest. Equally impressive was the December 26 issue of the *World* which presented three full pages of letters from prominent men expressing their approval of the disarmament movement. The contributors included senators, governors, admirals, public leaders, and President Harding.[33]

Thus fostered, the movement rapidly gained headway. Men in high position also began to lend their weight to the crusade in public addresses. Among this number were General Bliss and General John J. Pershing. One of the most impressive of Pershing's speeches was delivered in New York at a dinner meeting for European relief. The terrible aftermath of war was graphically illustrated to one thousands guests who had paid $1,000 a plate for this dinner in the Grand Ball Room of the Commodore Hotel in New York City. The menu resembled the starvation diet of Europe and was served from an army mess wagon. In this dramatic setting Pershing called for a "drastic cut in armament." The General said that failure to achieve this reduction would send the nations rushing "headlong down through destructive war to darkness and barbarism."[34]

Borah's presentation of the disarmament movement soon won the support of the peace societies in the country who recognized in it an opportunity to advance their cause. A meeting, utilizing the typical procedures of these organizations, was held in Washington on Christmas Day. It was sponsored by the Women's Peace Society under the leadership of Mrs. LaFollette, wife of the Wisconsin Senator. She told the assembled women, meeting in the very shadow of the Capitol on the traditional day of peace, that they must use their newly acquired suffrage to stop war. They must vote, she declared, against those congressmen who were bent on militarism, and for those who favored peace and disarmament.[35]

Other organizations not primarily peace societies registered approval of the movement to limit armament. Notable as an example was the statement by C. J. Murphy, the Leader of Tammany Hall.

53

He declared that his organization, which had long favored disarmament, had even urged the Democratic Convention to include it in the platform of 1920.[36]

Despite this growing public interest there was little official comment on the subject in the Senate. The most significant statement was made by Senator Johnson. This arch foe of international cooperation termed disarmament the only practical step that could be taken toward peace and declared himself in favor of a conference of the five associated and allied powers for armament limitation.[37] The two most irreconcilable Republican foes of the League, Johnson and Borah, were now openly advocating a joint conference for disarmament. This development made it appear that the Senate could be counted on to support the disarmament resolution. The indication of the Senate's probable approval was corroborated by numerous unofficial polls taken by various newspapers. The *Philadelphia Public Ledger* canvassed all of the senators and senators-elect as to their positions on the limitation of armament and the establishment of a world organization based on law. When this poll was completed on January 3, 1921, it revealed that 98 per cent of the next Senate was in favor of limitation of armament, and a majority favored some sort of international organization.[38] The results of this survey were substantiated by a similar poll conducted by the *New York World* which indicated that Congress was strongly in favor of limitation of armament and was anxious to proceed at once to working out the details of a disarmament conference.[39]

Perhaps the inspiration of the moment would have been sufficient to secure a conference immediately had the diplomatic relations of the nation been entirely in the hands of newspapers and senators. The executive branch of the government was to be considered also, and there the enthusiasm for disarmament was marked by qualification and caution. Secretary Daniels, the spokesman for the outgoing Wilson administration on its policy toward disarmament, favored the movement. He hoped that a plan might be rapidly perfected for its accomplishment. Daniels was willing to see Harding call a disarmament conference, a move that would become imperative if the United States continued outside the League. Still, the Secretary felt that disarmament would be safe only when agreed upon at a conference of all nations. Otherwise, disarmament would be a "blunder equal to a crime. . . ."[40] A more practical plan, Daniels felt, would be to invoke the congressional resolution of 1916 providing for a conference of all nations as a preliminary step to disarmament. Later, the Secretary of the Navy elaborated his objections to Borah's plan. If put into effect, the Borah Resolution would halt building at a time when England had a navy almost twice the size of any other in the world. In addition, the English sea strength was augmented by the Anglo-Japanese Alliance which conversely strengthened the Japanese fleet. The outgoing administration looked upon the Borah Resolution as a menace.[41]

Of more importance, for the future, was the opinion of the incoming administration. Here there was evidence of caution, although the principle of disarmament was warmly approved. Just shortly before the announcement of the Borah Resolution, Harding had given a clue as to his position. Speaking in Norfolk, Virginia, the President-elect declared: "I believe in partial but not permanent disarmament, and I see a time when this will be realized." Nevertheless, he did not think the time for disarmament was at hand, and advocated, for the present, a policy of naval supremacy.[42] This speech was in accord with Harding's record in the Senate where he had favored a big navy. Although his position was not clear by December, 1920, Senator Borah felt that the incoming President was not enthusiastic about immediate disarmament. He wrote to Frederick L. Allen, late in December, asking that the latter write to Harding about limitation of armament. "I am exceedingly anxious," said Borah, "to have him get interested in this matter."[43]

Thus, the immediate reaction to the Borah Resolution for the limitation of armament was general public approval and some organized support. The Senate, apparently, was ready for action; the administrations, both outgoing and incoming, were inclined toward caution. The *Literary Digest,* in surveying press opinion in America, Japan, and England at the close of the year, found that the *New York World's* crusade had created international interest and approval. The London correspondent of the *New York Tribune* reported that British papers "without exception" supported the proposal that Britain, Japan, and the United States lead the way to disarmament by agreeing to reduce their navies. The British Navy League embraced this sentiment, calling disarmament the only alternative to world suicide.

55

Even more striking proof of England's willingness to participate in the reduction of armament was given by Lloyd George. Before the announcement of the Borah Resolution, the English Prime Minister had ordered a 50 per cent reduction in the military and naval estimates for the coming year.[44]

Many leading newspapers in Japan also endorsed the idea of a three power naval agreement. The *Jiji-shimpo,* a big-navy paper, declared that there was no reason for Japan to continue its building program if a joint agreement could be reached. Other Japanese newspapers maintained that Japan was building a navy only because it felt it necessary to keep pace with the United States.

In the United States, a survey by the *Literary Digest* found strong opposition to armament, with much of this objection arising from its expense. Typical of this attitude was a statement quoted from the *New York World:*

The United States is spending more money today on preparations for future wars than any other country in the world, and it is useless to talk about economy in the administration of the Federal Government if this wanton waste is to continue at the expense not only of American labor and capital, but at the expense of the labor and capital of all civilization.

The *Washington Herald* emphasized the same theme, insisting that the disarmament problem was economic as well as moral:

A world brought to poverty, hunger, and dire want by war is still taxed the bread it must have to live, the clothes to cover its nakedness, the fuel to keep it from freezing, the materials to give it honest employment, and is kept in that state by the taxes to maintain war-armaments.[45]

The *Literary Digest* sanctioned this opinion by featuring a cartoon on government expenditures. It depicted a pie being sliced by the agencies to which the government contributed. Sixty-eight per cent of the pie went to "Past Wars," 25 per cent to "Future Wars," and the remaining 7 per cent to all other causes. The case against the economic waste of military preparation was made more striking by General Bliss, who stated: "Disarmament is the only means of preserving the world from bankruptcy and civilization from ruin." [46] All evidence demonstrated that the demand for disarmament was sincere, insistent, and universal.

Thus, by the end of 1920, the public appeared to be aroused to

56

the need for disarmament. In the Senate the irreconcilables, formerly the obstructers of administration policy, were in the forefront of the movement for the limitation of naval armament. The situation demanded action, and apparently the Senate was ready to assume leadership in formulating a positive foreign policy.

Congress Debates the Borah Resolution

♦ ♦ ♦ WHEN Congress reconvened in 1921, the problem of the limitation of armament demanded solution. The urgency of this issue arose from the public demand created by the Borah Resolution and from the duty of Congress to determine, before the end of the session, March 4, the size of a building program for the navy. Many of the advocates of disarmament, placing their faith in newspaper polls, predicted that Congress would meet this situation by calling a conference immediately. They were to be disappointed. The Senate did pass the Borah Resolution as modified by Senator Edge, but it died at the close of the session with the Naval Appropriation Bill to which it was appended.

The Senate at the beginning of the session did not consider the problem of disarmament immediately, since the Borah Resolution was still in the hands of the Committee on Foreign Relations. The first action came in the House of Representatives on January 11, when the Committee on Naval Affairs opened a series of hearings designed to clarify the relation of disarmament to general naval policy and to the naval building program for the current year. A second motive, according to the Chairman of the Committee, Representative Butler, was "to keep the subject of disarmament before the people and keep it up to fever heat." [1]

There was no difficulty in achieving this latter aim, for the Committee attracted much interest by calling before it many prominent men, including: Acting Secretary of State Norman H. Davis, Secretary of the Navy Daniels, General Bliss, General Pershing, career diplomat and commissioner to the Paris Peace Conference Henry White, as well as the directors of peace societies and leaders of public opinion at large.

These hearings were of even greater importance as a forum for discussing the problem of effecting disarmament. The most impor-

58

tant questions were the advisability of holding a conference for the limitation of armament, the most propitious time to call such a conference, the number of nations to be invited to the proposed conference, and the effect of these plans on the naval policy of the United States. As to the advisability of a conference, the experts who testified before the committee were in general accord. For the most part, they agreed that the conference should be called soon. General Bliss, one witness who held this opinion, told the committee that there was much talk of disarmament at the Versailles peace conference: "Everything that I heard confirmed my opinion that the general sentiment was ripe for a settlement of the matter." [2]

There was some disagreement as to just how soon the conference should be summoned. Mrs. Henry Villard, spokesman for the Women's Peace Society, recommended that President Wilson call a conference as soon as possible. [3] Senator Borah also regarded any delay in effectuating the conference as an effort to defeat disarmament.

On the other hand both major political parties favored delay in convening the conference. The Democratic leaders in Congress did not want the matter to be presented before the Wilson administration. It would only serve, they felt, to embarrass the administration which had been rejected at the polls and was now practically powerless. Furthermore, the Democratic party might suffer. President Wilson had established his opposition to disarmament while the United States was not a member of the League. Consequently, he would refuse to call a conference. Thus the party as a whole would be placed in the politically dangerous position of opposing the popular demand for disarmament.

In the Republican camp there was more agitation for immediate action. However, this enthusiasm was soon stifled by political expediency. The party's elder statesman, Elihu Root, in a letter to Chairman Butler, recommended that no definite plans be made until the Harding administration had taken office and could assume responsibility. [4] This pronouncement by Root apparently served to discourage the movement toward an immediate summoning of the conference. Agitation subsided and the advocates of disarmament began to look to the incoming administration to initiate a disarmament conference.

The hearings before the committee revealed that another problem on which the experts could not agree was the number of nations to

59

participate. The Borah Resolution and the recommendations of some experts called for a conference limited to a few powers. In defense of this policy, it was pointed out that the competition in armament was a problem confined to the great powers alone. Furthermore, the chances of reaching an agreement for effective curtailment of armament lessened as the number of powers represented at the conference increased.

The opposing school of thought favored a conference in which all countries would be represented; only thus would significant progress be made. It also maintained that a conference of a few powers, as provided in the Borah Resolution, would stir the suspicion, if not the active opposition, of the nations which it did not include. A prominent exponent of this plan was Secretary Daniels, who restated before the committee the policy of the Wilson administration—disarmament on a world-wide scale.

On the vital question of the size of the American Navy the experts were in agreement for the most part. They asserted that the United States should take no steps to reduce its armament until after an international conference had reached a definite agreement regulating the size of all fleets concerned. In the meantime, they advised that the nation continue without abatement its naval building program.

As important as were these findings of the House Committee, perhaps more significant was the discovery of the keen interest in disarmament among the voters and in Congress. In this regard, one of the members of the committee stated that the hearings had shown that: "The sentiment of the country is unquestionably in favor of an international conference," and "every Member of this Congress" is in accord with the public on the matter.[5]

While the hearings before the House Committee on Naval Affairs were bringing out these facts, Congress resumed its debate on the Naval Appropriation Bill. If enacted as presented, it would have enabled the United States, by an early date, to reach absolute supremacy on the sea. The optimism engendered by the hearings before the committee was quickly dissipated by the tone of the House debate on this appropriation measure. It had been expected that the House, following the precedent of 1916,[6] would temper the passage of a large appropriation bill for the Navy by appending a definite proposal to amend the program, if a conference for the limitation of armament by international agreement could be arranged. This was not done, although several resolutions for limitation of armament were offered.

As to the advisability of such a resolution, the House was divided along party lines. The Republicans while professing to favor limitation of armament questioned the propriety of fostering it by means of a congressional resolution. They felt it would constitute an unjustifiable invasion of the President's prerogatives in foreign affairs, would limit unduly the authority of the incoming President, and would be unnecessary.

The debate on the last of these contentions was warm, involving as it did the administration's future policy on the limitation of armament. Several Republican members of the House assured the body that Harding's advocacy of disarmament made the passage of a directive resolution ridiculous. Representative Oliver, a member of the House Naval Affairs Committee, testified that an interview had shown the President-elect so strongly in favor of the limitation of armament that he planned to call a disarmament conference shortly after assuming power. Thus, a resolution in the House directing Harding to call a conference was officious and improper. It questioned the integrity and high purpose of "a man of vision . . . imbued with noble ideals" and alive to "the highest conception of the obligations of humanity in its sweep onward to loftier planes." [7] Chairman Butler of the House Naval Affairs Committee testified that he, too, had talked to Harding. The President-elect, declared Butler, intended to call a conference for disarmament "before the next harvest time in Pennsylvania, or the next cotton picking in the South. . . ." [8]

The Democrats in the House, less certain of Harding's devotion to disarmament, felt it would be wise to withhold a part of the funds to be appropriated for an expanded navy until after the President had actually issued invitations for such a conference. Representative Brooks incorporated this idea into a resolution, suspending $90,-000,000 of the appropriation until after the President had issued the invitations for a conference. The Democrats disagreed with the contention of the Republicans that a congressional resolution was an invasion of the President's prerogative in foreign relations or in any sense an improper limitation of his authority. The Republican majority in the House steadfastly rejected all such resolutions which

61

might embarrass or restrict the President-elect in the discharge of his constitutional duties.

In addition, there was opposition to armament limitation on other grounds. Representative Britten, for example, favored disarmament and felt the American people wanted it. At the same time, he feared that the immediate enacting of such a policy would relegate the United States to a secondary position. Indeed, some nations favored disarmament because it would weaken America. "There is no human way for the English Navy to retain the supremacy of the sea without this naval holiday. It will insure to England permanent leadership of the seas," concluded Britten. His resolution opposed any limitation of the Navy, recommending instead the completion of all naval building in the shortest practicable time.[9]

As a consequence of these factors, the House passed the Naval Appropriation Bill, February 15, without qualifying it by any resolution providing for a reduction in naval building. This decision by the House clouded the bright prospects which had encouraged the advocates of the limitation of armament. While there was no opposition to the principle of disarmament among the members of the House, the majority wished to defer definite action until the United States had become either the greatest naval power in the world or had reached parity with the British fleet. Republican leaders in the House seemed determined to leave the formulation of policy on disarmament to the President-elect. According to rumor, Harding, like the leaders of the House, felt that naval supremacy, which could not be attained in less than three years, was a prerequisite to disarmament.[10] These rumors were offset by the frequent assertions in the House that Harding favored immediate disarmament. His attitude, when defined, would be the key to future policy, since the House had decided, apparently, to leave the matter to the discretion of the President-elect.

While the House was taking this cautious stand, Senator Borah kept the issue of disarmament before the members of the Senate, although his original resolution was still in committee. He introduced a new resolution in which he questioned the value of the battleship as the basic unit of the fleet and requested an opinion from the Committee on Naval Affairs as to the wisdom "of suspending the present naval building program for six months to the end that investigation may be had as to what constitutes a modern fighting navy."[11] Borah stated that this resolution was not intended to relate to the question of disarmament. It was only prudent to make certain that the new and bigger navy be composed of the most efficient units which could be built.[12]

The suggestion seemed logical because there had been much speculation since the advent of the bombing plane as to the future usefulness of the battleship. The American Navy, led by Secretary Daniels, was convinced that the battleship, impervious to air attack, would continue to be the backbone of the fleet. To substantiate his faith the Secretary issued a challenge to the chief exponent of air supremacy, Brigadier-General Billy Mitchell. So great was Daniels' confidence in the battleship that he offered to man the bridge of an obsolete war vessel while Mitchell attacked the ship from the air with bombs.[13]

The General Board of the Navy in replying to the Borah Resolution vindicated the battleship as the basic element in the fleet of the future. In the same report the Board attacked the disarmament movement, calling it a menace to the nation's security and an ideal that could be attained only in the distant future. Consequently, the General Board favored the continued use of the battleship in the construction of the strongest fleet which the country could possibly build.[14]

Even though Senator Borah did not profess to aid the disarmament movement by the introduction of this resolution on naval building, it became significant in the campaign for the limitation of armament. While inquiring as to the value of the basic and most costly unit of the fleet, the resolution stirred, in the mind of the public, the suspicion that the unlimited building of battleships, at $40,000,000 apiece, might not actually guarantee America's security in the future.

Even more important was the immediate and widespread disapproval engendered by what came to be known as the "General Board Document." Evidently, the public was in no mood to accept the Navy's dictum that no limitation of the fleet was practical. The newspapers of the nation also joined in castigating in numerous editorials the skepticism of the Board. The general tenor of the opposition was exemplified in an article in the *Scientific American,* usually classed as a pro-navy periodical. The editor condemned the General Board for its failure to say "a word of sympathy with the request of a war-weary world to be relieved, at least in some measure, of the burden of naval and military armaments under which it labors."[15] Another critic was Senator King who condemned the Board's recommendation as a fatalistic acceptance of militarism out of keeping with the traditions and current opinion of the American people.[16]

On February 15, the Senate began consideration of the Naval Appropriation Bill and with it the Borah Resolution of December 14, 1920, providing for a tri-partite naval conference. As had been the case in the House, much of the debate was devoted to the proper relationship between the President and the Congress in the conduct of foreign affairs. Thoroughly debated were the questions of the optimum size of the pre-disarmament Navy and the exact form in which a congressional resolution on the limitation of armament should be expressed.

The Republicans opposed any resolution by the Senate pertaining to foreign affairs. Many of them had only recently been engaged in rescuing the nation from a one-man government and denouncing the Executive usurpations of President Wilson.[17] Nevertheless, the Senate Republicans maintained the President should be independent of the Senate in calling international conferences.[18] Senator Miles Poindexter, who had charge of the Naval Appropriation Bill in the Senate and who was very close to the President, was the spokesman for the Republicans. Poindexter declared that the Borah Resolution was in purpose "an act of supererogation," although in practice it would be of value only "as an expression of opinion." The Resolution, Poindexter explained, was valueless, even as an expression of opinion. The congressional resolution on disarmament adopted in 1916, still in force, completely covered the fundamental features of the resolution by Borah.[19]

Senator Borah, contradicting these charges, maintained that he had "no desire to embarrass the incoming President," or to limit him in the discharge of his executive duty. The resolution would in no way curtail the President's authority. He would still be "free to suggest a wiser and better program." Borah admonished the Senate to exercise independent judgment on important issues. It had been charged, said Borah, that the Senate had abdicated not only its judgment, but also its functions during the previous eight years. It had reached a point where it feared to act "until the President-elect nods." If it was important, as the Republicans maintained, for the President to protect his prerogatives of office, it was equally important for the Senate to

64

protect its rights. The Senate must actively discharge its duties, asserted Borah, and not "loiter around like satellites of royalty until we are bid to act and to profess and pretend to think." [20]

The size of the navy was also the subject of much of the debate in the Senate during this session. The majority of the Senate approved the continuance of a naval building program providing for increased naval strength. Senator McCormick, an outstanding spokesman for this policy, declared that it would serve to stabilize international relations, encourage commerce, and strengthen America's position as a world leader. To curb the naval building program, he felt, would surely result in a loss of all of these advantages. [21]

Senator Borah, again speaking for the opposition, agreed in general with this reasoning. He felt that the effort in the Senate to add $100,000,000 to the Naval Appropriation Bill approved by the House went far beyond the demands of security. These professed champions of security were actually seeking to destroy the disarmament movement by means of the Naval Appropriation Bill. The bill would destroy any hopes for immediate economy in government even though disarmament might eventually be achieved. Accordingly, Borah assumed the leadership of a filibuster to prevent the passage of the Naval Appropriation Bill. [22] As a means to this end, he concentrated on arguments regarding the adoption of a resolution for the limitation of armament. He succeeded so well that during the last few days of the session, ending March 4, most of the time had to be devoted to reaching an agreement on a disarmament resolution. Only after this was done could a vote on the appropriations bill be taken.

At the time, Borah's task in getting a filibuster underway was simplified by the fact that there were three resolutions before the Senate, in addition to his, providing for conferences for the limitation of armament. One of these was Senator Walsh's resolution for cooperation with the League of Nations. Another, presented by Senator Pomerene, authorized the President to delay the naval building program for six months "in order to enable him to arrange for a conference with the governments of Great Britain, Japan, and such other powers as to him may seem proper. . . ." [23] The last resolution, an elaborate scheme based on the ideal of proportionate reduction of armament, was introduced by Senator France. It provided that the largest navy on July 1, 1921, was to be taken as the maximum stand-

65

ard for the navies of all the powers. Those countries which were inferior to this standard would be granted a period of time in which to expand to this maximum point. The difficulty in arriving at unanimity became apparent after some debate. The advocates of each of these various resolutions were staunchly opposed to vital features in the other plans.

In an effort to promote harmony among the warring peacemakers, Senator Edge offered, under a Senate rule for unanimous consent, still another resolution for disarmament. In its original form it was almost identical with the Borah Resolution.[24] An attempt was then made to graft to this proposal the modifications necessary to make the finished resolution acceptable to all the advocates of disarmament.

Senator Williams began the debate on the Edge Resolution with the suggestion that France and Italy be included in the proposed conference along with England, Japan, and the United States. This suggestion led to a lengthy discussion in which the principal arguments were presented by Williams and Borah. Williams maintained that the exclusion of Italy and France would render worthless any agreement reached by the other powers. Borah, in rebuttal, declared that France had already demonstrated that she would not agree to a limitation of her army. The inclusion of France would doom the conference to failure from the start. Eventually, Borah prevailed and the names of Italy and France were stricken from the Edge Resolution.

The next phase of the debate was dominated by Senator Walsh who sought the adoption of his proposal for cooperation with the League of Nations as an amendment to the Edge Resolution. Walsh consumed much of the Senate's rapidly diminishing time in presenting the advantages of his plan, but meeting with no success, finally withdrew it. Immediately he introduced a new measure, which was a restatement of the resolution previously offered in the House by Representative Brooks, providing for a meeting of all leading nations to consider ways and means of bringing about joint disarmament.

Borah found ample opportunity to filibuster in opposing this suggestion. He reiterated, at great length, his fundamental hypothesis that a conference of more than three powers was foredoomed to failure. Walsh upheld the principle, previously defended in the debate by Senator Williams, that the only practical solution to the armament problem was a worldwide agreement. Finally, after hours of argument, Walsh's proposal for a disarmament conference of all nations was voted on as an independent resolution. The results showed twenty-eight in favor and thirty opposed to this proposal, while thirty-eight did not vote. The floor was then cleared for a vote on the Edge Resolution, which was unanimously adopted with a tally of fifty-eight in its favor, none opposed, and thirty-eight not voting.[25] The attempts of Senator Edge to bring harmony into the discussions on disarmament had succeeded. However, so much time had been devoted to this effort that the naval bill to which the resolutions was to have been appended was never brought to a vote. The Borah Resolution, as reworded by Senator Edge, was adopted, only to be nullified almost immediately.

Despite this disappointment, the debate in the Senate was more encouraging to the advocates of disarmament than the House debate. The Senate, while casting no votes against a disarmament resolution, apparently was determined to adopt a tremendously expanded appropriation for naval armament. Like the House, it seemed more concerned with establishing supremacy on the seas than in bringing about disarmament. There was no suggestion in Congress, either in resolutions or speeches, that the United States jeopardize the position of pre-eminence in naval power which it was rapidly achieving. The consensus of the press was that the Sixty-sixth Congress favored the completion of the 1916 naval building program. The *New York Tribune* declared that this policy on the part of Congress was a true reflection of "the country's wish to have an adequate Navy as the first line of national defense." [26]

The *Nation* asserted that Congress was not unfriendly to disarmament, but felt it desirable to have the biggest navy on the earth before a proportional reduction of armament was instituted. The *New York Times* supported this view, stating that "it is the part of wisdom for the United States, while working for concord and amity, to maintain its present armed forces. . . ."

On the other hand, the more ardent advocates of disarmament saw in this seeming prudence of Congress an attempt to postpone, discredit, and ignore the disarmament movement. One journal charged that Congress was in the grip of the "great business interests that push us irresistibly forward on the path of imperialism, armament, and war." Many papers agreed that Congress left to its own devices

67

would never consent to disarmament. The only hope for armament limitation was to muster a popular demand "so overwhelming and so insistent" that the congressmen could not "dare to disregard it." The polls in late December had indicated that Congress would readily accept the responsibility for armament reduction. It now appeared that rather than leading the disarmament drive, congressmen were subtly working for its defeat.[27]

The attitude of the Senate as a whole probably lay closer to a compromise of these extreme positions. President Wilson's alternative to the League, supremacy on the sea, had been quietly accepted; the majority in Congress favored a navy unsurpassed in strength. If supremacy might be attained more cheaply by an agreement for joint reduction of the major fleets, Congress, it seemed, would accept such a course.

The high hopes of the leaders who favored disarmament had not been fulfilled by Congress. Immediate disarmament, a possibility in January, had fallen prey to a congressional tendency to procrastinate. It appeared in March that Congress would continue to delay, unless forced to take action in response to presidential leadership or popular demand.

Harding's Foreign Policy

⋄ ⋄ ⋄ THE majority in the Senate, thus far, had been cautious in approving a policy of limitation of armament and careful to pay all deference to the chief executive in matters of foreign policy. This consistently timid attitude on the part of the Senate consequently increased the significance of Harding's opinions regarding international affairs. Yet, by the time he assumed office no clear cut definition of his views had been made public. In order to foster party unity, Harding avoided making any definite commitments in foreign affairs.

While running for office he conducted a campaign calculated to win an election rather than to educate the people in the fundamentals of foreign policy; he had oscillated between the opinions of the factions within his party. In the weeks following his election no specific statement of policy on the principal issues, the League of Nations and plans for disarmament, was announced. Party unity continued to be a problem and Harding, by his delay and confusion, succeeded in convincing each of the factions that eventually he would espouse its doctrine and repudiate the others.

The more fundamental of Harding's two major problems was the attitude which the United States should adopt toward the League of Nations. During his campaign Harding extended promises to the pro-League faction, but he was careful that his practices remained in conformity with the wishes of the Senate irreconcilables.

In August, Harding, with the aid of George Harvey and Richmond Washburn Child, had drawn up a complicated and ambiguous plan for international cooperation which was designed as a straddle by which Harding would be able to placate the irreconcilables and the liberals. In short, he promised to work with the "best minds" in the country after his election in order to establish "a society of free nations . . . so organized as to make attainment of peace a reasonable possibility." [1] Later in the campaign Harding's ideals gravitated closer

69

to the opinions of the irreconcilables, and on October 8 he declared:

This issue does not present to the American people the question whether they shall favor some form of association among the nations for the purpose of preserving international peace, but whether they favor the particular League proposed by President Wilson. . . . We shall have an association of nations for the promotion of international peace, but one which shall so definitely safeguard our sovereignty and recognize our unlimited and un-mortgaged freedom of action . . . that it will have back of it the united support of the American people. . . .

Harding stated again that in order to perfect the form of this organization, he would "advise with the best minds in the United States. . . ." [2]

Immediately after his election Harding declared that the League of Nations was "deceased." The press and the public now assumed that he would carry out his pledge to provide for world peace by the establishment of an "association of nations." [3] Apparently Harding planned to do so. Relinquishing his seat in the Senate, December 6, he retired to his home in Marion, Ohio, for the reported purpose of deciding upon a basic course of action in foreign affairs which would be acceptable to the Senate, to himself, and to the country. During the following two weeks Harding held consultations at his home with a number of men prominent in the Republican party.

One of the first visitors was Charles Evans Hughes, rumored to be a possible choice for a cabinet post, who talked with the President-elect for more than two hours. While no details of the meeting were released to the press, it was assumed that the discussion concerned international affairs, the League of Nations, and the "association of nations." Harding's interest in the "association of nations" was publicly confirmed a few days later after a discussion with George Harvey. Harvey, an inveterate foe of the League and author of many of Harding's equivocal campaign speeches on that subject, declared himself to be wholeheartedly in favor of an "association of nations." Also, he suggested that no nation in the new association declare war without first gaining the sanction of a popular referendum. [4]

In view of Harding's indebtedness to and sympathy with the Senate, an interview of far greater significance was with Senator Albert B. Fall. The Senate irreconcilables had stubbornly opposed any recognition of the League during Harding's campaign. Yet, Fall, who was one of that Senate bloc, asserted that the irreconcilables were in favor of some sort of association of nations. In explaining his view Senator Fall declared in a statement typical of the opinion of the Senate, "I was an irreconcilable and still am. I believe we owe a duty to the other peoples of the world, but I always have thought we could do it without surrendering any part of our sovereignty." The irreconcilables, he continued, wanted peace and recognized that international cooperation was necessary to maintain it. However, they did not believe that cooperation should be carried to the extent of sacrificing American rights and sovereignty. Fall concluded his comments with the prediction that in a few months the United States would be host, at Washington, to a peace conference of all the nations of the world.[5]

Another notable who called on Harding was Nicholas Murray Butler. Harding told Butler that he felt the American people wanted an "association of nations," but did not want to have anything to do with the League of Nations. Butler urged the President-elect to reconsider this view and take the nation into the League after the way was prepared by suitable amendments. If Harding could not follow this course, Butler favored, as the next best solution, a conference at Washington. This meeting would serve to clear up the problems left by the war, bring about a reduction of armament, settle the problems of Far Eastern policy, and provide a proper setting for the launching of an "association of nations."[6]

Many other notables conferred with Harding during the ensuing days. On December 18 the *New York Times* headlined the news: "Harding Has Plan for World Peace Already in Mind." It was revealed at this time that he had discussed this plan with all of the "best minds" who had visited him at Marion during the previous two weeks. Although no definite details were given to the public, the information released indicated that the plan included an "association of nations." There appeared to be general agreement among Republican leaders, including the irreconcilables in the Senate, that such an organization should be established.

During this same period Harding also made statements, more inclusive than precise, as to his attitude on the second of his two major problems, the limitation of armament. In accepting the nomination he had declared, "I can hear in the call of conscience an insistent

71

voice for the largely reduced armaments throughout the world—we must give of American leadership to that invaluable accomplishment." [7] However, in the same speech he also asserted, "We hold to our right, and mean to defend, aye, we mean to sustain, the rights of this nation and our citizens alike, everywhere under the shining sun." [8] This note was reflected in a typical campaign speech made in September. Harding stated that he hoped for peace and a measure of disarmament, but, until such a time as disarmament could be reached by mutual agreement, he felt the United States should maintain the most effective and dependable navy in the world. After his election the President-elect continued to espouse this theory and, in December, delivered a pugnacious speech in which he praised the navy. He desired a nation "righteous in its purposes and righteous in its commerce," with the ability and willingness to defend these interests. [9] An editorial which appeared in his own paper, the *Marion Star,* on December 31, probably was most representative of the real convictions of the President-to-be. Here it was noted that the United States could reach supremacy on the sea by 1924 in spite of all efforts of Japan or Britain to match America's building; therefore, the wisest policy was to attain supremacy before attempting any reduction of armament.

Early in 1921, Harding apparently clarified his foreign policy when, in an interview with Jacob Gould Schurman, he announced that the problems of establishing an "association of nations" and of convening an armament conference were closely related. The President-elect, according to Schurman, felt at this time that the basic problem in policy was the establishment of the "association of nations." When this step had been successfully carried out the "association" would work for disarmament, codify international law, establish a world court, and organize world conferences to settle disputes which were beyond the scope of international law. [10] Harding further elucidated his policy three days later. He would not call a separate disarmament conference, but would leave that problem to the "association of nations." [11]

Subsequently this policy outlined to Schurman was befogged by conflicting reports in the press. One of these stated that Harding would call a conference for disarmament soon after becoming President. Full details of this plan would be made public in the inaugural address. Harding himself was quoted, a few days later, as hoping a conference for disarmament could be called. However, he denied he had gone so far as to contact foreign nations as to their attitude toward such a proposal. Speculation on the President-elect's policy was brought to a standstill on January 24 when Harding refused to answer questions saying that he did not want to worry about anything and was going to Florida for a two weeks' vacation.[12]

After this enforced respite, the press took up once again the problem of determining the President-elect's policy. Chairman Butler of the House Naval Affairs Committee, citing Harding as his authority, told the press, February 5, that the President-elect definitely would call a disarmament conference. A week later Harding announced that he would make no preparation for a conference until after taking office. He re-emphasized his earlier policy that disarmament was to be dealt with by his "association of nations." These views precluded definite steps toward calling a conference until sometime after he assumed office.

In spite of these rather definite statements, there was continued speculation as to Harding's policy on disarmament. A Canadian paper expressed the opinion: "There is reason to believe that President Harding intends to call a conference on general disarmament early in his administration." [13]

As a result of these conflicting reports, the public's understanding of Harding's foreign policy was almost as muddled on the eve of his inauguration as it had been before the President-elect began "clarifying" it. The press, which had tried hard to ascribe a definite policy to him, was becoming discouraged. The *New Republic,* for example, doubting that Harding had any policy at all, characterized his position as one of "honest bewilderment." He had agreed to do everything "becoming" to bring about disarmament, which meant "I may do everything, or I may do nothing, but whatever I do it will be becoming." [14]

This failure to define a policy increased the interest throughout the country as to what the President might say on foreign affairs when the day for his inaugural came. However, Harding's address, while defining the general scope and direction of foreign policy, did little to clarify his position on specific issues. The postulate on which his policy was to be founded was complete independence for the United States in its international relations. America would "enter into no political commitments nor assume any economic obligations or subject our decisions to any other than our own authority." Even more specific in defining this ideal was the President's statement that "the League Covenant can have no sanction by us." He added that world "super-government" was "contrary to everything we cherish"; the policy of independent action was "patriotic adherence to the things that made us what we are." The President hastened to qualify his views on isolation. The United States, he declared, stood ready to associate itself with the countries of the world in conference "to find a way to approximate disarmament"; also "to suggest plans for arbitration and the establishment of a world court"; and to make offensive war so hateful that those who resorted to it would stand "as outlaws before the bar of civilization." This cooperation would not violate his basic postulate, for: "Every commitment must be made in the exercise of our national sovereignty." [15]

The *New York Times,* in summarizing the President's position in foreign affairs, stated: "Harding says we are ready to associate ourselves with the nations of the world, but at the same time we want to have nothing to do with them." [16] The *Newark News* complained that "The mists that all along enveloped his intent have not been dispelled"; the *Springfield Republican* commented that the President's program was too vague in its outlines to permit any profitable discussion.

The journals more in sympathy with the President's point of view did not attempt to show that he had any well defined policy. They praised instead his sound judgment in steering a middle course which made it possible to "espouse any form of international agreement to prevent war, which, in his judgment, may appear practicable and hopeful." [17]

For more than a month after the inaugural Harding gave no further elucidation of policy. His only important step in this direction was to select and to gain Senate confirmation for his Cabinet. Its personnel was of vital significance since Harding, aware of his limitations, envisaged himself as a conciliator between "best minds" rather than a dominant leader. While he was often described in contemporary journals as a man of homely virtue and common sense, it was seldom maintained that he was a man of outstanding ability. He was the candidate who favored "normalcy rather than nostrums," and who was selected to be an errand boy for the Old Guard in the Senate. Indeed, the people had become so surfeited with outstanding ability in public officials, as exemplified by Wilson, that Harding's very mediocrity had been transformed into a vote-winning virtue. Under the circumstances, Harding's policies in foreign affairs and in other matters were expected to be set by his advisors in the Cabinet and in the Senate.

For the vital post of Secretary of State, Harding, after much deliberation, chose Charles Evans Hughes, former Supreme Court Justice and Republican candidate for President in 1916.[18] He was acclaimed the strongest man that Harding could have picked for the office and the ablest man in the Cabinet. His selection was interpreted, especially by those who favored such a policy, as an indication that the administration intended to foster international cooperation. Hughes had favored entry into the League of Nations modified by reservations; his appointment was opposed by the irreconcilables in the Senate. It was reported that he had accepted the cabinet post only upon condition that he was to have a free hand in the management of his affairs.[19] After his appointment the President asserted that the Secretary of State would run the Department and manage the country's foreign affairs. Finally, it was believed that Hughes would be his own master rather than a tool of the Senate; his past record indicated that he was insensitive to political considerations and fearless in carrying out an independent course of action.[20]

In spite of these factors, as the first weeks of the Harding administration passed, it became evident that the new Secretary of State was not disposed to clash with the Senate on the question of the League of Nations. At this time, and for the next six months, Hughes ignored the League of Nations so completely that he did not even acknowledge its communications. They were carefully filed, but never read by his Department.[21] Whatever his personal feelings were, the new Secretary, who was ever the realist, apparently felt the League issue too hopeless to merit a struggle.

Another event early in the Harding administration, vital to foreign policy, was the announcement, on March 15, that the new President would address the special session of Congress which would convene in April.

The speech made by Harding on this occasion constituted his most complete and considered statement on foreign policy prior to the calling of the Washington Conference. For the greater portion of the speech the President dealt with domestic affairs. He emphasized that the Republican administration, in solving the problems facing the country, would begin with "our problems at home." The latter part of his address Harding devoted to the problems of foreign affairs, defining in greater detail his policy—the general outline of which had been revealed in the inaugural address.

In regard to the League, Harding followed the course already established by Secretary of State Hughes, when he declared, "In the existing League of Nations, world governing with its superpowers, this republic will have no part . . . the League Covenant can have no sanction by us." This pronouncement was greeted with a great demonstration of enthusiasm by the Senate Republicans. Harding, as in earlier addresses, maintained that the United States although rejecting the League was still anxious to aid the cause of peace by international cooperation. The campaign pledge by the Republican party to establish an "association of nations" would be faithfully kept, the President assured the people. The new international organization would be "conceived solely as an instrumentality of justice, unassociated with the passions of yesteryear." It would be carefully designed to guarantee the ideal of American independence in foreign affairs, and to prevent "the surrender of national sovereignty." The United States should never be a party to any plan which required the use of force in unknown contingencies, the recognition of a superauthority in government, or the enforcement of the Versailles Treaty.

In this exposition he neglected to explain the positive attributes of this new organization to secure the peace, but stated that he would continue to work to achieve its establishment. The most tangible evidence was his assertion of the willingness of the United States to cooperate with other nations to settle specific problems.[22] In short, the President with "the advice of the Senate" would, in a strictly limited way, enter the field of international cooperation in the solution of world problems through conferences and the "association of nations."[23]

Harding turned then to disarmament, which he recognized as one of the pressing problems for the "association" to solve. He sounded a note of caution when he declared, "The Government is in accord with the wish to eliminate the burdens of heavy armament . . . and stands ready to cooperate with other nations to approximate disarmament, but prudence forbids that we disarm alone."

The appraisals in the press on this address were divided. The *Chicago Evening Post* commented that Harding evidently planned to control his own foreign policy and praised him for his determination to take foreign affairs "out of the hands of the world-hating Senators." On the other hand, the President's "association of nations" was characterized as "a toothless whatnot, with no power to promote peace except to talk about it." The *New York World* denounced Harding's whole policy as "nothing better than an attempt on the part of the administration to compromise the foreign affairs of the United States in order to vindicate the partisan record of the United States Senate during the last two years." [24]

Harding, after two months in office, appeared to be gradually evolving a foreign policy. As his plans took form it became clear that American traditions in foreign affairs, as he interpreted them, were to be preserved. For this reason the League of Nations had been rejected finally, and in its place an "association of nations" more in keeping with American traditions had been promised. As to disarmament, the President had repeatedly declared himself in favor of it provided the United States first became supreme on the sea. Furthermore, he objected to the Borah Resolution on the ground that it was an invasion of executive authority. Indeed, the "wooden Indian" President, who had been destined to be the antithesis of the dominant Wilson, seemed to be coming to life and assuming leadership.

Public Opinion and the Borah Resolution

. . . By the spring of 1921 many leaders of public opinion had become convinced that the limitation of armament rather than the establishment of a world league for peace was the fundamental solution of America's problems in foreign relations. The public, thus influenced, grew to believe that disarmament should precede the establishment of an "association of nations." President Harding's plan to put the "association" first would delay disarmament while necessitating the development of a complex organization whose benefits would seem remote and abstract. By contrast, disarmament could be achieved in one conference. Its practical and tangible benefits would soon become evident in a reduction of taxes and a warless world.

The public, as a result of these factors, was unworried by Harding's failure to produce an "association of nations" immediately after his inauguration, but was disappointed by the President's vague, inconsistent, and procrastinating policy toward disarmament. Public opinion, as yet weak, was taking form. While individuals favored disarmament, this sentiment was mostly scattered, diffused, and lacked coordinated support.

The only organized groups favoring disarmament in December, at the time of the introduction of the Borah Resolution, were the various churches in the nation. With the return of peace, church leaders were somewhat embarrassed by the militarism which they had often exhibited during the course of the war. Consequently, they were very anxious to prove their adherence to the traditional Christian ideal of peace on earth by showing their zeal for disarmament. A symposium on disarmament, which appeared in the *New York World* shortly after the first of the year, revealed that "all shades of religious belief take up the new crusade [for disarmament] with the unanimity of spirit with which they answered the call to arms in 1917."

This finding was borne out by public expressions from the churches of various faiths during the next few months. The *Reformed Church Messenger* was typical of many church groups when it stated:

Now is the time for the Churches of Christ to speak in favor of a 'naval holiday' and the reduction of armaments in general. . . . It does seem as tho [*sic*] one theme concerning the application of Christian principles to present-day duty on which all American preachers should be able to unite at the beginning of the new year is in a demand for American leadership in this duty of hastening disarmament.

For the Catholic Church, the Pope, through Cardinal Gasparri, approved the principle of world disarmament stating that he had suggested it himself in August of 1917. The *Jewish Voice* expressed the opinion of the members of that faith in an article favoring disarmament which closed with the observation that "a weapon in a man's hand was the best seed of hate that could be invented." [1]

This sentiment on the part of the various sects was quickly directed into organized channels. The Federal Council of Churches meeting in Boston, December 1920, adopted a resolution expressing concern over the problem of competitive armament. The Administrative Council of this organization requested the churches on April 8, 1921, to urge that the United States government initiate a world conference for the limitation of armament. Almost simultaneously another church group, the Church Peace Union, lent its influence toward arousing the public to the need for disarmament. It set up a special committee on disarmament representing Catholic, Jewish, and Protestant faiths, which went to work immediately for the cause. [2]

Another important factor in developing public interest was the leadership of Senator Borah. With his resolution in December Borah had captured the public's imagination and crystallized the people's desire for disarmament. The Senator had been gratified by the instant enthusiasm which his proposal had created, yet he had realized from the first that to be effective public opinion must be continually stirred. Once aroused it must be directed and integrated. [3] To this end Borah worked unceasingly in the Senate. In addition, he gave numerous public addresses, gave interviews to the newspapers, and sent telegrams to public meetings in the interest of disarmament when he was unable to attend. Not the least of his contributions was his vast personal correspondence with people in all walks of life throughout the United States. He received hundreds of letters approving his work for

79

the limitation of armament, replying to each one with a personal note of thanks and exhortation to continue the work.[4] To the people at large, Senator Borah became a combination of a knight errant, championing their cause in the halls of Congress, and kindly grandfather, ready to hear and sympathize with the aspirations of the weak.

The Senator's diverse following was well illustrated in a letter he received which read as follows: "My family consisting of my father, manager of the Henry George Lecture Association, my brother, a university student, my mother, a busy house wife and myself, a school boy, wish to show our appreciation of your effort for universal disarmament."[5] To letters such as this a typical reply from Borah was, "The longer I am in public life, the less I think of the vision and patriotism and good faith of leaders and the more profoundly I respect the wisdom and patriotism of the masses. Therein lies the hope, and the only hope, for disarmament."[6] Borah constantly reiterated the opinion that the people must lead the way to disarmament. Frequently he declared, "There is no way to prevent this competitive armament race except through the power of public opinion, through and by means of the activities of the people who pay the taxes."[7] If the people did not prevent it, Borah constantly warned, the disarmament movement would be shunted aside by "sinister and unseen forces."[8] He therefore urged his correspondents to write members of the House and Senate and other men in public life requesting their influence to help bring about the limitation of armament.[9] On one occasion he asserted, "Unless we build up with tremendous effect the public opinion of the country and keep it alive and sustained, there is no possible hope of accomplishing anything."[10] Partially as a result of Borah's efforts, definite steps to turn mass opinion into organized opinion were taken in the first few weeks following Harding's inauguration.

Borah's leadership encouraged various national groups to oppose officially the continued building of naval armament. One of the first of these was an insurgent branch of the National Women's Party. This faction favored disarmament as the primary objective of the national unit. When this minority failed to win the support for its program from the group as a whole, it left the parent club and reorganized as the Women's Committee for World Disarmament. This group, which soon gained the blessing and support of Senator

Borah, declared March 12, that its purpose was to "organize the mass sentiment for disarmament and bring it to bear on Congress." [11] Thus was inaugurated a new phase in the disarmament movement.

The influence of the Women's Committee soon became widespread. Its initial step had been to constitute itself as a national coordinating committee on disarmament for all of the major national women's organizations in the nation, including the League of Women Voters, the Women's Christian Temperance Union, and the Federation of Women's Clubs. The Committee soon began to marshal its resources in order to challenge an even larger public by dramatizing the cause of disarmament. This campaign was launched by a mass meeting held in Washington at the National Theatre. Appropriately it was addressed by Senator Borah. In a stirring oration he declared:

It would seem perfectly clear that it is the duty of our Government, of our people, to demonstrate beyond question our good faith in bringing about a conference and an agreement for disarmament. To urge disarmament upon our part, with corresponding action upon the part of other naval powers, would be at once to discredit the whole movement. But to urge a conference, or an agreement, through, and by means of which, this competitive naval building program will cease and naval competition have an end, is the part of enlightened patriotism. To procrastinate in regard to such a program is to make it all the more difficult to effectuate when we come to take it up.[12]

One of the organizations in this group which was especially active in leading the popular demand for the limitation of armament was the League of Women Voters. When the annual convention of this group was called in Cleveland, in April 1921, Senator Borah, in an interview released by the *Philadelphia Public Ledger,* expressed the hope that disarmament would be a prominent subject for discussion at the meeting. Whether in compliance with Borah's suggestion or not, a much discussed issue at the convention was disarmament. Enthusiasm of the delegates was raised to a climax by the veteran suffragette, Mrs. Carrie Chapman Catt, who discarded her prepared address and delivered an impassioned extemporaneous plea for disarmament. She declared that "there isn't anything that can't be done in this country as a result of popular opinion." Thus, emphasizing the power of the people and the need for disarmament, she concluded her appeal with the command, "For God's sake, do something." [13] Her plea was heeded, for before the close of this convention a resolu-

81

tion calling for disarmament was passed by a unanimous vote. A committee was appointed to present this petition to President Harding.

This quickening interest, fostered by women's organizations, began to manifest itself in Washington early in April. Before the month was over the President had been fairly inundated by petitions demanding immediate disarmament. On April 19, a typical day, Harding was host to the Women's Committee for World Disarmament, the League of Women Voters, and a deputation including among its members representatives of the General Federation of Women's Clubs, the National Consumers League, the National Council of Jewish Women, and the Women's Christian Temperance Union.

Harding at first attempted to cope with this insistent demand by agreeable evasiveness. The task was too great—even for one with his outstanding talent in obfuscation. The President finally told the Women's Committee for World Disarmament that no positive steps toward disarmament could be taken by the United States until a peace treaty with Germany had been drawn up and ratified by the Senate.[14] Even so, he assured these citizens they "would not be disappointed."

The President only a few days later seemed to have forgotten this promise or to have become bolder once the ladies were out of sight. He publicly stated that he did not favor curtailment of the 1916 naval building program, and felt that the limitation of armament should not be undertaken until after the completion of the naval building program late in 1924.[15] It began to appear that Senator Borah had been correct when he advised the Women's Committee on World Disarmament that the new administration was absolutely opposed to his resolution. The President and to a lesser degree the Senate now became the objects of renewed and vigorous attacks by the advocates of disarmament. These efforts were given further incentive because Congress, during May and June, was considering the Naval Appropriations Bill and the accompanying disarmament resolutions. Public interest was attested by the fact that more than five hundred petitions for disarmament were recorded in the *Congressional Record* between May 5 and June 22.[16]

Prominent in this accelerated drive was the Washington Committee, as the Women's Committee on World Disarmament was now designated. One spectacular accomplishment of this group was the proclamation of a National Disarmament Week for May 22-29. This idea was not formulated until May 2, yet thirty-three states united in the observance of the occasion. As a climax to this event, numerous petitions for disarmament were sent to Washington. This demonstration offered Senator Borah an opportunity to exhort the people further. He publicly commended the committee and restated his belief that unless the public interest was maintained, no progress would be made toward disarmament. If the government were left to itself, it would fall into "the old practice and system of postponing and procrastinating . . . trusting and believing that the people will forget about it and that the cause will be killed through discouragement and delay." [17]

Eventually, the Washington Committee was able to expand its program into thirty states. In many states, groups of women, known as the "Women's Flying Squadrons for Disarmament," toured from town to town attempting to arouse popular demand for a conference. The League of Women Voters also lent its influence to this drive. In addition, by May 25, it had worked out the internal organization necessary to enlist the full cooperation of all of its local branches.

Although it would be impossible to estimate the relative value of the work of these organizations, numerically speaking the greatest force was exerted by the churches of the United States. The Church Peace Union, one of the leading organizations, sought the advice of General Bliss while planning its campaign for disarmament. The General replied:

> If the clergymen of the United States want to secure a limitation of armaments they can do it without any further waste of time. If, on an agreed-upon date, they simultaneously preach one sermon on this subject in every church of every creed throughout the United States, and conclude their services by having their congregations adopt a resolution addressed to their particular Congressmen, urging upon them the necessity of having a business conference of five nations upon the subject, the thing will be done.[18]

Subsequently, a group of churchmen held a Congress on the Reduction of Armaments in Chicago from May 17 to May 19, 1921. This group adopted unanimously a resolution calling on President Harding to invite Great Britain immediately to a conference for the limitation of naval armaments by mutual agreement. It was decided at this meeting to follow the advice of General Bliss in setting aside

83

one Sunday for nation-wide emphasis on the cause of disarmament. A letter was prepared and distributed to thirty thousand churches in which the principal Protestant, Catholic, and Jewish organizations urged the pastors to exhort their congregations to send petitions to their senators. Each pastor was invited to place his signature on a national petition addressed to the President and the Congress, recommending a conference for the reduction of armament at the earliest possible date. This plan was carried out. On June 5, the appointed Sunday, the Senate was deluged with resolutions from churches all over the country. Three weeks later the petition of the clergymen, which carried more than twenty thousand names, was presented to Harding by a delegation of churchmen.[19]

Numerous other groups effectively expressed their opposition to armament before the calling of the Washington Conference. Both management and labor agreed on this issue. The American Federation of Labor, June 18, presented Harding with a petition. They also rendered vital service for the disarmament movement in the months immediately preceding and during the conference. Business groups were not actively engaged in petitioning the government for a conference; however, men holding responsible and influential positions approved disarmament in statements which carried weight with official circles.

When Harding issued an invitation for a disarmament conference on July 11, these organized blocs of public opinion saw their aim achieved. The influence of the public in securing this result was of great, though indeterminable, significance. The insistent public demand was to a great degree the work of Senator Borah. So outstanding was his contribution that even a Democratic senator declared, "More than any other man in America he crystallized sentiment for the limitation of armament." [20] Yet it was largely a blind movement by the public insofar as the real issues in international affairs were concerned. A study of the petitions of the people and the speeches of senators show that both were chiefly concerned in defeating, as easily as possible, two old enemies, war and taxes. A shrewd contemporary observer summed up the situation by stating that Americans were sincere in their desire to bring peace, but, in advocating disarmament, they sought it down the pleasant road of tax reduction rather than down the painful path of sacrifice and justice.[21]

84

9 ...

Adoption of the Borah Resolution

. . . CONGRESS, with the convening of the special session of April 11, resumed its consideration of the still unsolved problem of national defense and the limitation of armament. Although there was much sentiment in Congress favoring the Borah Resolution, it was steadfastly opposed by the President and his followers in both houses. They continued, as in the previous session, to assert that it was a usurpation of Executive authority, and was impractical due to its limited scope. This opposition, so the leaders of public opinion maintained, dissolved only because of mounting popular demand for disarmament.

The House began consideration of the Naval Appropriation Bill with the presentation of four resolutions for the limitation of armament.[1] As the debate developed, the relation of disarmament to national defense became the primary issue. The fundamental difficulty was the relative status of the United States Navy at the time disarmament was to be undertaken. By its decision on this issue Congress would determine whether a conference for the limitation of armament would be called within a few months, or postponed for three or possibly four years.

The administration's position of naval supremacy first and disarmament second was well expressed by Bourke Cockran. "Second-best armament," he told the House, "is like the second-best hand at poker. It serves no purpose except to get its holder into mischief and bring him to disaster if not ruin." The only safe course for the United States was to build the greatest army and navy in the world. Then, declared Cockran, this country could say to the nations, "We will be first in armament if you make us; we will be first in disarmament if you let us."[2]

The opposing factions, largely Democratic, felt that if supremacy were stressed disarmament would be sidetracked. They distrusted

85

Harding's devotion to the cause, and intimated that the administration's real purpose in stressing naval supremacy was to delay disarmament until it died. The Democrats asserted that the wisest course was to call a conference immediately for the limitation of armament. To assure Harding's compliance with their theory they sought to pass a resolution which would withhold a part of the naval appropriation until after the President issued a call for a disarmament conference.[3] This division of opinion, which was partisan in nature, led to an acrimonious debate in the House. The Democrats charged that the Republican majority was weak and uncertain in its leadership to secure the disarmament conference demanded by an overwhelming majority of the American people. The Republicans were anxious to talk about disarmament but very cautious about procuring it.[4] In this respect, Harding was classified as the arch offender. Representative Eugene Black summarized his party's opinion when he declared, "The President has told us over and over again that he favors disarmament but the trouble about it is that we have got no further than the telling and the time has come when the American people want something done on this important question." In a final thrust of irony, Black suggested that the House ought to pass a resolution on disarmament as an aid to the President "because of the great difficulty that he has thus far had in making up his mind on this vital and important question."

The Republicans denied all these charges, defending with great eloquence the sagacity and nobility of purpose of their President. Frank W. Mondell spoke for his party when he accused the Democrats of pandering to the public's ill-conceived wishes. "The trouble is that you gentlemen want, apparently, to have the credit of being a little more anxious than the rest of us to do something about disarmament just at this time, whether it is sound or otherwise, whether or not it is sane or sensible."[5] The Democrats, he implied, were politicians catering to the whims of the public, while the Republicans were statesmen concerned with the public's ultimate welfare.

The debate resulted in a Republican victory. The House defeated all resolutions to effect disarmament which were offered as amendments to the Naval Appropriation Bill. The bill itself passed by a vote of 212 to 15.[6]

The press interpreted this decision by the House—for naval supremacy before disarmament—as a personal victory for President Harding. Certainly it was commensurate with the ideals which the President had recently proclaimed. Reviewing the Atlantic Fleet at Norfolk, he had delivered what was described as a "fighting speech to fighting men." He declared that this country coveted nothing which was not rightfully its own, but it meant to keep, at all cost, that to which it was entitled. The *Washington Post,* which often reflected the administration's policies, called this speech a blow at disarmament, crediting it with great influence in the House's decision to defeat proposals for disarmament.[7]

Apparently encouraged by this event, and more determined to forestall immediate disarmament, Harding announced publicly, May 3, that he was opposed to the Borah Resolution. It constituted, he felt, an improper invasion of the President's prerogatives in the management of the nation's foreign policy.[8] This attack by the President assumed increased importance since the Senate had just taken for consideration the Naval Appropriation Bill recently passed by the House. Further significance was to be found in the recommendation by the Senate Committee on Naval Affairs: This committee recommended that the huge Naval Appropriation Bill just passed by the House, without any provision for disarmament in the future, be increased by $100,000,000. When the debate opened in the Senate, Miles Poindexter, an administration Republican, gave a typical defense of the policy of supremacy when he declared:

The existence of the Navy, whether it is used or not, will do much to bring about such an agreement [disarmament] and to secure justice for the national interests and protect the welfare of this great Nation and its people. If it is not in existence the United States will be compelled to accept the terms of foreign countries with whom we are negotiating.[9]

The opposition did not lose faith despite the apparent hopelessness of its cause. Senator Borah and Senator King led the attack. While in favor of a sound policy as to naval strength, they maintained that the proposed building program for the navy was useless as a security measure and dangerous in its implications. Borah protested that the United States did not need to expand its navy. It was already on a basis of equality with England, who had ceased building capital ships. Senator King agreed, in general, with this view but questioned the evidence cited by Borah. The British, said King, had stopped building naval craft in 1920. As a direct result of American naval expansion the English had recently authorized the building of four new battleships.[10] If the United States would reduce its building program, disarmament might be effectuated eventually. On the other hand, if America insisted on expansion to the point of supremacy, the suspicion and fears of foreign nations would be aroused. An unending spiral of competitive building would be set in motion, at unending cost to taxpayers.

A decrease rather than an increase in military expenditure should be planned, for the economy made possible by disarmament was badly needed. Senator Borah pointed out that even at that time 93 per cent of the government's income was being devoted to war. In contrast to this huge sum, only one per cent was allotted for the purposes of education. Security, said the Senator, was of paramount importance, but security lay in the character and intelligence of the people as well as in armament. Republican government itself might fail, Borah warned, unless this oppressive and inequitable policy were quickly altered.[11] Senator Lenroot summarized this argument by stating that "this Government must reduce its expenditures. If we do not do so, the people of the United States will find somebody who will. Expenditures can be reduced." [12]

Furthermore, it was charged that the huge expenditures for armament were encouraged by selfish interests which would profit by orders for naval armament. Senator LaFollette, to substantiate this indictment, presented to the Senate an elaborate chart showing the total profits and the percentage of profit of the nineteen leading steel companies in the United States for the period 1912 to 1918. The United States Steel Company, according to this chart, made a profit of 6.1 per cent on its capital investment from 1912 to 1914, and a 24.3 per cent return for the war years 1916 to 1918. The Bethlehem Steel Company in the same period had advanced its profits from 14.3 per cent to 48.8 per cent. LaFollette presented a detailed account of an investigation by the House Naval Affairs Committee in 1894. As a result of this investigation two prominent officials of the company had been charged with fraud in the fulfillment of government contracts. These and many other officials were guilty, according to LaFollette, who asserted, "Instead of being in their palatial offices . . . they ought to be in the penitentiary, wearing stripes." The evidence indicated unmistakably that the great interests which profited by the manufacture of armaments had international agreements as to the price of the materials of war, enabling them to place each country at their mercy. These interests, united with each other throughout the world, encouraged competitive building of armament between nations in order to increase the business of the armament trust in each of the competing countries.[13]

Meanwhile the demands of the public for immediate disarmament were becoming more and more insistent. The anti-administration senators sought to utilize this sentiment to embarrass the Republican administration by showing that it was fundamentally opposed to the popular demand for disarmament. They charged that Harding himself was covertly thwarting the will of the people, while openly professing to desire the limitation of the navy. The debate on this issue grew warm when Senator King, a Democrat, asked Senator Borah if the newspaper reports of Harding's opposition to the Borah Resolution were true, and, if so, what reason motivated the President. Borah answered that he did not think the President opposed the resolution, for in that case he would have stated his position directly to the Senate:

My candid opinion is, from a conversation which I had with the President himself, that he has made no such statement, and I take this opportunity to say that if any gentleman wishes it to be understood that the President has said any such thing, he ought to be willing . . . to say it and say it publicly, and state when and how the message was given, and just what it was.[14]

At this point Senator Frederick Hale suggested that Senator Poindexter, who had been quoted as the authority for the President's statement of policy, should be allowed to speak for himself. However, Poindexter was not in the Senate chamber at the time. Hale undertook to clarify the situation. While Harding favored disarmament, he opposed the Borah Resolution, feeling it unnecessary and presumptuous of Congress to instruct him as to policy.

Borah hastened to challenge this logic, calling foolish and unfounded the charge that the Senate was exercising improper authority by attempting to instruct the President in his foreign policy. According to Borah, the Senate did not infringe on the prerogative of the President when it expressed, as it had the right to do, its own opinion

89

as to the proper course of action for the nation. Commenting iron-
ically on the fear of some senators lest they encroach upon the authority of the President in foreign affairs, he asked what had suddenly caused the thirty-seven senators who signed the "Round
Robin," sent to President Wilson, to become sensitive to Executive
prerogatives.

Senator Hale once again came to the President's defense by reiterating the right of the Chief Executive to full control of foreign
affairs. Even if the President needed congressional authorization before calling an international conference, the Borah Resolution was
unnecessary, because the 1916 amendment to the Naval Appropriation Bill had given the necessary sanction. The President was not
opposed to disarmament, Hale repeated, but felt that it should be
postponed, for "this is not the time to go ahead with a resolution of
this kind . . ." since "foreign relations at the present time are extremely delicate. . . ." [15]

With the pro-disarmament group refusing to admit the validity of
these arguments, the Democrats continued to press the charge that
the Senate Republicans, so recently zealous in upholding the independence of the Senate, were not acting as a sovereign body but in
subservience to the orders of the President.

In spite of these denials of Executive dictatorship, there was a rapid
shift in senatorial opinion regarding the Borah Resolution between
May 17 and May 25, when the resolution was adopted. The press
carried accounts of further visits by Senators Hale and Poindexter to
the White House during this critical period.[16] When the Borah Resolution was finally passed, by a count of 74 to 0, the Associated Press
reported that "the vote was in conformity with the understanding
reached last week by the administration forces to give their support
to Senator Borah's plan." By this agreement Borah dropped his opposition to the proposal to add $100,000,000 to the appropriation
for the naval program in return for the passage of his resolution.[17]

The Democrats continued to charge that Harding controlled the
Senate Republicans. Senator Pat Harrison asserted that there had
been a definite shift in Republican opinion on the Borah Resolution
just before its passage. This shift, he stated, was a direct result of instructions from the White House. Harding had opposed the measure
and had planned to defeat it. Then it became apparent that a solid

90

Democratic minority plus the more liberal Republicans had mustered enough votes to pass it regardless of Harding's wishes. Thus, seeing that opposition was useless, the President ordered a vote in favor of the resolution.[18] The vitriolic James A. Reed described the situation by declaring that "no more pitiable spectacle of complete legislative subservience, of legislative truckling, of legislative crawling upon the belly at the feet of a master and licking the boots of authority" had ever been seen than that presented by the Republican majority in the Senate.[19]

The Republicans refuted all of these charges. Senator Poindexter emphatically denied that Harrison's assumption was true. Referring to the favorable vote and how it was secured he declared, "What I did I did entirely upon my own initiative." When questioned as to the purpose of his conferences at the White House, he refused to answer specifically, reiterating that his action was not "influenced in any way whatever or changed, by any word from the White House." [20]

The success of the Borah Resolution, according to the newspapers, was the result of the overwhelming tide of popular opinion which could no longer be stemmed. As one editor expressed it, the resolution "finally fought its way through to acceptance because of the solid and cumulative pressure behind it of American sentiment." [21]

The public celebrated its victory in securing the passage of the resolution which it felt would soon lead to a conference. Nevertheless, the significance of this measure was questioned by those senators who had formerly opposed it. Senator Poindexter asserted, later in the year, that the resolution was of no actual value because Harding had already taken definite steps in accordance with his pledges to bring about a conference for the limitation of armament.[22] The semi-official *Washington Post* reminded the public that Harding was "enthusiastically in favor of a reduction of armaments, both as a step toward the goal of universal peace and to relieve the tax burdens of all peoples." It asserted that he was only waiting for the first opportune moment to issue his call. Consequently, the paper continued, "the advocates of disarmament in Congress have no monopoly on the desire to accomplish this step in the progress of civilization." [23] In another issue, the *Washington Post* minimized the importance of the Borah Resolution, calling it "one of the most conspicuous examples of supererogation of which the Senate has ever been guilty." It stated that

91

the resolution invaded the Executive authority in a field where the Senate had no right to speak by demanding that the President espouse a policy which he had already plainly declared he favored. Lastly, the resolution was of little consequence, for it expressed only the opinion of the Senate and was "not in any way binding upon the President." [24]

It soon became evident that the administration, whatever its attitude might be on disarmament, was still opposed to the Borah Resolution. The advocates of disarmament feared that the administration had agreed to let the Borah Resolution pass in the Senate only because it was certain that the House, which had already defeated disarmament resolutions on two occasions, would likewise defeat a third proposal. Secretary of War John W. Weeks did nothing to allay these fears when he stated in a public speech on June 1, "The present administration is desirous of disarming so far as it is safe to go, but it is not the time to make the move for everlasting peace." [25] The feelings of many friends of disarmament were reflected in a letter from Frank Cobb, of the pro-disarmament *New York World,* to Senator Borah: "I share your suspicion and have yet to see any evidence of good faith in this matter of the other end of the Avenue. Perhaps we can smoke them out, however." [26]

When the appropriation bill was introduced into the House, June 1921, the issue of limitation of armament was brought to the fore immediately. Notwithstanding, the Borah Resolution was overlooked, and new resolutions for disarmament were presented. The most important of these was drawn by the President and Representative Porter at a lengthy conference. This resolution stated that the House of Representatives concurred with the President in his declared purpose to call a conference for the limitation of armament.[27]

It was suspected that the Porter Resolution was designed to replace the Borah Resolution. This fear was strengthened when the House conferees on the naval bill gave their approval to Porter's proposal. In the House the advocates of limitation of armament regarded the Porter Resolution as pious in expression, but impotent in effect. They sought to pass a motion instructing the House conferees on the naval bill to support the Borah Resolution. In the debate on this motion the Republicans maintained that the Borah Resolution was "narrow and restricted." They favored a disarmament conference of all nations and of all forms of armament on land as well as on the sea. The

Democrats, in rebuttal, insisted that the Porter Resolution, by attempting to deal with all problems, would succeed in solving none. A vote for the Porter Resolution was a vote to slay, at one stroke, the Borah Resolution and the hope of a practical solution to the problem of armament. Eventually, this motion to instruct the conferees was defeated on points of order.[28]

The advocates of disarmament in the House continued their efforts to defeat the Porter Resolution. Under the leadership of John N. Garner they began a concerted drive to force the majority to allow a vote on the Borah Resolution when the naval bill was returned to the House.

Representative Patrick H. Kelley, co-manager of the naval bill with Mondell, refused to sanction such a proposal and in defense of his position declared, "I think the Borah amendment should be amended. . . ." Mondell opposed this motion because it constituted an attempt to instruct the House Committee, a procedure which had been used only rarely in the past. He continued his arguments against the Borah Resolution itself, asserting that it was not, as it was being represented, the most important feature of the naval bill. The vital issue was the increase in appropriation of $100,000,000, which the Senate had added after the bill left the House. In closing, he criticized the motives of the Democrats in supporting disarmament: "All that we hear from that side is a partisan attempt to make political capital out of the disarmament provision of the bill." [29]

Such arguments kindled rather than quieted the opposition. Garner quoted the *Washington Post* as evidence that the House leaders were opposed to the Borah Resolution and favored the flaccid Porter Resolution. Garner then questioned the managers of the bill as to which of the two resolutions they favored. Kelley refused to reply, but Mondell declared his preference for the Porter Resolution. To Garner, this was proof that the administration leaders hoped to quash the Borah Resolution and wished to keep the House from voting on it.

Representative Tom Connally, continuing the opposition's attack, declared that if the House failed to endorse the Borah Resolution, disarmament would become a lost cause. It would do no good to pass the Porter Resolution. It was a "colorless, vapid, denatured, one-half of one per cent . . . resolution." The House, he continued, could not concur with the President's "declared purpose, and intention to call

93

an international conference" as the resolution proposed, for it was impossible to show "where the President has ever declared his intention to call such a conference." [30] James F. Byrnes of South Carolina added that the Porter Resolution amounted to "the funeral exercises of the Borah Amendment." The administration had opposed disarmament at every step. Borah had "pushed them to the brink of disarmament even if he could not throw them into it." This view was reiterated by Cockran of New York, who declared, "The Porter resolution is nothing but an attempt to evade the question of disarmament." Another member warned the majority to cooperate in allowing a vote on the Borah Resolution, or "make ready your answer to the people of America."

In reply to the avalanche of charges, Hamilton Fish of New York stated that the Porter Resolution was not an attempt to sidetrack disarmament. "It is an improvement upon the Borah Amendment, and is meant as such." The Porter Resolution went much further in achieving the real aims of those who favored disarmament than did the more restricted proposition of the Senator from Idaho, he declared.[31] The result of this debate was the defeat of the motion to let the House vote directly on the Borah Resolution.

Although the pro-disarmament members of the House were unable to carry any motion to guarantee them the right to vote on the Borah Resolution, other factors gave them this opportunity. The first indication the administration's position was crumbling came with the announcement that the House conferees on the naval bill had not opposed the Borah Resolution, as recommended by the House Foreign Affairs Committee. House leader Mondell, fearing that this action might result in overriding the administration, called for a vote on the Porter Resolution in the House, June 20. He hoped for a favorable vote which would counteract the revolt of the House conferees. However, June 20, Mondell announced that no vote would be taken. He explained that many of the members were out of the city and would be unable to vote unless the original date were altered.

Those members of the House who opposed the Porter Resolution were much encouraged by this development. The real cause of the postponement, they said, was Mondell's realization that he could not carry enough votes to pass the Porter Resolution, which they called "a legislative soft drink absolutely lacking in influence." [32]

More encouragement was soon offered by the Senate conferees on the naval bill. They dealt the Porter Resolution a mortal blow by agreeing to vote for a reduction of the $90,000,000 figure for supplies requested by the House, on condition that the Borah Resolution be subject to a direct vote in the House. This assured the members of the House the opportunity which they had been unable to secure by direct means.

Just before this vote was taken, Representative Mondell read a letter from Harding clearing the way for his supporters in Congress to vote for the Borah Resolution. In explanation, Harding noted the difficulty in "arriving at a satisfactory agreement with regard to the language to be used in expressing the favorable attitude of the Congress toward efforts to secure international agreements for the limitation of armaments." While expressing his appreciation to those who had sought his advice as to the form of expressing this attitude, he declared "that it is not of particular concern to the Administration what form the expression of Congress shall take. . . ." The administration favored "the broadest and most general terms," but the wording was not important, because the "favorable attitude of the Congress on this question . . ." was of more importance than "the form of expressing that attitude." The President further deprecated the efforts of Congress, and the significance of any resolution it passed, by stating, "I think it has been pretty well understood that the Administrative branch of the Government has already been seeking information with regard to the attitude of foreign nations on the general subject of disarmament." [33]

House leader Mondell in elucidating the President's letter stressed that the administration did not approve the Borah Resolution. The administration sanctioned a vote for the resolution despite its flaws. It was a prerequisite to the adoption of the appropriation bill, which had to be approved within the next two days. Furthermore, the Borah Resolution had little significance; the President for the previous six weeks had been carrying on the type of negotiations authorized by its terms. [34]

The supporters of the Borah Resolution were unimpressed by this reasoning, and in the final debate contradicted Harding's presentation of administration policy. Far from working to bring about disarmament, they asserted, the administration had never favored the cause, had opposed it at every opportunity, and had finally yielded only because popular demand became overpowering.

At the close of this debate the much contested Borah Resolution was voted on in the House. It was approved amidst cheers by a majority of 332 to 4, on June 29, 1921.[35]

10 . . .

The Administration and the Calling
of the Washington Conference

. . . DURING the first six months of 1921 the Harding administration had steadfastly opposed the Borah Resolution while constantly asserting its devotion to disarmament if it could be postponed
until after the United States had reached naval supremacy. However,
late in June the President assured the Congress that he not only favored immediate disarmament, but had already been negotiating for
some months to attain it. This sudden reversal of policy, so the pro-
moters of the resolution maintained, was a response to Senate and
public demand. The administration denied this, asserting that it was
completely independent of the Senate in formulating policy on the
limitation of armament.

Whether the Harding administration would have summoned a
conference had it not been for the public's demands and the insistence
of Borah and his followers in the Senate is a question of motives—a
field beyond the historian. The administration did delay and obstruct
the passage of the Borah Resolution. This might have been done, as
Borah charged, to kill disarmament by endless postponement. On the
other hand, it could have been the means to gain time needed to
solve difficult and complex diplomatic problems that stood in the way
of a conference. Congress had given little attention to questions of
this nature. Much of its time had been devoted to the technicalities
of congressional prerogatives in foreign policy. In international affairs
it had confined itself to the general questions of world peace and
naval supremacy. While Congress debated these general issues, the
administration worked diligently to clear the specific issues that stood
in the way of a conference.[1]

It was the more diligent in this respect because of the desire of the
Harding administration to assure the success of any conference it
sponsored. The Republicans made political capital by charging the

Democrats with failure at the Paris Peace Conference. Furthermore, the Republican party, in the presidential campaign of 1920, had challenged the theory of international relations espoused by the Wilson Democrats and had promised a plan more practical and more American. Senator Lodge reflected the attitude of his party when he wrote to Ambassador Harvey that the Washington Conference would accomplish a great deal and plainly demonstrate the wisdom of rejecting the League of Nations.[2] The emphasis on "success" became so pronounced that it drew criticism. During and after the Washington Conference it was frequently charged that the administration, intent upon giving the appearance of achievement, had made unwarranted concessions. In any event, the administration in its preliminary planning was cautious. It sought to limit the scope of a conference and made every effort to avoid being hurried into a meeting that would have little chance to succeed.

Among the problems which confronted the administration in its preparation for a conference for the limitation of armament were two which had been outstanding since the close of the war—the reconstruction of America's Far Eastern policy and the establishment of a new naval policy. Both issues had become progressively serious as the United States continued to drift outside of the League of Nations with none but a wavering foreign policy.

The need for a reaffirmation of American Far Eastern policy was emphasized by an increase in the chronic disorders in China. Two rival governments were contending for authority while civil strife rent the country. The United States recognized the government at Peking in preference to the one in Canton, but was constantly embarrassed by the failure of the Peking government to restore order in China, exercise its authority, and meet its obligations to foreign countries. An illustration of this latter difficulty was the failure of the Republic of China, at Peking, to meet the payment on loans extended to it by the Continental and Commercial Trust and Saving Company of New York. This company requested the State Department to interpose its authority, and Secretary Hughes responded with no less than nine notes on the matter.[3] The Secretary's concern was not limited to the financial welfare of the New York company alone. He recognized that the failure of the Peking government to meet this obligation tended to destroy confidence in China as a field for invest-

98

ment. Consequently, it would become more difficult to practice dollar diplomacy in bolstering Far Eastern policy.

Another complication, troublesome to the Republican administration, was the Chinese Eastern Railway. This line was in financial difficulties. Hughes feared that Russia or Japan would take advantage of this situation to proffer a loan, thereby gaining control of the railway which was the key to the control of Siberia. Hughes felt that this possibility should be counteracted by extending the scope of the recently organized Consortium. He believed control of the railway was a "matter of fundamental and urgent importance for the stabilization of the situation in the Far East." [4] Hughes was not able, however, to put this plan into effect, the American members of the Consortium disapproving of the suggestion as being unsound financially. The English, while favoring restraint of Japanese ambitions, were unwilling to aid the United States actively in making an issue of the control of the railroad. [5]

Added to the inherent complexity of the situation within China was the fact that the United States had to measure the need for cooperation with various other powers which maintained interests in the Far East. In dealing with a semi-colonial state, such as China, the American government was obliged to take into account the approval of France, England, Japan, and other powers.

The policy of the United States was complicated by the apparent ambition of the Japanese to establish an exclusive control of the Orient, a policy referred to by the Japanese as one of "special" or "paramount" interest. The basic conflict between the United States and Japan in the Far East, emphasized once again by the above mentioned disagreement over the Chinese Eastern Railroad, was of utmost importance in shaping the naval plans of the two nations. Americans feared that Japan was building an expanded navy, experimenting with submarines, and fortifying Pacific islands to establish its policy of aggression toward China. Likewise, in Japan it was asserted that the United States was building an increasingly large navy in order to have available the force needed to thwart the legitimate aspirations of Japan.

In addition, a serious obstacle to disarmament was the traditional composition of the Japanese government. The parties struggling for political supremacy—the Satsuma Clan, which controlled the navy;

the Choshu Clan, which controlled the army; and the liberal civilian party—would all be gravely affected by it. To limit the navy would ruin the Satsuma Clan politically. This powerful group could scarcely be expected to accept such a development without a struggle. Joint limitation of both army and navy as a compromise would redress the balance between the two older clans. Such a solution was not feasible, because it would result in a loss of power by the military caste, while increasing the power of the party representing civilian elements. Matters were complicated further by Japanese mistrust of American willingness to effect disarmament. This suspicion was fostered by the early enthusiasm for but subsequent rejection of the League of Nations by the United States. When this distrust was augmented by the constantly mounting tension between the two nations, it was relatively easy for the militarist to convince the Japanese people of the need for increased armament.[6]

Kiroku Hayashi, a leading Japanese statesman, asserted that the League of Nations had not met the problem of disarmament, this failure being largely a consequence of the United States' refusal to join the League. Because America realized its responsibility for this failure, it was now proposing a separate conference for disarmament. A wiser course of action, according to Hayashi, would be for the United States to join the League. A separate conference for disarmament would not prove practicable.[7]

In February, Yukio Ozaki, a member of the Japanese Parliament, introduced a resolution providing that Japan, after consultation with England and the United States, limit its navy and army. This proposal was rejected by an overwhelming vote, 285 to 38, which, according to the American ambassador in Japan, clearly represented the attitude of the governing classes on disarmament.[8] It was reported by a Tokyo newspaper that the parliamentary fight for immediate reduction of armament had been defeated. As a result the construction of naval vessels was being rushed at maximum capacity.[9] This meant that Japan would continue her "eight and eight program" (designed to give her by 1927 eight battleships and eight cruisers, all of which would be less than eight years old).

Nonetheless, in Japan, as in the United States, the popular movement for disarmament was reported to be gaining strength during the late spring of 1921. Marquis Shigenobu Okuma, a distinguished

100

elder statesman of Japan, noted for his devotion to nationalism (and baseball), asserted that Japan would join in a plan of disarmament, if the United States and England would take the lead. He added further, "If the Great Powers could mutually agree to reduce their armies and navies it would indeed be a blessed thing for Japan as well as for this war-weary world." [10] Despite the popular demand in Japan and the United States for disarmament, it was obvious to governmental leaders in both nations that no disarmament would be successful or possible until the fundamental problems of Far Eastern policy were stabilized. So long as rivalry and suspicion were rampant, no agreement to disarm would be observed long enough to be of significance.

The third nation whose cooperation was vital to any plans for disarmament was England. Again, the Far East was of paramount consideration by reason of the Anglo-Japanese Alliance. The United States government felt that, if the Anglo-Japanese Alliance could be broken and a joint Anglo-American Far Eastern policy substituted, America's problems in the Orient would be largely solved. Furthermore, there could be no disarmament until the United States and Britain reached an agreement on naval policy. Here again, the Alliance was vital, for the American Navy would agree to no curtailment of its forces, until the Alliance was abrogated. In the spring of 1921, Britain, still refusing to renounce the Alliance, provided for a great expansion of its navy. Relations between the two countries were further complicated by the problem of British policy toward Ireland and by popular American interference in the solution of this matter. Fortunately for the future success of the United States in solving its international problems, the British government, despite these facts, was very anxious to cultivate American friendship. It began to sense the possibility of serving this end, while stabilizing its own naval and Far Eastern policy. Under these conditions the success of the administration, in working out a joint Far Eastern policy and in reaching a compromise on sea power with England, would determine the degree of progress toward calling a conference for the limitation of armament.

No conference could be called until an understanding was reached on these matters. Yet there are no records in the files of the State Department to indicate any negotiation from the time Harding became President until the date on which the invitations to a disarmament conference were issued in July.[11] Obviously the two governments did work together for they had reached a mutual understanding by the latter date, but because of the diplomatic problems involved in American efforts to abrogate the Anglo-Japanese Alliance, the negotiations had to remain confidential.

In these circumstances unofficial communications between the British and American governments, for the purpose of seeking a common ground of understanding on these matters, might well have been exchanged. Supporting the thesis that such conversations did take place is an impressive array of evidence.

In July, 1921, the British Foreign Office was quoted in the London papers as follows:

Our whole attitude with regard to a conference amounts to this—that the idea of a conference has been canvassed in America during these last three or four months; ever since President Harding came into office. We have repeatedly informed the United States, both publicly and confidentially, that we should welcome a conference and we understand that the other countries concerned are of the same mind.[12]

Other officials of the two governments substantiated the existence of negotiations. In his letter to Congress, late in June, President Harding had asserted that the administration had been working to bring about the type of meeting that the Borah Resolution envisaged. Many years later Secretary of State Hughes declared that plans for a conference were taking definite shape during May and June.[13]

Further evidence appears in articles published in the *New York Times* in January and February, 1921. It was reported, January 18, that the British Ambassador Geddes had been recalled suddenly to England. The purpose of this hurried visit, according to the press, was to inform the ambassador as to Britain's latest plans in regard to disarmament and to instruct him to survey American opinion on disarmament when he returned.[14] Subsequently, it was asserted that Geddes was returning to the United States with full authorization to treat with the American government relative to the organization of a conference on disarmament.[15]

In the House of Representatives notice was taken of this mission. Representative Britten denounced all plans for immediate disarmament, including the Geddes mission, as attempts by the British to

102

maintain naval superiority without building costly ships.[16] The mission was also noted by President Harding, who was quoted as saying that Ambassador Geddes's conference with United States officials would have an important bearing on American decisions as to the advisability of a conference for the limitation of armament.[17]

A positive indication that the British were willing to reach an understanding regarding disarmament was the appointment, February 22, 1921, of Lord Lee as the First Lord of the British Admiralty. Since Lee was well known as an advocate of Anglo-American cooperation, his promotion was interpreted as part of a British policy of cooperation with the United States. This seemed to be confirmed when he spoke, March 16, before the Institute of Naval Architects, proposing a naval understanding with the United States. Britain was willing, declared Lee, to forsake its cherished tradition of naval supremacy and accept parity in order to prepare the way for an agreement which would eliminate the possibility of naval competition between the two nations.[18]

Although this speech created "something of a stir" in England, it provoked little reaction in the United States. It was accorded routine notice in the press, with only one popular magazine devoting a feature article to it.[19] The Senate appeared to be more impressed with the action of the British Parliament, late in March, in voting an appropriation for four new dreadnaughts, than by the words of the First Lord of the Admiralty. Even so, the statement of such an important official could not have been overlooked by the administration or have failed to influence its thinking. Lord Lee's speech was soon followed by renewed rumors that the two powers were conferring on matters relative to a conference for the limitation of naval armament.[20]

Later, publisher Adolph Ochs of the *New York Times,* who was in England on a visit, conferred with Lee on naval matters and agreed to act as an unofficial envoy. When Ochs returned to the United States, he informed Secretary of the Navy Edwin Denby, through a reporter, that Britain was willing to accept naval equality with the United States and to concentrate its fleet in the Atlantic.[21] This was a most important communication, since the American cabinet had been reported, only a few days before, to be studying naval policy, with particular emphasis on the practicability of placing the entire fleet of battleships in the Pacific Ocean.[22] Secretary Denby made no

103

reply, officially or unofficially, and did not immediately relay the information to the State Department. Lee's work was, however, of importance since it acquainted the administration with England's expressed willingness to work toward a satisfactory settlement of the naval problem.

Another hint of diplomatic activity was the report that American Ambassador George Harvey was holding conversations with the British government officials on the advisability of joint action for limiting naval building. This report was published June 1, five days after the Borah Resolution passed in the Senate. Any connection between the President's orders to the ambassador and the Senate's resolution was denied. Instructions to Harvey, according to this report, had been dispatched prior to the passage of the Borah Resolution.[23]

The next development of importance was the convening of the British Imperial Conference, June 20. Lloyd George, in a speech before the first meeting, declared:

There is no quarter of the world where we desire more greatly to maintain peace and fair play for all nations and to avoid a competition of armament than in the Pacific and in the Far East. . . . We desire to work with the great Republic [the United States] in all parts of the world. . . . Like it, we desire to avoid the growth of armaments, whether in the Pacific or elsewhere, and we rejoice that American opinion should be showing so much earnestness in that direction at the present time. We are ready to discuss with American statesmen any proposal for the limitation of armament which they may wish to set out, and we can undertake that no such overtures will find a lack of willingness on our part to meet them.[24]

Willingness to consult with the United States on matters concerning disarmament was even more emphatically expressed by Prime Minister Hughes of Australia at a later meeting of the Council. In his view, there would never be a time more favorable to disarmament than the present. He suggested that Lloyd George, on behalf of the Council, take the initiative toward bringing about disarmament:

Let us give the world, weary of war and staggering beneath its crushing burdens, a lead. Invite the United States of America, Japan and France to meet us. We cannot hope that the world will beat its sword into a ploughshare but at any rate it can stop building more ships. . . . Such an invitation issued with such authority behind it would, I think, find great support in America, and I hope and believe in Japan too.[25]

Efforts to establish an Anglo-American naval policy were being

104

made in the spring of 1921. Evidence indicates that the initiative for this movement came from the Senate resolutions on disarmament to which the British government responded promptly, though unofficially. The Harding administration had little to do with this phase of the preparation for a conference.

Concerning the Anglo-Japanese Alliance the situation was reversed. The Executive took the lead, stating the position of the United States and pressing the British government for a satisfactory settlement. The Alliance was of primary importance to the formulation of American plans, for it not only was the key to the Far Eastern policy of the nation, but also to disarmament.[26]

The American ambassador to England had been instructed to lose no opportunity to protest the renewal of the Alliance in unofficial statements, casual conversation, or by other informal means.[27] Meanwhile, the State Department was employing a similar policy in its dealings with the British ambassador.[28]

Opinion that the Alliance should be abrogated was strengthened by State Department reports from Japan. Its foreign policy, according to one of the reports, was in a state of flux, and aggressions in China and in Siberia might be redoubled with the renewal of the Alliance.[29]

The Japanese were thought to be desirous of continuing the Alliance. The wave of protest against it in 1915 and 1916 had subsided with the close of the war. A leading Tokyo paper reported in 1921 that the popular consensus in Japan favored its renewal. Other newspapers also advocated renewal. This sentiment was shared by many high officials in the government.[30] The Tokyo *Yorodzu,* in support of this opinion, declared that Americans who opposed it failed to understand that the Alliance was "necessary for the maintenance of peace in the Orient, and that it makes the functions of the League of Nations more effective locally." The official Japanese attitude was indicated by the ambassador to England, Baron Hayashi. He was strongly in favor of a renewal. To support his contention he made several public addresses in which he attempted to quiet the fears of the United States by demonstrating that the Alliance was not inimical to American interests in the Far East; it contained no threat to American security.[31]

The Japanese government also made direct attempts to improve relations with America. Late in June 1921, Ambassador Kijuro

Shidehara held conversations with Secretary Hughes relative to negotiating a treaty to cover the principal matters in dispute between the
two nations. He sought to gain approval of a statement on the Anglo-
Japanese Alliance which his government wished to publish. This
note stated that negotiations had not yet been undertaken to renew
the Alliance; it was in no way directed against the United States—
either for aggression or defense—and its chief purpose had always
been to preserve and consolidate the cause of peace in the Far East.[32]

In Britain, the government began to doubt the value of the Alliance as American opposition to it became apparent. While it was
expedient to meet this American view, it was inadvisable to sacrifice
Japanese friendship to this objective. As a solution, the English began
suggesting unofficially that the United States be invited to join the
Anglo-Japanese Alliance. This was not a new plan. It had been suggested in 1905, 1911, and 1917. The possibility of such an entente
was discussed with increasing frequency in 1920 and 1921. One of
the first of these discussions was reported to the State Department by
U. S. Smith, of the American mission in Budapest. He stated that the
June 19, 1920, issue of *Nepszava* carried an article on the possibility
of an American-Japanese-British alliance to replace the Anglo-Japanese Alliance. England, according to the report, was anxious to
establish such an agreement in order to eliminate herself as a factor
in the event of a Japanese-American war.[33] The inclusion of the
United States as a party to the Alliance was proposed from various
other quarters. The British periodical, *Round Table,* suggested in December 1920, that it be expanded into "a four-cornered entente" including, in addition to the original members, China and the United
States. The tripartite plan was approved in the various dominions
of the British Empire.

This plan was suggested directly to the American government late
in May by Sir Arthur Willert of Great Britain. The American Under
Secretary of State, who talked with Willert, felt that such a solution
was not feasible. The American people, he felt, would never consent
to join any alliance.[34] This conversation and the American objection
were not made public. Suggestions for a pact that would include the
United States continued to spring from various parts of the British
Empire. Prime Minister Hughes of Australia again presented the plan
early in June 1921, adding that any request by Japan for a renewal

of the Alliance should be countered by a British demand for the limitation of armament. The Prime Minister's perfected plan suggested the adoption of a modified alliance, providing for the limitation of arms to which the United States and France should be parties along with Japan and England.[35]

As the time for the meeting of the British Imperial Council drew near, there were renewed evidences that the British government and the dominions were willing to meet American demands in regard to the Alliance. Typical of the attitude of the premiers was the remark made by Hughes, of Australia. In regard to the Japanese question, Australians and western Americans "for all practical purposes view this problem eye to eye." In this statement just before the conference, Hughes demanded that the Alliance be modified into a form "acceptable to the United States." [36] With the British public the most popular solution of the problem was the often proposed tripartite pact. This suggestion was reiterated so frequently as to merit a satirical cartoon in the *Literary Digest,* July 2, 1921. A tripartite pact, however, aroused little attention and almost no enthusiasm among the people of the United States.

With the convening of the Imperial Council of the Empire in June, Britain began work toward a solution of the problem of the Alliance. At the opening session of the Imperial Council, Lloyd George referred to the Alliance in broad terms stressing the desire of Britain not only to consider the wishes of the United States, but also to meet the obligations which his nation felt toward Japan. He stated:

We look confidently to the Government and people of the United States for their sympathy and understanding in this respect. Friendly cooperation with the United States is for us a cardinal principle, dictated by what seems to us the proper nature of things, dictated by instinct quite as much as by reason and common sense.[37]

The next day, June 21, Prime Minister Hughes dealt with the Alliance. In general, Hughes declared himself to be in favor of renewal, yet in a form so modified as to make it perfectly clear that the United States was not jeopardized by its military clauses. He continued by asserting, "It is vital in the interest of civilization that a good understanding should exist between America and ourselves; we should endeavor to do everything in our power to ascertain exactly what it is to which America takes exception in this Treaty." He then added:

107

Whether it would be wiser to invite a Conference with America and Japan, to ascertain what would be mutually acceptable, is a suggestion which I throw out. If one were quite sure that America desired, or was prepared to accept, what would form a reasonable basis of an Alliance with Japan, then I certainly would strongly press the suggestion.

In any event, thought the Australian leader, the conference should obtain for its guidance a precise statement as to American objections to the Anglo-Japanese Alliance.[38]

In other speeches at the opening of the Council, Prime Minister Smuts stressed the need of friendship with the United States, asserting, "It seems clear that the only path of safety for the British Empire is a path on which she can walk together with America." Prime Minister Massey did not disagree with this point of view, but reviewed in detail the important service rendered the British by the Japanese during the First World War. In view of this record, he intimated that the friendship of Japan was perhaps as vital as the friendship of the United States. A more compromising tone was struck by Arthur Meighen. While he hoped to represent the prevailing opinion of the people of Canada, he was determined "to reach, if it can be reached, common ground with all representatives here."[39]

The next important step toward bringing about a conference for disarmament was the result of a conversation between British Ambassador Geddes and American Secretary of State Hughes. Ostensibly, this conversation was arranged to consider the report released by the Associated Press, June 22, and denied by the State Department, that the United States was being informed as to every move in the negotiations between Britain and Japan relative to the renewal of the Anglo-Japanese Alliance.[40] Whether this visit by the British ambassador was the result of the request at the Imperial Conference that the exact position of the United States in regard to the Alliance be determined is not demonstrable. In any event, Geddes did succeed in acquiring the information which the Australian Prime Minister had desired.

Secretary Hughes, during this conversation, informally and confidentially revealed the precise nature of America's objection to the Alliance. He did not even mention the possibility that it might bring Britain to the side of Japan in a war against the United States, (a fault which Australia had announced its willingness to rectify).[41] The

American Secretary declared that his country objected to the policy of exclusive control which Japan was establishing in the Far East. Hughes stressed the idea that:

. . . if Great Britain and Japan had any arrangement by which Great Britain was to support the "special interest" of Japan, the latter might be likely, at the instance of the militaristic party, to be led to take positions which would call forth protest from this Government, and that in making such representations this Government might find itself virtually alone. . . .

The policies of the United States and Great Britain in the Far East were similar, he added. It should be possible for the United States in executing its policy to have the support of Britain. Ambassador Geddes was warned subtly that failure of the British to comply with the American position might result in unpleasant repercussions in Congress when the resolution for the recognition of the Irish Republic was presented for consideration.[42] Hughes also emphasized that Congress was overwhelmingly opposed to renewal of the Alliance, with public opinion no less emphatic in its opposition.[43]

Geddes replied that Britain and Japan would not reach a decision on the Alliance by the July 13 deadline. Consequently, they would postpone for another year a final arrangement as to renewal of their pact. In the interim a modification of the Alliance, one acceptable to the United States, might be worked out.[44] Britain's position, according to the ambassador, was delicate. Japan could not be summarily dropped. If this were done, it would appear that England had used Japan, repudiating her as soon as her usefulness was at an end.

The remarks did not satisfy the American Secretary who wanted nothing less than an immediate denunciation of the pact. The British ambassador suggested a tripartite agreement, an idea popular throughout the empire. This, he felt, "might prove to be the best solution of the question." Japan would oppose such an agreement but could be persuaded to acquiesce. The entire matter could then be settled by an exchange of notes between the powers.

To this suggestion Hughes gave his personal but qualified approval. The agreement must not constitute an alliance; its principles must be in harmony with United States traditions in foreign policy. The American Secretary promised to discuss the matter with President Harding the same day, and to write to Geddes the official opinion of the United States. The British ambassador, Hughes continued, was free to quote the Secretary's personal views on the proposed tripartite pact. He stressed again that before any final settlement was made "the question would remain as to the essential character of the declaration." Also to be considered was the "practical application of the principles it would embody. These matters would probably determine the attitude of our Government toward it." [45] In short, Hughes felt certain that the United States would cooperate with the Japanese and the British, provided the agreement were drawn in a form which would meet the Senate's objections—prejudice against alliances, commitments, and obligations. This same day Hughes, after conferring with MacMurray, gave the Ambassador an official note confirming the opinion he had stated. [46]

The administration had maintained, in the face of an impetuous Senate and public, that it was not forestalling a conference but awaiting the first favorable opportunity for convoking one. [47] With the conclusion of the conversation with Geddes, Hughes had completed one of the most vital steps in preparation for a meeting. He now waited for the final adoption of the Borah Resolution and a definite reply from the British on the modification of the Anglo-Japanese Alliance. On June 29, Congress adopted the Naval Appropriation Bill to which the Borah Resolution was attached. Technically it was inoperative until the bill became law with the President's signature, on July 12. Hughes apparently would have preferred to wait for this event before issuing invitations to a conference, [48] for such a course would have avoided any possible offense to the Senate. Hughes recognized that it was imperative that the United States take the initiative in calling a conference and defining as its chief purpose the limitation of armament. Failing in these objectives there would be no possibility of Senate support for a conference. The rapid development of events in Great Britain made it expedient to act without official approval of the Senate in order to establish conditions which would assure success.

Between June 28 and July 1, the Imperial Council, meeting in London, agreed to modify the Anglo-Japanese Alliance, which was to remain in force for another year, beginning July 13. [49] In order to deal with the problem of redrafting the Alliance, the Council agreed, by July 2, that a conference should be held "to consider all essential matters bearing upon the Far East and Pacific Ocean with a view to

110

arriving at a common understanding designed to assure settlement by peaceful means, the elimination of naval warfare, consequent elimination of arms, etc." [50] To this end, the British Secretary for Foreign Affairs was instructed to inquire of Japan, China, and the United States, as to their reaction to this suggestion by the Imperial Conference. Lord Curzon discussed the matter with Harvey on July 5. However, Harvey had not been informed of the negotiations between Hughes and Geddes in regard to the Anglo-Japanese Alliance. [51] The Ambassador was so misinformed in general as to declare to the British that the Alliance was a matter of no concern to the United States. [52] He did not recognize the urgency of the situation or forward Curzon's request to Hughes. Curzon interviewed Harvey again explaining that Lloyd George was being hard pressed in the House of Commons for information regarding the Alliance and the possibility of a conference on Far Eastern affairs. The Prime Minister had promised to make a complete report in Parliament on July 11. [53] Harvey was goaded into action by this news. The next day, July 8, he cabled Hughes.

In the meantime the International News Service asked Hughes, July 7, to confirm a report that Great Britain and the United States had made an arrangement to take the place of the Anglo-Japanese Alliance. When Hughes protested that this was not accurate information, the reporter retorted that it had come directly from Downing Street. [54]

The same day Lloyd George, in giving the speech to which Curzon had made reference, declared that the nature of his address on July 11 would depend "upon the replies received from the United States, Japan, and China." [55] The rumor now gained credence that Great Britain was about to call a conference. The American press even charged the State Department with suppressing news which the British government was releasing to the newsmen of that country. [56]

Before hearing directly from Harvey as to these British plans, Hughes issued a dispatch instructing the ambassador to ascertain informally whether the British government would accept an invitation to participate in a conference on the limitation of armament to be held in Washington. [57] Apparently the rumors were sufficiently well substantiated from other sources to convince the Secretary that he must act immediately if American aims were to be achieved.

111

Harvey, in his dispatch of July 8, asserted, with unintentional irony, that it was important for the United States to gain the initiative in instigating the conference. He suggested that the President issue a statement to the press before Monday morning, the date scheduled for Lloyd George's speech to Parliament, declaring that he had received favorable replies to American inquiries concerning a conference. If the President merely replied to the British proposal, wrote Harvey, Lloyd George would appear to be solely responsible for initiating the conference whether he wished to take the credit or not.[58] It appeared that Harvey's fears were unfounded, for the British did not desire to claim the initiative. The *London Times* denied that a reply was expected from the United States in regard to a British inquiry for a conference. Lloyd George's statement before Parliament, July 7, that the nature of his speech on Monday, July 11, would depend "upon the replies received from the United States, Japan and China," said the *Times,* "may be regarded as officially non existent." [59]

To these messages Hughes replied that the United States' proposal for limitation of armament would stand, but, in order to lend additional strength to the President's initiative, a supplementary cable would be sent. It would include the original American proposal and also, as suggested by the British, the questions of the Far East. The President, in announcing to the press on Monday morning that the cable had been sent, would state that "on his own initiative he has asked the powers whether they would welcome such an invitation." [60]

The dispatch was followed shortly by another giving the complete text of the statement which the President was to release on Monday. Hughes requested that Harvey present this document to the British officials and have them make any suggestions which they thought advisable.[61] The Prime Minister, Harvey reported, felt the statement was admirable, approving it in its entirety. The *Times,* in an editorial which he had seen in advance of publication, was "splendidly appreciative of the President taking the initiative so opportunely and strongly."[62]

The text of Harding's message treated the American invitation to a conference for the limitation of armament as the primary issue. The Far East and Pacific problems, the chief concern of the British invitation, were included also, but only because it was "manifest that the question of limitation of armament has a close relation" to those problems.[63]

Acquiescence in this grouping of problems indicated that the English were completely aware of the importance of American initiative in sponsoring the conference. The British, from the time of Lord Lee's first attempts to gain an agreement on fleets, had recognized that a conference openly instigated by England would have slight chance for success. Such initiative would arouse the opposition of the numerous anti-English elements in the American population. At the same time it would incur the wrath of Japan by making it seem that England was anxious to forsake the Alliance. While willing to relinquish the honor of instigating the conference in order to smooth the path of diplomacy, England felt, with considerable justification, that the conference was primarily the result of her own efforts.[64]

The idea of a conference was not popular with government leaders in Japan. They had not shared in the preliminary planning and apparently felt that they were being summoned to account for their policies by an all-powerful and unsympathetic Anglo-American tribunal. They delayed in accepting the invitation while seeking to limit the scope of the conference.[65] These efforts failed, for the popular insistence on the conference was so great in all countries that Hughes was able to use it to bring pressure on Japan and win her agreement to support the conference. In a long series of negotiations the American Secretary resisted all efforts by the Japanese Ambassador to gain a specific definition of the meaning of "Pacific and Far Eastern problems." [66]

The popular approval of the conference in Japan and all other countries was overwhelming. Press dispatches from Paris, Rome, Tokyo, and Berlin, as well as London, told of cheering parliaments, approving statesmen, and civic leaders joining together in a world-circling chorus of approbation. "At last," said one of these enthusiasts, "we have set foot upon the road that will lead us to the era when the world's battleflags will be furled." Lloyd George called President Harding's act "one of far-seeing statesmanship"; French Premier Briand thanked the President for taking such a "noble step . . . which the world will hail with joy." The congratulations from the British Dominions and from Japan were equally warm. Throughout the world plans for disarmament were welcomed with

113

more enthusiasm and relief than any event since the signing of the armistice.[67]

When it is recalled that these events were taking place while Congress debated the resolution for disarmament, the apparent hesitancy of the administration to call a conference becomes understandable. Harding had, as he stated to Congress, June 29, been negotiating for a conference. The contention, by the leaders of public opinion, that the administration completely opposed disarmament but was forced to espouse the cause by the pressure of public demand, was overdrawn. The administration, it is true, gave precedence in its planning to sustaining America's commitment in foreign affairs, rather than to achieving disarmament. It was determined that American interest and rights should not be sacrificed to an impatient and imprudent desire for disarmament. In addition, there was a less laudable tendency to heed the importunities of the pressure groups favoring a big naval building program. Because of its preoccupation with the overall policy and its subservience to the "big navy" group, the administration probably would not have made the necessary effort to prepare the way for a disarmament conference had it not been for the insistent goading of the public. In the final analysis, it could not be maintained that public opinion, the Borah Resolution, the American administration, or the British government was the sole or even the principal factor in bringing about the Washington Conference. The conference was the result of the fortunate coincidence of the divergent aims of all of these indispensable factors.

The Senate and the Preliminary Preparations for the Washington Conference

. . . AFTER the convocation of the Washington Conference was assured, the Senate's influence on the foreign policy of the Harding administration immediately increased. The traditions of the Senate and the nature of the proposed conference made it practically certain that any international agreements which resulted would have to take the form of treaties which would be faced by the two-thirds rule. In this circumstance, the administration prepared for the future by paying deference to the known prejudices of the Senate.

The general expectation, both at home and abroad, that the Senate would exercise the right to pass judgment gave rise to many misgivings. The attitude of the Senate in the debate on the League of Nations and the Treaty of Versailles had given foreign nations little reason to believe that the present conference would see its efforts materialize, even if it were to succeed in formulating a possible solution for some of the issues before it.

This distrust of the Senate reacted in a manner detrimental to the interests of the United States. Foreign delegations proceeded very cautiously and withheld their full cooperation in planning for the conference. They feared that they might be humiliated by having any agreements with the United States repudiated by the Senate.[1]

The role of the Senate was overlooked neither by the administration nor by the American delegates. In the pre-conference preparations of the American delegation almost as much care was devoted to the demands of the Senate as to the demands of some of the foreign countries represented at Washington. In this respect, the Senate occupied a role not unlike that of a foreign state.

Secretary Hughes had planned to delay issuing confidential invitations until after the Borah Resolution had been finally adopted in order to avoid irritating the Senate needlessly.[2] The need for immediate action by the United States, after it received the British proposal, forced Hughes to abandon this scheme. Thus the invitations were issued after Congress passed the Borah Resolution, but before the President's signature had implemented it. The circumstances of international affairs further modified this invitation, making it appear that Harding was ignoring the will of the Senate. The President's proposal expanded the Senate Resolution to include land armament and the problems of the Pacific on the agenda of the conference. Also, he proposed to invite France and Italy. The press had commented at the time: "President Harding, in acting before the Borah Resolution came to him, and in going far beyond the scope of that resolution, ignored the Senate and Congress."[3] The debates in the Senate on the Borah Resolution had shown that its author specifically opposed the inclusion of France and Italy and a discussion of land armament. Apparently he carried the majority of the Senate with him in these views.[4]

These slights were not unnoticed. Many Senators, including Borah, criticized the President's action. Borah wrote a friend that France was in the grip of militarists. A decision to invite her and to discuss land armament would present to the conference problems sufficient to frustrate it. He added that he was "utterly opposed to the old system of diplomats, to wit, to settle everything before you talk about disarmament. I am in favor of disarmament and then adjust these questions afterwards in the court of reason and conscience."[5] He stated that France would wreck the conference because she would be satisfied with nothing less than a guarantee of her borders. As to the Far Eastern problems, the Senator felt that they could never be solved. Discussing them would serve no purpose other than complicating negotiations and perhaps preventing agreement on disarmament.[6]

Other senators were afraid that broadening the agenda was unwise in that it might entangle the United States in numerous international problems. Said one proponent of this theory, "There is no Far-Eastern question that does not have an end in Europe. The discussion, therefore, must bring up Persia, Mesopotamia, Egypt, and even India." This senatorial group felt that the European situation, particularly the strained relations between Germany and France, would

116

make it very difficult for the powers at Washington to reach any agreement on disarmament. Like Borah, they believed that France would insist on the security of her German border. Several senators asserted publicly that the limited scope of the Borah Resolution would have been much more practical than the expanded proposals of Harding. An important leader espousing this opinion was Senator Henry Cabot Lodge, who said that the administration proposal would have been more sound had it been limited to naval questions alone. Hiram Johnson, another Republican leader, likewise felt that any hope of success would depend on directing all of the efforts of the conference to disarmament.[7]

The objection to the announced purpose of the Washington Conference by Lodge, Johnson, and Borah was a matter of concern to the administration. They had demonstrated in the debate on the League their effectiveness in defeating Executive plans which did not meet with their favor.

In dealing with this nascent rebellion on the part of the Senate it seemed advisable for the administration to select senators as official delegates to the conference. The success of President McKinley, who had placed senators on the delegation that drew up the Treaty of Paris, and the failure of President Wilson, who had ignored the Senate in selecting his delegates to the Versailles conference, were precedents which seemed to demonstrate the advisability of this policy.

Executing such a plan was difficult. Senator Borah, by reason of his leadership in the disarmament movement, would have been the logical choice as a delegate. Yet from the administration's standpoint he was not a desirable co-worker. One of Harding's advisors, Charles D. Hilles, in a letter to the President stated some of the more important objections to Borah's selection as a delegate. It was expedient that Harding maintain his initiative in calling the conference, at home as well as abroad. The President should indicate that the disarmament conference was a part of his larger plan for an "association of nations," rather than the result of coercion by the Senate. The selection of Borah, according to Hilles, would tend to give undue importance to the Resolution passed by the Senate as a factor in bringing about the conference. Furthermore, Hilles said, Borah did not possess the necessary attributes of a delegate. He had demonstrated on numerous occasions that he could not work well with other

117

people. He was too independent, impulsive, and unpredictable to serve the needs of the administration. Still it was important to keep his good will by finding a plausible reason for not including him on the delegation. To accomplish this purpose, Hilles suggested limiting the delegation to those men who held important offices, such as Chairman of the Senate Committee on Foreign Relations, Minority Leader in the Senate, Secretary of State, and former Secretaries of State. Since Borah held none of these offices, his omission from the delegation could be explained tactfully.[8]

This plan was followed. Borah was not chosen as a delegate. To the country at large and to Borah's friends this was a shock. In response to his brother's query as to whether he had been asked to serve as a delegate, Borah answered that he had not been invited "loud enough for me to hear it, although I wasn't expecting to hear anything of that kind and I might have overlooked it." He philosophized, "No, brother, I have not been offered a place, did not expect to, do not feel badly about it, and anticipate I will find something to do in connection with disarmament nevertheless." [9] Moreover, Borah was not considered because, as he put it, "Naturally I incurred the displeasure of some in high places because of my persistent urging of the resolution. Besides I am not supposed to be able to work in double harness." [10]

With Borah eliminated, the most prominent Republican senator was the Chairman of the Foreign Relations Committee, Henry Cabot Lodge. As leader of the majority party in the Senate, his positive value to the administration could not be questioned, while the extent to which his opposition might be carried had been amply demonstrated in the past. After Hughes, Lodge was the first delegate chosen. His pleasure in being selected was made apparent in a letter to Henry White acknowledging congratulation. "The President," wrote Lodge, "has only decided on two members of the delegation—the Secretary of State and me—and I naturally was very much gratified by his doing so." [11] This gratitude proved to be of great value to the administration, for Lodge was a staunch advocate of the conference from this time on, doing much to secure its success.

By this time it had been decided to keep the delegation small, probably no more than four members.[12] The next selection was Elihu Root, whose claims were overwhelming. As the elder statesman

118

of the Republican party his influence was tremendous; his judgment was highly respected. He had much experience in government service as well as knowledge of the problems of the Far East. During his career he had served as Secretary of War, Secretary of State, and senator. He was a very close friend of Senator Lodge. In addition, he was congenial with Hughes—both socially, and in his outlook on governmental problems.

Hughes, for his part, felt that the fourth place on the delegation should be offered to the leader of the minority party in the Senate. In the event that this officer refused to serve, he recommended that the position be granted to another Republican, Senator Philander C. Knox, formerly Secretary of State.[13] However, Senator Oscar W. Underwood, minority leader in the Senate and a member of the Senate Committee on Foreign Relations, agreed to serve. He was considered in some quarters to be the official head of the Democratic party. His selection was further justified by reason of his interest in the cause of world peace and the belief that he would be able to subordinate partisan gain to the common good.

The press, in general, approved these nominations in such commendatory statements as: "The shining quality of the President's selection is clear to all eyes" and "will gratify those who are earnestly hoping and expecting great results from that epochal gathering." The apparent motive back of the choices was not unnoticed. Harding's decision to place senators on the delegation was characterized as "a stroke of simple common sense." It was a "demonstration of political sagacity which might well have been shown in the selection of delegates to the Versailles conference. . . ." The choice of Lodge was applauded because of his great influence in the Senate.

Criticism of the President's selection of delegates centered around his decision to include Lodge and to exclude Borah. The appointment of the latter, according to the press, would have been a guarantee that the conference would have made a more earnest and determined effort for disarmament than might be expected under the leadership of Lodge. The selection of Lodge was attacked by Democratic papers because he was held to be the chief factor in the Senate's defeat of the League. One typical editorial castigated the gentleman from Massachusetts as "an incurable malignant, a partisan scold, and in no sense a diplomat." [14]

The appointment of senators on the commission representing the United States was not challenged on constitutional grounds at the time. Subsequently, there was some objection in the Senate itself. Hiram Johnson, in the debate on the Four-Power Treaty, stated: "Senators ought not to be appointed; and I hope, sir, that this is the last time that upon any such commission or conference Senators will be appointed." [15] Later in this debate, Senator Joseph T. Robinson attacked the selection of senators, declaring that the function of the Senate, in regard to a treaty, was entirely separate from the Executive in the view of the Constitution. Commissioners from the Senate, by aiding in the negotiations of a treaty, committed themselves to its support in the Senate. Particularly was this true when the senators chosen were the leaders, as in this case, of the majority and minority in the Senate. This, in effect, committed the entire Senate in advance, voiding its duty under the Constitution as a check on the Executive.[16]

The influence of public and senatorial opinion continued to be of significance in shaping the administration's plans in regard to the conference. This was well illustrated in the negotiations with Britain relative to a preliminary conference. The issue was first raised by Lloyd George in his speech to Parliament, July 11, announcing the invitation from the United States. He declared that President Harding also had suggested calling a preliminary conference to treat with matters pertaining to the Far East. This invitation England would gladly accept. After this address Lord Curzon discussed the proposal for a preliminary conference with Ambassador Harvey, and the latter forwarded the proposal to Secretary Hughes. In reply, Hughes denied that the United States had suggested a preliminary conference, adding that such a plan would be impractical. Japan and China could not get authorized representatives to a conference by August 15, the date suggested by the British. A conference devoted entirely to Far Eastern affairs would arouse immediately the suspicion of the public, which would assume "that limitation of armament had been sidetracked. . . ." It would be charged, Hughes felt, "by those who are now unable to voice effective criticism that the entire plan had been arranged with this in view." A conference held in London would not meet with administration approval, for only a conference held in the United States would elicit the wholehearted cooperation of the American people. Finally, Hughes reminded the British government that it had specifically endorsed President Harding's invitation both before and after it was issued to the public. This invitation, he reemphasized, had called for one conference in Washington.[17] American cooperation with other powers must conform to conditions set by the public and the Senate. In these circumstances he felt that if the United States were to participate in an international conference, it must be called by the United States, meet in the United States, and be under the leadership of the United States.

This attitude did not please the British. The premiers of the Dominions, who had recently agreed to modify the Anglo-Japanese Alliance, were anxious to be present at the conference which assumed that task. Most of them had to return to their own countries after the middle of August. Unless a conference were held by that time, they could not attend. Subsequently, on July 15 and on July 19, the British again pressed the plan for a preliminary conference. Secretary Hughes remained adamant, stating that a preliminary conference was not possible, and that "this must be regarded as this government's final attitude."[18]

The British, not dissuaded after two refusals by Hughes, reintroduced the subject on July 27. At that time, the British ambassador presented Hughes with a message from his government. "Some doubt appears to exist as to nature and locality of preliminary consultations or conversations which United States Government has signified its willingness to hold before meeting of Pacific conference at Washington later in the Autumn." The British government regarded this preliminary conference with the United States and Japan as being of the utmost importance. Also submitted was a complete itinerary for the British representatives to the proposed conference which was to be held in America.[19] Hughes, equally obstinate, refused to yield, emphasizing repeatedly the position of his government: "Opinion in the United States is decisively against a preliminary conference at London."[20]

For the third time, it seemed to the American Secretary of State that the matter was settled, but such was not the case. About the middle of August, Prime Minister Lloyd George in an address before Parliament renewed the British demand for a preliminary conference, also suggesting a solution to the problem of the Anglo-Japanese Alliance. He declared that if "the alliance with Japan could emerge into a greater understanding with Japan and the United States on all problems of the Pacific, that would be a great event which would be a guaranty for the peace of the world." Also, if a preliminary conference on all Far Eastern problems could be held, it would do much to insure the final success of the forthcoming disarmament conferences.[21]

The American public in its reaction to Lloyd George's speech showed decisive opposition to both of his suggestions. The American press had approved the inclusion of Far Eastern problems on the agenda of the conference, because it was realized that they were inseparably linked with the problems of disarmament. There was general agreement in the United States that the Anglo-Japanese Alliance would have to be modified before disarmament could take place. In the eyes of the Senate and the public, however, disarmament was the prime consideration of the conference. Far Eastern problems were included only because they could not be excluded. As to the suggestion for a tripartite agreement, Senator Borah spoke for the majority when he detected in this plan the germ of an alliance. It was "fundamentally wrong in principle."[22] The press all over the country took note of Lloyd George's plan. In numerous instances it was interpreted as being an invitation to join an "entangling alliance," a move inconsistent with and fatal to America's long cherished ideals in foreign affairs. These sources indicate that there was almost no sanction for American participation in an alliance regardless of its purpose. Nevertheless, there was some question as to whether the broad terms of the English Prime Minister's suggestion actually called for an alliance or merely provided for an "understanding" between the countries. If the entente were not an alliance, it might be entirely compatible with American traditions. In elucidation of this view, the *New York Globe* explained that the Monroe Doctrine and the Open Door policy were examples of an "understanding" between nations. It was observed further, by this editor, that "without some 'understanding' between the powers the attainment of the long sought goal of disarmament would certainly be impossible." In New York City, a reporter questioning people on the street found them solidly opposed to American participation in any sort of alliance. A typical justification of this conviction was given by a pedestrian who said, "I don't believe we should in any way affiliate ourselves with the yellow race, or in any way bind ourselves with European diplomacy." The *Boston Transcript* assured its readers that nothing said by Harding or Hughes indicated they had any idea of having the United States join the Anglo-Japanese Alliance. It further declared that:

If they [the American people] get it in their heads that the English premier is coming to the United States in quest of such a bargain his mission will be foredoomed to failure and the Conference of Washington, instead of commanding the support of American opinion, will from the very start excite American suspicion.[23]

The American Secretary of State, while evidently cognizant of the importance of the Far East in American policy-making, realized that disarmament was the cause that had awakened public and senatorial enthusiasm. Therefore, the American government, if it were to maintain the interest and good will of the public along with the support and approval of the Senate, had to place the emphasis on disarmament. Hughes was willing to treat with the British regarding the Far East, but he insisted on discussing the matter later on when the Senate and the public could be better prepared for it. Hence in this phase of policy-making, the Senate was a powerful factor in a negative and static way.

In regard to some other matters of policy at the conference, the Senate took a very active and positive role. Most important of these matters was the effort to keep the conference free from "secret diplomacy." The Republicans in the Senate had often condemned the secrecy which had shrouded the negotiations on the Treaty of Versailles. The Treaty was faulty because the public had no voice in, or knowledge of, the negotiations at Paris. The Senate determined that it would attempt to forestall any such tendency at the forthcoming conference on the part of the administration by adopting a resolution demanding open diplomacy.

Leading this movement was Senator Borah, who did much to direct the attention of the public to the importance of an open conference. One of his first moves, early in August, was a telegram published in the *New York World* calling for an open conference.[24] The Idaho Senator explained the reason for his campaign when he confided to one of his correspondents, "I haven't a particle of confidence in these diplomats who close the doors and write agreements." [25] This feeling was shared by many people who wrote Borah in the days before the conference. A typical letter expressed the hope that Borah

123

could succeed "in prying the doors of the conference chamber from their hinges, so that the sun of righteousness may warm the hearts and enlighten the minds of those who are again given an opportunity to lessen the World's woe. . . ." [26] Elsewhere in the Borah correspondence are numerous letters thanking him for his efforts to open the conference to the public. [27]

On the floor of the Senate, the attempts to secure open sessions were led by Senator Patrick Harrison of Mississippi. On August 17, he introduced a resolution as an amendment to the urgent House Deficiency Bill. It provided that delegates representing the United States at the conference exert all proper influence to provide that the business of the conference be transacted in open sessions. [28] This proposal was subsequently offered on September 21 in an expanded form. At this time Harrison emphasized his desire to see the work of the conference culminate in complete success. He felt that success would be probable if the press were allowed free access to all the sessions, with an exact record kept of all of the proceedings of each meeting of the delegates. Furthermore, Harrison was desirous that both the press reports and the minutes be free from any censorship which would result in giving the people an inaccurate opinion as to the progress of the conference. [29]

There was no debate on the proposal at this time, but the subject was revived near the end of October. Senator Robert L. Owen, in a short speech favoring open sessions at the conference, noted that:

If the discussion and decisions be made behind closed doors, in extreme secrecy, and the world is then faced with the "accomplished fact" and must take it or leave it, the United States Senate will have another Versailles treaty to consider and the world may again be disappointed because its statesmen, acting as rulers, behind closed doors may again be moved too far by national and commercial ambitions rather than by the American ideals of full justice and the golden rule.

After asserting that only by the force of world opinion could the doctrines of true democracy and equal justice be upheld, Owen declared, "World opinion cannot exert itself if the conference on limitation of armament is behind closed doors." [30]

The final debate on the resolution, November 8, was the scene of a sharp exchange of views between Harrison and Lodge. The Massachusetts Senator maintained that the Harrison Resolution "would be very much out of place." He felt that the Senate ought not "to offer suggestions as to the procedure to be followed by the conference," for this would amount to instructing the delegates of foreign countries. Harrison denied these charges, maintaining that the resolution pertained only to American delegates. Foreign delegates were not addressed in the resolution, and certainly were not to be instructed by it. The Senate, he continued, did not wish to exercise undue authority or act in an improper manner, but sincerely wished to do what it could to assure open diplomacy. It hoped that a senatorial resolution would carry some weight in attaining that purpose. Harrison added that Lodge was attempting to prove that the resolution was designed to embarrass the delegates and humiliate the Republican administration. This charge was entirely false, for the conference was sponsored by Democrats as well as Republicans. Indeed, continued the senator from Mississippi, the Republicans had often been reluctant in their support of the cause of disarmament. The Democrats had "on every proper occasion voted to bring about a disarmament conference. . . ." There could be no political advantage in hindering the work of the conference, Harrison asserted, for it had been at all times a subject free of politics. Senator Lodge immediately denied that he had any intention of casting Harrison in the role of a partisan politician. He opposed the Harrison Resolution solely because it was an act of bad manners.[31]

In reply Senator Harrison inquired if Lodge had not thought it entirely proper, at one time, for the Senate to instruct American delegates to international conferences. Had he not voted for the resolution requesting the United States delegation at Versailles to use its good offices for Ireland? Lodge countered that he had voted for the Irish Resolution, but did not feel it represented an analogous case. Senator John Sharp Williams, a Wilson Democrat, came to Harrison's aid with the observation that the resolution on Ireland dealt with a situation in which the United States had no direct interest and no authority. That resolution had been a definite case of "bad manners." The action by the United States was as uncalled for and as unjustified as would be the passing of a resolution in the House of Commons calling for the independence of the Philippine Islands. Lodge, ignoring this charge, reaffirmed his sympathy with the motion for full publicity. Yet he continued to insist that it was improper for

125

the Senate to dictate to foreign delegations the manner in which their business was to be conducted. It would be embarrassing, he explained, to meet the nations coming to the conference at "the threshold with a Senate resolution, which, . . . intimates indirectly that we doubt whether they are going to desire publicity, that we suspect that they wish to conduct the conferences in holes and corners and behind curtains."

Senator Hiram Johnson joining the debate upheld the right of the Senate to recommend to the American delegates a course of action. He reminded Senator Lodge, "We had no hesitance in doing it when our representatives were at Paris. We had the right, and we did it." Johnson gave eloquent expression to the importance of open diplomacy, declaring that President Wilson failed at Paris "not because his intentions were not good, but because he was locked in a room in secrecy over there, and his idealism finally was broken and destroyed and secrecy rendered nugatory every good intention that he had." Johnson admonished Lodge and Underwood that publicity would be their strongest weapon in seeking to guarantee the success of the conference. "You will not obtain success by locking the door and keeping from the people of this and other lands what you are doing," he warned. In a final flight of oratory the senator from California, leader of the irreconcilables, summed up the importance of open diplomacy:

You will witness with publicity the peoples of all the world behind you praying, fighting, advocating disarmament; but if you shut the door and divest yourselves of this one great weapon, just that instant you are powerless; just that instant you come upon the peril which the President came upon at Paris; and just that instant you endanger that which all the world desires. I beg and I plead with the Senator from Massachusetts and the Senator from Alabama, when you go into that conference, go there not alone the delegates of the United States, but go there representing the hopes, the aspirations, the prayer of the peoples of all the world, peoples who desire disarmament, though rulers may not. Let peoples operate upon that conference, and they can operate in just one way, by publicity, and publicity will enable an overwhelming righteous public sentiment of the peoples of the world to compel delegates there to do the peoples' will.[32]

At this point the debate was interrupted by consideration of other bills. When the discussion was resumed, Harrison announced that he was willing to amend the resolution into a form acceptable to Lodge.

126

This being done, the resolution was passed by unanimous consent. As amended, it requested the American delegation to use its influence at the conference to discourage censorship, which would prevent the public from gaining through the press a correct opinion of the attitude of the delegations and nations at all sessions. The resolution requested also that the press be admitted to meetings of the full conference, and a complete record be kept of the proceedings.[33] Lodge, even after this concession, continued to emphasize that "the resolution constitutes merely a request."

Certainly the Senate, in adopting this resolution, was in accord with the opinion of a large proportion of the public. The Committee on General Information for the Washington Conference received petitions representing more than a million people advocating open sessions at the conference. William Allen White reflected the popular spirit. "What right," he asked, "have any four American commissioners . . . to sit in such a council behind closed doors with the gamblers of Europe and hazard our destiny?" He urged that the conference be the "Town Meeting of the World."

Until the world does have a town meeting, it will not be safe for democracy. And we Americans who have staked our whole fortunes upon democracy, must stand for the publicity which sustains democracy. In secret the same forces that wrote the treaty of Versailles will write the disarmament pact, and it will be just as miserable a hobble upon the feet of men as the thing the devil devised at Paris. . . . America's one hope is in an open conference. The world must have faith before it can resume the business of civilization—faith of men in men, faith of nations in nations, faith of all of us in the general decency of mankind and the changeless goodness of God. But faith never grows behind closed doors and in secret conclaves. Men make their noblest professions and square them with their greatest deeds while they are being watched. Open diplomacy is the safest diplomacy.[34]

About the middle of October the Senate completed the separate peace with Germany. The attitude and demands of the Senate on this matter were important to the Washington Conference, for they clearly indicated the limits to which the administration could later go in cooperation with other nations.

Hughes at the outset of his administration held informal discussions with Senate leaders regarding the League of Nations and the Treaty of Versailles. The irreconcilable bloc, so vital to Republican unity, reaffirmed its adamant opposition to American participation in

127

either. It convinced Hughes that opposition to this view would lead to prolonged controversy and eventual failure for the administration's program both at home and abroad.[35] The administration forthwith shunned the League and pacified the internationalists with the promise of an association of nations. While the issue of future peace could be postponed, the problem of present peace with Germany could not. Some method of bringing the war to an official close had to be developed.

To this end Harding in his address to the special session of Congress, April 12, recommended the ratification of the Treaty of Versailles with ". . . such explicit reservations and modifications as will secure our absolute freedom from inadvisable commitments and safeguard all our essential interests."[36] Hughes soon found that this compromise would not satisfy the Senate. Borah felt that the Treaty was even more dangerous than the League of Nations. Lodge expressed the hope that the administration would free itself of all of the works of Wilson and start afresh.

Rejecting the Treaty of Versailles completely, Congress adopted the Knox-Porter Resolution early in July. This repealed war legislation, specified the conditions of separate peace with Germany, and reserved to the United States the rights of the other victorious powers.[37] Hughes objected to the last provision as being meaningless. The Senate had reserved rights; it had created no rights. With the approval of Congress he added to the resolution the provision that the United States claimed all rights and privileges stipulated for its benefit in the Treaty of Versailles despite the fact that this country had not ratified it.[38]

Still the Senate was not satisfied. Many felt that unless this nation met with the powers of Europe, it must be willing to let its destiny under the Treaty be determined without its consent. If the United States agreed to meet with these powers, then the Treaty was an entangling alliance.[39] To clear this point a reservation was added which stated that the United States should not be represented or participate in any body, agency, or commission authorized by the Treaty, nor should any person so represent the United States "unless and until an act of Congress . . . shall provide for such representation or participation."[40] Even with these elaborate precautions Borah and La Follette voted against it as unwise. The administration had learned what to expect from the Senate on the question of association with foreign powers.

The Senate, despite Harding's attempts to maintain independence and leadership, continued to seek the initiative in foreign affairs. Secretary Hughes in these preliminaries indicated the course which his administration would follow. Quietly he laid the foundation for a countermove toward administrative direction. To this end he exerted every effort to win the cooperation and support of the Senate, as well as the approval and backing of the public. Superficially, the administration appeared to be subordinating itself to the wishes of the Senate. Actually, as subsequent events demonstrated, Hughes was making the necessary preparations to extend the scope of the conference beyond the narrow limits envisioned by the Borah Resolution.

The Conference Begins

. . . THE Senate and the public did not lose interest in the disarmament conference after its convocation had been assured. Indeed, interest continued to increase and national committees were organized which integrated this sentiment, making it far more articulate than it had been while the Borah Resolution was before Congress. The administration realized that in its contest with the Senate for control of foreign relations the public represented the balance of power. Secretary Hughes never underestimated the power of public opinion, and in this respect was one of the most adept managers in the history of the affairs of the State Department. He influenced opinion so skillfully that it became the decisive force enabling him to gain Senate approval for the policies which the administration deemed necessary to the success of the conference at Washington.

One of the administration's initial steps toward gaining public support was to extend recognition to the representatives of organized public opinion and to provide an opportunity for these groups to have a voice in the work of the conference. To accomplish this purpose a committee of twenty-one members known as the Advisory Commission was appointed under the directorship of former Senator George Sutherland. Other members were well known figures in finance, commerce, labor, agriculture, and in the three great religious faiths. Care was exercised in these selections to represent all geographical sections of the country. This commission thus granted representation and recognition to prominent men and organizations that could not be included on the small, official delegation to the conference. In addition, it was hoped that the commission would serve a practical purpose by acting as a liaison agency between the public and the government. To aid in this work, a Committee on General Information, a subsidiary to this Advisory Commission, was created to receive, digest, and submit to the official delegation all suggestions,

130

appeals, and resolutions submitted by the American public. Also, it was to survey and summarize press opinion of the conference, issuing this information in a printed bulletin once every two weeks. An additional service of this committee was a periodic compilation of the appeals and resolutions sent into the official delegation and the Advisory Commission.[1] Working with these committees was a vast network of organizations which, in their coordinated function, approached the efficiency of a well directed presidential campaign.

Partially as a result of the work of this organization, the government was deluged with petitions from clubs, churches, mass meetings, and individuals demanding that the conference bring about disarmament, establish peace, and effect a reduction in taxes. A representative petition addressed to Secretary of State Hughes read:

My Dear Sir—I am but a little girl, but I have two brothers whom I love dearly and I don't want either of them to go to war. I know you are trying to have war impossible and I want to thank you and President Harding. Your sincere friend Barbara Dillon.[2]

Petitions were sent to the Senate from many different groups. The Akron Typographical Union declared in sentiments characteristic of many similar unions, "Nothing but less army, less navy and less taxes will do." The Reno Chamber of Commerce wired Senator Key Pittman to exert his influence for disarmament, because business would profit by the resulting reduction in taxes. Similar petitions were sent by the Chambers of Commerce from all parts of the country. The Child Conservation League of America, the Women's Nonpartisan League Club, and the Sons and Daughters of Liberty were other organizations which sent stereotyped petitions from their chapters all over the United States. Petitions came also from the National Federation of Business and Professional Women's Clubs, the Military Sisterhood of the World War, the Federal Council of the Churches of Christ in America, and from local organizations, such as the Ypsilanti Study Club, of Ypsilanti, Michigan.

An eloquent example of these petitions was offered by the Woman's Home Mission Society of Altoona, Kansas. In a plea sent to Senator Arthur Capper, this organization called for peace, "knowing that war violates every instinct of a woman's heart, that it mutilates and kills the beloved of our hearts, that it is followed by an aftermath of crime and violence in all countries that have shared in its

131

turmoil. . . ." The Parent-Teachers Association of Mystic, Connecticut, recommended that the Senate promote "all efforts toward peace—especially the abolition of illegal warfare." The International Longfellow Society of Portland, Maine, stated that its total membership, numbering one hundred thousand,

in the light of the record of centuries showing the horrible futility and atrocious crime of war, URGES as the first essential of WORLD PEACE, AN INTERNATIONAL AGREEMENT FOR THE IMMEDIATE AND PERMANENT ABANDONMENT OF ALL FURTHER ARMAMENT AND MUNITIONS CONSTRUCTION; . . . PEACE ON EARTH GOOD WILL TO MEN.

In addition to these organizations, many informal groups drafted petitions. One petition was from the women citizens of Albany, Georgia, to Senator William J. Harris. Another sent in was drawn up at a mass meeting of citizens in Little Rock, Arkansas, and signed by the mayor of Little Rock and the governor of the state. Students at universities passed resolutions. In some instances the grand juries of counties adopted recommendations in favor of disarmament.

National magazines printed petitions for disarmament in the form of ballots. The public took advantage of this service; many such ballots reached the files of the Senate Committee on Foreign Relations. One periodical which took a most active part in work of this type was the *Farm and Home Magazine.* It printed a very elaborate petition which stated that the people would not be satisfied with the work of the conference until military expenditures were cut in half and taxes reduced in like proportion. The allied nations were admonished: "Disarm and pay up. Americans Won't be Taxed to Support your Armaments." At the head of the petition was the command: "Let the voice of the masses speak as the voice of God!" At the bottom of the ballot was a space to which a sheet of paper could be attached to include additional signatures. The editor promised to print, in the next issue, the name of the county in each state sending in the largest number of signatures; special mention was to be accorded the most extensive lists in each state. Provided these entries were accompanied by ten cents to cover postage, they would be forwarded to Congress by the magazine. The editor reported more than two million of these petitions in circulation at the time the conference opened. One of the most imposing of these ballots found in the Senate files was from Ingham, Michigan, and bore 128 names. These petitions, many of them on cheap tablet paper with the names laboriously entered in pencil, were sufficient to confirm the universal concern for the disarmament conference.[3]

Another magazine which conducted an active campaign for disarmament was *Collier's Weekly*. It printed a ballot for the convenience of its readers which was very specific in its demands. In part it read: "It is my request, as a taxpayer and a citizen, that the November conference on disarmament be opened with a concrete proposal on the part of America to stop the building of war ships." [4] A later issue stated that the American people expected a detailed plan for the cessation of naval building to be presented on the opening day of the conference. This idea appeared to have the approval of the public, for more than a thousand of these ballots reached the State Department each day in the weeks just before the conference was convened.

From the poorest citizens to the men at the top of the great financial structures of Wall Street, disarmament appeared to be the unanimous wish. Charles M. Schwab, of the Bethlehem Steel Company, declared, "I am at the head of the largest war materials manufacturing works in the world, but, gladly would I see the war-making machinery of the Bethlehem Steel Company sunk to the bottom of the ocean . . ." if thereby the burden of armaments could be lifted from the nations. Judge Gary, of the United States Steel Corporation, agreed with this opinion, stating that disarmament would be good for all businesses, including the steel business.[5]

Apparently America was unanimously in favor of disarmament. So insistent became the clamor that Secretary of State Hughes began to fear that "too powerful and irresistible a demand from the American people" might result in hindering rather than in helping the movement to secure an international agreement for disarmament. One method used to meet this problem was the establishment of the aforementioned committees to guide the popular will. Samuel Gompers was influential in this instance. He did much to direct the opinion of American labor, while urging a definite demand for disarmament by labor in Japan, England, Italy, and France. These steps improved the diplomatic position of the United States, relieving it of the embarrassment of being the foremost advocate of disarmament.[6]

133

In addition to the interest of the labor unions in disarmament, women's groups over the world enthusiastically championed its cause. British women held, at Central Hall, Westminster, a large mass meeting to voice their approval of armament limitation. Frances Balfour acted as chairman, with speeches by Lady Astor and Maude Royden. At the close of the meeting a message advocating disarmament was sent to women's organizations in the United States.[7] A great deal of publicity was accorded Mme. Kaji Yajima, the foremost woman educator in Japan. Despite advanced years, she journeyed to the United States to present a petition for disarmament signed by more than ten thousand of her countrywomen. This petition was rendered more impressive by the fact that the names were inscribed on a scroll more than one hundred yards long.[8]

By the time the conference opened, newspapers and magazines in the United States reflective of public interest devoted a tremendous amount of space to the forthcoming meeting and its plans. The *Literary Digest,* the week before the conference convened, devoted almost an entire issue to it. Even advertising space of newspapers was given to presenting the aims of the conference in bold letters, with those of the commercial sponsors in more modest type.

The opening day of the conference was to be devoted to burying the unknown soldier at Arlington. The Senate recognized the importance of the occasion by passing a joint resolution authorizing the President to "declare November 11, 1921, a holiday as a mark of respect to the memory of those who gave their lives in the late World War, as typified by the unknown and unidentified American soldier who is to be buried in Arlington National Cemetery on that day...."[9] A few days later President Harding proclaimed November 11 a national holiday. He directed that chimes be played in Washington for fifteen minutes, business houses closed, and the day observed by the churches as an occasion for prayer and religious observance. Every fifteen minutes throughout the day November 10, organizations filed by the tomb of the unknown soldier to place floral tributes of honor.[10] The Senate itself was one of these many groups. Interest over the nation mounted steadily. A day was set aside for prayer throughout the country. Madison Square Garden was sold out completely for a mass meeting on disarmament sponsored by the Central Trades and Labor Council, and addressed by Samuel Gompers.[11]

November 11, 1921, found the country wrapped in religious fervor which was raised to a climax when President Harding, standing before the tomb on which were engraved the words, "We highly resolve that these dead shall not have died in vain," closed an earnest speech with the Lord's Prayer. In his address Harding expressed the belief that there must be and would be an overwhelming voice speaking from the conscience of civilization and denouncing armed warfare. Alluding to the World War and to the unknown soldier, representative of the many lives lost in that conflict, he asserted solemnly and repeated for emphasis, "It must not be again." [12]

A most eloquent description of the mood of the moment was given by Senator Frank B. Willis who declared later:

I thought as I looked out over that vast crowd of 50,000 people that there were others there in spirit, even though we could not see them. I thought that I saw standing out in the mists the figures of the 100,000 boys who gave up their lives over yonder that there might be peace and the preservation of free government. I thought I saw those boys standing there at "Present Arms" to do honor to the memory of this soldier, the unknown dead.

The spirit of the Washington conference was born in that solemn hour when with bated breath and tear-dimmed eyes a sobbing, heartbroken world stood on armistice day at the grave of the unknown soldier at Arlington. In high, solemn purpose this Nation then and there resolved that it must not be again.[13]

The spirit engendered by this service was further manifested by a demonstration in Washington the next day, just before the conference met for its first session. Two thousand women marched down Pennsylvania Avenue carrying banners denouncing war. One of these proclaimed: "We will not give our children for another war." Another advised: "Scrap the battleship and the Pacific problems will settle themselves." Among those in the line of march were Gold Star Mothers of the First World War, as well as many women prominent in society and club work.[14]

The stirring events of the Armistice Day ceremony might well have marked the peak in public fervor. However, the leaders of the conference held in reserve an even more striking event. William Allen White, seventy-five years of age, surveying a career in newsgathering which had taken him to most of the great events of his time, declared that the opening day at the Washington Conference "furnished the most intensely dramatic moment I had ever witnessed." [15]

135

The first session, and the plenary sessions which followed, were held in Continental Hall in downtown Washington. Long before 10:30 A. M., November 12, the streets were crowded with throngs of people waiting to get a glimpse of the great and near-great as they filed into the hall. The building itself was not large, holding a little less than a thousand people. Admission for all, including senators and congressmen, was by special invitation. Near the center of the first floor was a large rectangular table around which the delegates of the countries were seated. At the head of the table was the American delegation with the British to its left and the French to its right. The rest of the first floor was filled with special advisors to the delegations, and prominent newsmen. The balcony, the back, and one side of the auditorium were reserved for the Senate and the House of Representatives, while members of the cabinet and the diplomatic corps were seated on the other side.

Shortly before time for the session to begin the prominent delegates made their appearance, each being greeted with applause. Just before 10:30 A. M., President Harding entered amidst a loud demonstration. Hughes, as temporary chairman, rapped for order. A prayer was offered and Harding arose to make the opening address. He delivered a routine speech of welcome which confirmed the general opinion that the opening day would not afford the occasion for any dramatic action. The President described the meeting as "an earnest of the awakened conscience of twentieth century civilization. It is not a convention of remorse, nor a session of sorrow. It is not the conference of victors to define terms of settlement. Nor is it a council of nations seeking to remake humankind." Harding assured the nations of the determination of the United States to cooperate toward reducing the evils of armament and wars. He was, however, careful to qualify this cooperation by adding:

I do not mean surrendered rights, or narrowed freedom, or denied aspirations, or ignored national necessities. Our Republic would no more ask for these than it would give. No pride need be humbled, no nationality submerged, but I would have a mergence of minds committing all of us to less preparation for war and more enjoyment of fortunate peace.

The President hoped the conference would bring an "understanding which will emphasize the guarantees of peace, and for commitments to less burdens and a better order which will tranquilize the world." [16]

136

Contrary to diplomatic precedents, there was a round of applause as the President concluded his address. Secretary Hughes took the floor. After disposing of several minor matters, he began his address. The relaxed expressions of the delegates afforded evidence that they expected nothing more exciting than words of welcome and planning for the general conduct of the business of the conference. After offering his greetings, Hughes declared that the world looked to the conference for a practical solution to the problem of armament. Probably the delegates felt that he would stop at this point. Hughes, however, continued by giving a short account of the historical precedents for disarmament. The aim of this rather dry recital became dimly apparent when he concluded this phase of the address with the observation that the failures of the past must not be repeated:

Competition in armament must stop. We can no longer content ourselves with statistics, with reports, with the circumlocution of inquiry. . . . The world wants a practical program which shall at once be put into execution.

This pronouncement brought a round of applause from the gallery led by the members of the House and the Senate. Hughes had the rapt attention of each of his auditors. He proceeded to increase the sudden tension by asserting that the United States would be pleased with nothing short of a naval holiday. His startled audience gasped as he recommended that "for a period of not less than ten years there should be no further construction of capital ships." The excitement increased when Hughes announced that the United States stood ready to destroy thirty battleships; it reached a climax with his suggestion that Britain and Japan follow suit by sinking thirty-six battleships, thus establishing a ratio in battleships of 5-5-3. So great was the wave of emotion which this statement elicited that spontaneous applause was sustained for many minutes. His auditors felt that Hughes in less than thirty minutes had sunk sixty-six battleships, thereby transposing disarmament from idealistic theory to practical reality. They were engulfed by the assurance that the millennium was not simply to be planned, but was to be ushered in immediately. Such determination to limit armament at a conference called specifically for that purpose was so entirely unexpected that it literally startled the world.[17]

The impact of Hughes' speech was increased by the element of surprise. No delegates from foreign nations had been previously informed of his thunderbolt. Only nine men including President Harding knew the exact nature of his message. Copies for these men were mimeographed by an admiral. No printed copies were made until the day of the speech. Hughes had originally planned to give his address at the first plenary session on Monday or Tuesday. However, his determination that the message be a surprise prompted him to give it on Saturday and avoid the possibility of a leak. Borah might complicate matters, he feared, by offering a resolution in the Senate similar to his proposal.[18] The only clue to its nature had been a report on October 26 that the United States had worked out a complete but secret plan for the limitation of armament. To this hint was added the information, November 4, that Hughes would recommend a drastic reduction of armament when the conference convened.[19] These foreshadowings, however, were not featured, and in no way prepared the public for what took place.

Overnight Hughes became a national hero, talked about "like a man who had saved a city." It was generally felt that in one short speech he had wiped out navies, war, high taxes, and the old method of diplomacy. All of Washington hummed with his name. Across the nation the next day the pastors of churches hastily changed their Sunday morning sermon topics to hail him as the savior of civilization.[20]

An informal poll of Congress showed almost unanimous approval of his plan. It appeared practically certain that a treaty embodying these suggestions would sweep through the Senate with no difficulty. Elsewhere, the address was praised as truly significant, a speech which would force action. Its greatness lay in its "unanswerable righteousness," its "wedding of an exact program to a high theory." It was called "the most important public utterance made by an American during the last hundred years. . . ."[21] So great became the popular fervor inspired by the address that the president of the American Civic Association proposed that all decorative cannons in parks be destroyed.

Insofar as the conference and the opinion of the United States Senate toward the conference was concerned, the Secretary's dramatically presented plan was a vital matter in practical politics. Lord Balfour declared, at the end of the conference, that much of what had been accomplished was a result of the inspiring way in which the conference was opened and world opinion focused on the meeting. Fear of incurring public wrath should the conference fail was a restraining factor on the actions of the delegates.[22]

Although the apex of popular interest was reached on the opening day,[23] the public continued to follow closely the rest of the sessions. To cultivate this interest, civic leaders conducted a program of public education on a large scale. The governor of Massachusetts suggested that all schools and colleges study the progress of the disarmament conference. The *Literary Digest* championed the idea, telegraphing the governor of each state of the union for his opinion on this proposal. Acknowledgments from thirty-eight governors were received. These indicated in all cases great enthusiasm for the proposal. Illustrative of all the replies was that of Governor Edwin P. Marrow of Kentucky. The conference deserved all the study that could be devoted to it, he believed, for it was "a drama as great in its possibilities for the children of men as the crucifixion of the Son of Man. . . ."[24] Public interest was stimulated by the Council of Churches' suggestion that Christmas be observed as a day of prayer for the success of the conference. It recommended that urgent appeals be sent the senators who were delegates requesting them to use their influence for disarmament.[25] These and other efforts resulted in keeping the public interested in the work of the conference throughout its duration.

Subsequently, this aroused public opinion was vital in shaping the attitude and determining the policy of the Senate. The advocates of the conference treaties never tired of reminding the Senate that the public was unanimously in favor of the disarmament movement. The failure of senators to meet this demand by ratifying the work of the conference would be disastrous to the political future of the obstructionists. Seldom had a Secretary of State, in peace time, been able to mobilize and utilize so well the force of public opinion toward the solution of the problems in diplomacy. The public was so satisfied with the administration's policy that it placed no faith in senatorial criticism. Thus, the Senate from the start of the conference was outmaneuvered by an administration which had won the implicit trust of the public.

13 . . .

The Association of Nations

◦ ◦ ◦ THE administration while gratified at its early success did not fall into the error of overestimating the strength of its position. It was recognized that the progress made was in large measure the result of a policy of cooperation with the Senate. Evidence of continued prudence and caution was the approach to the matter of activating the long awaited "association of nations." Here Secretary Hughes followed the spirit of the Borah Resolution—positive action on a strictly limited number of problems. Preliminary soundings had indicated that the Senate would not favor an "association of nations." To arouse the opposition of the Senate was to endanger the entire program of the Washington Conference. The administration, apparently at the insistence of Hughes, concluded that the doubtful possibility of gaining an "association" should in no way jeopardize the relative certainty of establishing an agreement on the limitation of armament. Hughes subscribed to the theory that a bird in the hand is worth two in the bush.

The public, because of Harding's statements of policy early in the year, expected disarmament to follow the establishment of the "association." However, in the months immediately preceding the conference, the administration gave little indication that it intended to fulfill this hope. Many interpreted this silence as evidence that the administration had not altered its original policy and still planned to carry out its campaign promise for an "association." Surveys of opinion indicated a demand that this be done.[1] The logical time for this step would be at the Washington Conference—the administration's first official gesture of cooperation toward the outside world.

Possibly Harding, and certainly some of his advisers, actually contemplated such a course of action after the conference was called. Nicholas Murray Butler, while consulting with Harding on policy at Marion, Ohio, in December 1920, suggested the launching of an

140

"association of nations" as a vital part of a conference for the reduction of armament and the solution of problems in the Far East.[2] Charles D. Hilles was another adviser who subscribed to this theory. In August he wrote a confidential letter to the President suggesting that the conference be a part of his larger plan for the "association of nations" rather than simply an independent conference on disarmament. This plan, he asserted, would enhance the impression of Executive leadership.[3] Chandler P. Anderson, staunch Republican and one of the legal advisers to the American delegation, wrote Hughes early in September proposing "to work out . . . the framework of an association of nations as an agency for what might be called international administrative rather than executive action. . . ." Anderson was willing to develop the plan even though he understood that it had not been decided whether the conference would consider this matter.[4] Hughes, who waited for more than a month before replying to this offer, advised Anderson that the policy regarding the "association of nations" was very indefinite. The matter would not be considered until the right moment presented itself. Anderson's offer was welcomed, however, and he was told to proceed with his work toward developing a definite basis for an "association of nations." Incidentally, this statement by Hughes was made only two weeks before the opening of the conference at a time when other major policies had been reduced to definite form.[5]

Speculation that the real purpose of the conference was to launch the "association" was not confined to the United States. The League of Nations became apprehensive over the possible aims of the Washington Conference. One of its spokesmen charged that the United States had blocked the League's effort at armament limitation. Then it had called the Washington Conference in order to compete with the League in securing disarmament. Finally, with the prestige which it hoped to acquire in solving the armament problem, the United States planned to kill the League of Nations and establish a thoroughly "American" association under the complete domination of the United States.[6]

As the time for the opening of the conference approached, American citizens, who were hopeful that an "association of nations" would be established, had reason to be encouraged. Harding declared late in October that it was "inevitable that the United States participate in world affairs." [7] This hope was further stimulated when Secretary Hughes, in his opening speech, made it plain that the conference was bent upon taking definite action to meet the problems before it. He did not specify by what method this was to be done, however. Surveys of the press, after the opening of the conference, showed that the public overlooked this fact, and expected daily the announcement of a plan for the establishment of an "association of nations." [8] Such hopes developed from the widely held opinion that the success of the conference in meeting its limited objectives had already been assured. There was an optimistic feeling that America had already triumphed over armament and would add to this accomplishment the glory of establishing a practical peace-keeping organization.

The assumption appeared to be justified and hopes near fulfillment when President Harding, shortly after the opening of the conference, began to "hint" that the Washington Conference was to be the foundation of a larger "association of nations." The President, it was said, felt that the meeting in Washington would be the first of a series of conferences. In the course of time, these meetings, including all nations, would be called whenever a specific international problem demanded solution. [9] The *New York Times* headlined this proposal: the "Germ of New 'Association' Seen in Suggested Annual Meetings." This possibility, it declared, dwarfed all other matters taken up by the conference. [10]

Harding did not deny that the "association" might at last become a reality, yet he refused to define his plans. He had "tried to keep his proposals as free as possible," he stated, "with the deliberate purpose of reducing to a minimum the probable causes of complication." His only clarification was the suggestion that when the new plan was announced, it would constitute a "meeting of minds" on a world scale. [11]

Harding's proposal, even in so indefinite a form, awakened the greatest enthusiasm since the sensation of the opening day at the conference. There was a general plea from all sides for more information on the plan. In this vaguely defined form it was discussed in Congress where it won the unofficial approval of the pro-League senators and also the majority of the Senate, according to some estimates. The foreign delegates to the conference, all representing nations who were members of the League of Nations, likewise gave their sanction to

142

Harding's nebulous notion. The reaction of René Viviani of France was typical. He called Harding's suggestion "a high thought" and "a practical solution of a world problem." [12] The American press was somewhat more cautious than the Senate and the foreign delegates; it preferred, for the most part, to wait for further particulars on the President's organization before approving or condemning a plan as yet distinguished only by a great lack of clarity. [13]

Possibly more important to policy making was the fact that Harding's plan, even in this elementary form, aroused the ire and opposition of the anti-League senators. "The Battalion of Death" once more formed ranks at the sound of a trumpet call for international cooperation. Senator Tom Watson of Georgia dismissed the plan as being "just damned humbug." [14] The irreconcilables were more specific in their objections. Senator Borah, who had always registered opposition to "any international league, association, combination, or alliance of any kind" and who had not favored the Harding "association of nations" even during the most critical days of the presidential campaign, led the assault. In a speech that attracted headlines over the nation, Borah reminded the President that any such plan as he was reported to have in mind must have the consent of the Senate. This new proposal, said Borah, was even more dangerous than the League. The old League was defined in its powers, while the new "association" called for nothing but "a conclave of diplomats, sitting behind closed doors with nothing to direct or limit their powers save their own will and discretion. . . ." Harding's suggestion was superfluous, asserted the senator, because the new "league" was designed to do precisely the same kind of work that was already being done by the old League. No useful purpose could be served by the creation of the new organization. Finally, said Borah, "If we are going into Europe we ought to go in. If we are not we ought not to be handing her a new league every ninety days." [15]

The next day Borah wrote a friend: "The symptom around this morning *is* that the 'association of nations' languishes, and languishing, lives, but will likely die before a great while." [16] About this time, according to the press, Senator Johnson called on Harding to discuss the "association." Johnson reaffirmed his unswerving opposition and that of the "irreconcilables" to any sort of permanent international organization. His statement, it was reported, shook the Presi-

143

dent's resolve. When Johnson left he carried with him Harding's assurance that no further steps would be taken toward the organization of an "association of nations" at that time.[17]

Whether or not this interview was held, Harding had suddenly decided to become more cautious in launching his plan. The Department of Current Information of the State Department found a feeling in the foreign press that the Harding "hint" had gone too far for "a very powerful section of American opinion." There was active revolt against the President's plan, for "it must be recognized," the report continued, "that America is in a stage of transition between self-sufficiency and a need for expansion beyond her borders."[18]

On December 3, the Associated Press declared the accounts of Harding's world union baseless. The President, according to this source, denied that he had approached foreign delegates or members of the American delegation on the matter of an "association." Furthermore, the President declared that at no time during the preliminary planning for the conference had he broached the subject to the American delegation. The story of the "association," concluded the report, was like Ireland in that it simply "fell from out of the sky one day." This fiction served only to arouse Borah's disapproval and to embarrass the administration senators who were forced to explain why they enthusiastically supported the Harding "association," yet were firmly opposed to the Wilson League.[19]

Such a report from so authoritative a source should have settled the matter, but on the very same day that the Associated Press laid the ghost of the "association of nations," the *New York Times* quoted Harding as reaffirming his faith in the principle of small conferences—the foundation of "his proposal for an 'association of nations'. . . ."[20] Elsewhere in the press was the assertion that the plans for it had not been abandoned. The St. Louis *Globe-Democrat* endorsed the "association" because it would

accustom the people to the fact that we have, and always must have, international relationships, that we have international obligations, and that our own welfare is dependent upon the recognition and fulfillment of these obligations. . . .

Another editor called the proposal "the biggest thing that has come out of the Disarmament Conference." The *Washington Herald* thought that Harding's plan was in response to a public trend.

144

Americans were beginning to realize that "the most emphatic result of the conference so far has been to make evident that though conferences can initiate proposals, only alliances or world associations can carry them to effective conclusions and give them continuous operation." [21] The surveys of public opinion, which the Committee on General Information conducted, showed that the number of organizations over the country favoring an "association" was gradually increasing. Typical of the optimism shown in the press was the *New York Tribune's* opinion that "the Association of Nations, not yet achieved, seems about to be realized." [22] Despite this optimism subsequent events showed that Harding let the "association of nations" die, although the press refused to bury it.

There were a number of factors compelling the administration's decision. At the time the suggestion was first publicized, the delicate problem of establishing the ratio for naval armament was still under discussion. The equally intricate negotiations on the Four-Power Treaty were also underway. Far from being an inevitable success as the public thought, the conference was at a point where it could easily have fallen into complete failure. The administration was determined to accomplish the stated aims of the conference; to antagonize the Senate irreconcilables by forcing the issue of a permanent plan for international cooperation was to invite certain failure. Once again there appeared that sensitivity to the prejudices of the irreconcilables which had dictated the Republican platform and the choice of a candidate for the presidency. Since these "hints" by Harding, late in November, constituted his only steps to establish the "association of nations," it appeared that the President had subordinated his campaign promise to the interest of continued party harmony and the success of the conference. [23]

Another appraisal of the incident gave credit for the suggestion for an "association of nations" to Harding, but traced its defeat to Secretary Hughes. His primary objective at the conference was to carry it through to a conclusion that could be called successful. The guiding principle in reaching this goal was not to attempt too much at one time. Hughes felt that the most that could be expected of the Washington Conference was the creation of international good will—developing an atmosphere in which it would be possible to solve eventually the major problems of international affairs. Har-

145

ding's advocacy and denial of an "association" was explained by the frequent moods of enthusiasm and despondency which engulfed him. At such times he was likely to espouse projects which in the cold light of political interests were entirely impractical. Hughes, on the other hand, was noted for his ability to forge toward his goal without variation in mood or determination. The Secretary of State understood the complexity of the problem which would be presented by establishing an "association of nations." He felt that consideration of such plans at the Washington Conference would reintroduce the troublesome realities of European politics which had been excluded carefully from the agenda. Hughes was aware also of the hostility which the plan had awakened in the Senate and therefore vetoed the President's suggestion for an "association of nations." To avoid the possibility that Harding's periodic fits of unguarded enthusiasm would lead him again to make embarrassing suggestions, he forbade him direct contact with newsmen. From this time on, the President was to be questioned only by means of written statements so that there would be ample opportunity to prevent any imprudent answer.[24]

Later the *New York Times* attributed the failure of the "association of nations" to the foreign diplomats at the conference. These gentlemen, it was said, opposed the creation of a new "association" while the old League was still active. They had made their opposition known to Hughes, so the story went, who had quashed further discussion of the matter.[25]

Possibly all of these factors were significant. In any event the "association of nations" died quietly, obscurely, and completely. Its friends, planning for its future, wondered what had happened. President Harding paid his last respects to it in his final speech at the conference by a vague reference to the possibility of future meetings which would follow the pattern of the Washington Conference. Even the most resourceful commentators were forced to conclude that the relation between this statement and any future "association" would become apparent only after further developments.[26]

In the Senate, Fordney McCumber, a Republican who had voted for the League, in the course of the debate on the Four-Power Treaty asked what had become of the Republican party's pledge to create an "association of nations." He sought the answer to a question in the minds of many, but he received no answer to his query.[27]

146

Its demise was due to a variety of factors. Foremost among these was the quite evident opposition of a powerful bloc in the Senate to the "association" or any other plan for permanent and binding international agreement. An angry Senate might jeopardize all work of the conference and all other plans of the administration should it press the issue of international organization.[28] This rejection by the Senate of the Harding "association" was one of the most significant results of the conference. It indicated the extent of the growth of isolationism which had steadily developed since the close of the First World War. It also established definite limits to American cooperation in international affairs, making most difficult future enforcement of any agreement adopted at the conference.

The completeness of the defeat was not realized by the internationalists who continued to be optimistic. One of these, President A. Lawrence Lowell of Harvard University, wrote Hughes urging that the administration carry the "association" through to completion. Hughes, in reply, made it plain that the administration had no such plans. "We have been dealing with matters in a practical way and have accomplished a great deal. If there are those who think that they should renew a barren controversy, that is their right. Nothing good will come of it, and very likely it will stand in the way of much that might otherwise be accomplished." The Secretary added that the real difficulty was not in a lack of machinery "... but the attitude and opinion of peoples." [29] This statement was conclusive, but it was not made public. There was yet hope that the "association of nations" would become a reality eventually and would prove a link between the United States and the League of Nations. This hope was dispelled in large measure by President Harding who declared, in his address to the Senate at the presentation of the Washington Conference treaties, that "none of the treaties at the Washington Conference have any relation to the League except a desire for peace." [30] Notwithstanding these denials the pro-League newspapers continued to interpret the conference as a move toward the League. Others, who did not possess so much faith, still felt that the conference constituted "a long step toward the larger association that is essential to the maintenance of peace throughout the world and to which we must come." Much was written to this effect. Many felt that the conference had brought

147

the United States into an international partnership in which this Nation is certain to attain experience and confidence of a sort that will gradually allay American fears of larger cooperation in safeguarding of peace.... The first step is the hardest. At last we have taken it.[31]

Perhaps only a few men in the United States Senate knew how hollow was this hope.

14 . . .

The Four-Power Treaty

. . . FOR almost a month after the opening of the conference the problem of limitation of navies continued to hold the attention of the public. This work was approved by the Senate since it carried out the spirit, if not the letter, of the Borah Resolution. It was suggested by Senator Pomerene that the President would require authorization by Congress before he could execute the reduction in the navy as recommended by Hughes. The Senate, usually most anxious to assume all prerogatives to which it had a claim, demonstrated further its satisfaction with the administration's direction of the conference by failing to consider Pomerene's resolution.[1] Most Senators agreed with Borah's estimate of the conference: "It is a splendid beginning. . . ." Despite this seeming amity, the Senate still threatened the success of the conference. Far Eastern problems had not been included in the Borah Resolution. Senate opposition might be aroused easily when the conference turned to this part of its work.

Speaking on this possibility, Senator Borah confided to a friend that the conference had started well enough but he feared Far Eastern problems would be discussed before details of disarmament were worked out. If this happened, Borah felt the result would be interminable delay in arriving at an agreement on disarmament, leading, perhaps, to the collapse of the conference because of misunderstandings among the powers.[2] Subsequent events were to show that there was a solid basis for Borah's suspicion that Far Eastern policy was being considered.

Despite his desire to place the problems before the conference into separate categories and deal with them singly, it had been recognized officially, and in the press, that such a policy was impossible. The problems of the Far East, the Anglo-Japanese Alliance, and disarmament were no more divisible at the conference than they had been in the negotiations prior to its convocation. The American press at

149

the time Harding issued his invitations to the conference had expressed its approval of the inclusion of Far Eastern questions along with the discussion on disarmament only because the two were felt to be inseparably linked.[3] An American commentator, on the day the conference opened, wrote that the Anglo-Japanese Alliance was the "over-towering issue of the Conference" in the opinion of all of the delegates in Washington. It was recognized generally, he continued, that, while the Alliance was not an item on the agenda of the conference, the solution of the problems of the Far East and of disarmament was dependent on an early and satisfactory settlement of the issue of the Alliance.

Certainly this estimate was correct as far as the English and Japanese were concerned. The British had given ample evidence of their desire to reach an early settlement on the Alliance, insisting doggedly on a preliminary conference on Far Eastern problems in order to conclude discussions on the Alliance before the Washington Conference began. The press in Japan had conceded likewise that an understanding in regard to the Alliance would be a necessary prerequisite to the attainment of peace and disarmament. In addition, it was recognized in Japan that the United States would not consider disarmament until the Alliance had been abrogated or drastically modified. Both England and Japan, it was frequently rumored, were agreed that the Alliance ought to be modified, and that a tripartite pact would be the most reasonable modification.[4]

After the announcement of the Hughes plan for limitation of capital ships, the importance of the Far East and of the Alliance became increasingly evident. Said the St. Louis *Globe-Democrat*: "Obviously, the application of this program is dependent upon the settlement of Far Eastern problems." The *Chicago Tribune* feared that the disarmament plan would be of no value if the British-Japanese Alliance were continued. The Alliance, according to the *Tribune,* made possible the uniting of the British and Japanese navies. Consequently the ratio system, set forth by Hughes, would be nullified should the Alliance be renewed.[5] In addition, the American public had never liked the Alliance. Lord Bryce estimated that nine out of ten Americans opposed it at the time the conference met. He felt that this opposition was too deeply rooted to be satisfied by anything short of abrogation.[6]

In these circumstances, the problem facing the American delegation, and particularly its head, Secretary of State Hughes, was three-fold in nature: it was necessary at all times to keep the emphasis on disarmament; it was expedient to nullify the Anglo-Japanese Alliance; and it was imperative that this be done without involving the United States in an alliance. For various reasons, Hughes felt, these objectives could best be achieved through secret rather than open diplomacy. Hence, while the conference considered the Alliance, rumors and speculation were all that the practitioners of the "new diplomacy" allowed the public to glean. As was to be expected, there were numerous press reports on the matter—some of which contained elements of truth. None of these had official confirmation, and for this reason did not impress the public. Consequently, there was genuine surprise when it was announced that the Alliance had been replaced by a new agreement, the Four-Power Treaty.

The press reported negotiations on the Alliance, November 16, when it related that Senator Lodge was to confer with Arthur Balfour. It was thought that the result of these discussions would be the abrogation of the Alliance. Again, on December 1, it was reported that Great Britain, the United States, Japan, and France were on the point of signing a treaty. The exact nature of this agreement was unknown; it was thought to deal with Far Eastern problems, and probably with the issue of Russian territorial integrity. The same day, H. G. Wells declared that no lasting peace in the Pacific was conceivable without an alliance composed of America, Britain, and Japan.[7]

The number of rumors increased after December 1. The Associated Press reported, December 5, discussions relative to obtaining a suitable and practical substitute for the Anglo-Japanese Alliance. An English correspondent disclosed that an American-Japanese-British Treaty had been submitted to President Harding and would shortly be transmitted by him to the Senate. There was no confirmation of this report. An American correspondent commented that such an event was not even among the possibilities of the conference.[8] Nevertheless, rumors persisted in spite of denials. By December 7, all of the papers were discussing the nature of the "treaty," "agreement," "alliance," "compact," or "understanding" to which it was thought the United States had become a party. Harding, it was said, had refused to divulge the nature of the plan, but had asserted repeatedly

151

that it would be in a form acceptable to the American public. The Senate would be consulted on this and all other action taken by the United States at the conference. The Committee on General Information reported, the next day, that the papers of the nation were engaged in playing the game, "Treaty, Treaty, who has the Treaty?" [9]

By this time the press had what proved to be a fairly accurate—although still unsubstantiated—conception of the nature of the agreement and the obstacles which had delayed its announcement. It was thought to be a plan that would substitute for the Anglo-Japanese Alliance a four-power pledge to cooperation. Japan was delaying the final announcement of the pact, because that nation was satisfied with neither the naval ratio nor the proposed settlement of the problem of China. In addition, Japan wanted assurance that there would be no sudden attacks on Pacific possessions. These objections were countered by the rumor, December 8, that the Japanese government had given its assent to the pact on the previous day.

The period of suspense and speculation was brought to a close, December 10, with the announcement that four powers—England, France, the United States, and Japan—had accepted a pact which would be made public in a special plenary session to be called immediately.[10]

At the same time, it was explained by an official of the American government that the matter was to have been kept secret until all negotiations were complete. However, information had continued to reach the public despite all efforts to keep the sessions secret. The American delegates became concerned with the comments this information elicited from foreign powers. The frequent use of the word alliance in describing the pact and the rumors of secret negotiations leading to the drafting of an alliance had excited the suspicion of the Senate. It had conducted a veritable inquisition in its efforts to gain exact information from Secretary Hughes and President Harding as to developments.[11]

These questions can now be answered with much greater clarity than was possible in 1921. Inasmuch as the Four-Power Treaty which grew out of these negotiations was, in the estimation of the Senate, the most controversial phase of the Washington Conference, the real negotiations leading to the formulation of the pact merit examination. After Hughes and Geddes reached an understanding regarding the Anglo-Japanese Alliance in June, formal invitations to the Washington Conference were extended. The British then sought to arrange a preliminary conference to deal with the Alliance. Hughes, as has been shown, refused to cooperate with this plan. He also rejected suggestions by the British that Far Eastern problems be given first place on the agenda of the conference. In so doing, he proposed that Great Britain, Japan, and the United States discuss the Alliance in informal meetings during the conference and sought assurance that Britain would not support Japanese aggression and political domination.[12] The negotiations were resumed by Arthur Balfour, British delegate to the conference, on the night before its first session. Balfour said that the Japanese delegation had been looking for him the entire day. Its first question would concern the future of the Anglo-Japanese Alliance.[13] Therefore, the English delegate felt that it was imperative that he and Hughes agree on a joint policy with which to confront the anxious Japanese. If the Alliance was to be dropped, asserted Balfour, some new policy must be prepared immediately to take its place. For this substitute Balfour suggested a tripartite agreement dealing with the preservation of peace and the maintenance of the territorial *status quo* in the Far East, exclusive of the problem of China.[14] Secretary Hughes requested time to consider the aspects of this proposal in detail but immediately raised some objections to Balfour's plan. He felt it would be unwise to use such words as "treaty" and "alliance," suggesting the substitution of the less provocative term "arrangement."[15] Justifying these requests, Hughes explained that an "arrangement" might not be a treaty; if not, the problem of gaining Senate approval would be eliminated. Popular and senatorial prejudice would not allow the United States to join any alliance, but there would be a good possibility of joining an "arrangement."[16]

Hughes then suggested as a model for the new pact the Root-Takahira Agreement of 1908.[17] This agreement had been designed "to preserve the common interest of all powers in China by supporting by pacific means the independence and integrity of China and the principle of equal opportunity for commerce and industry of all nations in the . . . Empire." A second provision pledged the signatories to "maintenance of the *status quo* in the region of the Pacific Ocean." It had constituted a statement of friendship between the

United States and Japan at a time when talk of war was in the air. It had been designed to purchase security of America's Pacific possessions at the cost of recognizing Japan's "special position" in Eastern Asia.[18] Hughes hoped that the new arrangement entered into by the United States would partake of this same informality, express American friendship for Japan, and demonstrate America's willingness to recognize the "natural and legitimate economic opportunities for Japan." At the same time it would reassert American opposition to political control of Asia by Japan.[19] At this point the first conference ended. Subsequently, numerous discussions were held in which Hughes found additional faults in the tripartite agreement which Balfour had presented. The American secretary pointed out that the agreement did not definitely cancel the Anglo-Japanese Alliance. The weakness lay in the fact that any two of the high contracting powers when threatened by any other power could form a military alliance. Thus it would be possible for Great Britain and Japan to reactivate their old alliance without the consent of the United States. This provision would not aid the American people who would never give their consent to become party to an alliance. Furthermore, a tripartite agreement with Great Britain and Japan would be regarded as fatal to American interest. Hughes then suggested that the agreement be freed of the provision for a military alliance and broadened to include France. He also reemphasized that it must be called an agreement rather than an alliance. He felt that it would be improper for the United States, which was not a party to the Alliance, to press these suggestions. The next step was for Balfour to gain Japan's consent to these proposals.[20]

In the early stages of these negotiations Hughes worked with other members of the American delegation. On November 20, Root and Lodge in conference with Chandler P. Anderson, legal adviser to the American delegation, discussed the problem of United States policy on Far Eastern questions. Lodge, conference chairman of the committee on Far Eastern affairs, wanted the United States to keep the leadership it had so far maintained by making a definite statement on the position of the United States relative to the security of Australia and the Pacific Islands. He suggested that a treaty be drafted using the Anglo-Japanese Alliance as a basis.[21] In the new agreement, however, all reference to force was to be eliminated and the powers were to adopt a general statement as to mutual recognition of their sovereignty and rights in the Pacific area. This would have the effect, the American delegates felt, of "substituting a general and harmless international agreement for the Anglo-Japanese agreement," and would enable Great Britain to extricate herself gracefully from the Alliance without raising a direct issue with Japan.[22]

Anderson, with the aid of James Brown Scott, another legal adviser to the American delegation, proceeded to formulate a statement incorporating these ideas. The finished proposal provided for conferences when the general peace was in jeopardy, called upon each power to respect the territorial possessions of the other signatory powers, and provided that none of the signatories would enter into a separate arrangement with any other power or powers.[23] Anderson later discussed this draft with Lodge. The Senator now felt that the agreement should be limited to the area of the Pacific and Indian Oceans, excluding the mainland, in order to avoid the problems of domestic politics in China and India. "With this exception," Anderson related, "Lodge approved it without any material change, and expressed himself as very much pleased with it and greatly obliged to us." [24] Hughes did not share Lodge's enthusiasm for this treaty draft. His chief objections were that the proposal did not cancel the Alliance, and was indefinite as to the number of signatories.[25]

From this point on the negotiations progressed without the aid of any of the members of the American legal staff or any of the American delegation except Hughes.[26] The next draft considered by the Secretary of State was presented by the Japanese on November 26. Although not officially approved by the Japanese government, it did represent the personal views of the Japanese ambassador, Kijuro Shidehara, and was sanctioned by the other members of the Japanese delegation. Apparently it had the approval of Balfour who not only discussed the preliminary proposal with Shidehara but also made certain changes in the final draft.[27] It differed from the original Balfour version in that it covered both the territorial rights and the "vital interests" of the contracting powers,[28] a modification which was evidently included at the request of the Japanese. This draft did not please Hughes either, for it still contained the objectionable features of Balfour's proposal—it was tripartite in scope and did not definitely abrogate the Anglo-Japanese Alliance.[29]

155

Meanwhile no final steps toward the inclusion of France into the proposed agreement had been taken. The Japanese cable was heavily congested and no reply had been received from the Japanese government on this important matter. This situation worried Hughes since he knew that the French delegates were becoming restive because of inactivity. France was not destroying any battleships and consequently the French delegates did not meet with Britain, Japan, and the United States as they discussed a naval ratio. The French were thus reduced to the unwelcome role of spectators at the conference.

Hughes inquired of Baron Kato, December 2, as to the attitude of the Japanese delegation on the proposed quadruple agreement. Kato replied that he had telegraphed his government but had not received an answer. He believed that his government would be perfectly satisfied with the proposal. It would be safe to approach the French delegation on the matter. Hughes was too wise and cautious to take such a step before the position of the Japanese government became definitely known.[30]

The next day Senator Schanzer told Hughes that he felt Italy should be a party to the proposed quadruple agreement rumored in the press. Hughes explained that any such proposal would apply only to the territorial holdings of the four nations in the Pacific. Italy, having no such holdings, would be excluded from this agreement. In the larger matter of general policies toward China, said Hughes, Italy and the other nations present at the conference would be consulted.[31]

Shortly after this, word was received from Japan approving the inclusion of France in the proposed agreement. Arrangements were made for a meeting of the four powers. Secretary Hughes prepared from the earlier drafts his own version of the pact.[32] Although this draft was similar to the English and Japanese plans, it differed in several vital particulars. The scope of the agreement was reduced, guaranteeing "the insular possessions and dominions in the Pacific Ocean," whereas both the other powers had specified the area to be covered as the Far East and the regions of the Pacific Ocean.[33] Also Hughes omitted reference to the "vital interests" of Japan, limited the pact to ten years, and specifically abrogated the Anglo-Japanese Alliance. Copies of this draft were given Root and Lodge who approved it. Senator Underwood was not consulted as he was out of

Washington at the time because of the death of his mother.[34] Hughes also had the pact approved by Balfour, Shidehara, and Geddes. He incorporated the suggestions of all these advisers into a revised version presented to the French on the evening of December 7. When Viviani, the head of the French delegation after the departure of Premier Briand, read the agreement at this meeting, he was so pleased that he kissed Hughes on both cheeks.[35]

Further discussion of the act took place on December 8 and 9 at the home of Secretary Hughes. At the first of these meetings Shidehara presented yet another draft.[36] It contained the provision that two powers could "in mutual agreement with each other" invite the remaining contracting parties to a joint conference. This possibility of the continuation of Anglo-Japanese accord Hughes rejected once again. In further discussion of Shidehara's draft it was brought out that Hughes wanted to exclude from the scope of the agreement any question relating to the mainland of Asia, especially China. He insisted, however, that the act be interpreted as including the mandated islands. This definition of the area covered by the agreement to include insular possessions was not completely satisfactory since Japan was itself a series of islands in the Pacific.[37] Shidehara inquired whether Japan's home islands were to be considered in the same category with other island possessions. Hughes, in reply, asserted that the agreement did include the home islands of Japan. Shidehara objected on the ground that such an interpretation would not be satisfactory to his government. The homelands of the other signatories were not included simply because they were not islands in the Pacific. A long discussion followed in which an attempt was made to meet Japanese objections. Balfour observed that England would be presented with a delicate problem in dealing with Australia and New Zealand, which were island possessions in the Pacific, if Japan were accorded a special exemption from the terms of the treaty.

At the conclusion of the discussion on December 8, the delegates decided to consider a proposal to exclude the Islands of Japan from the treaty, and also to exempt from the action of the treaty any matter which, under the terms of international law, was a part of the domestic policy of the nation concerned.[38] However, at the beginning of the last session, December 9, Shidehara announced that he would abandon his demand for the exclusion of the main islands of

Japan. This proposal, having been accepted by the other powers, was incorporated in the treaty.[39]

This treaty, thus completed, was the handiwork of the heads of the delegations to such a degree that its real nature was unknown to the lesser members of the delegations and their official advisers. Anderson was shocked to hear that the agreement had been completed without his knowledge, and sought Root to find why the legal staff had been ignored. Its members, in appraising the Four-Power Treaty, had reached the conclusion that it had two serious defects: it failed to state definitely that in a conference of the powers action would be determined only by "adjustment by mutual agreement"; it implied, in the second article, that the powers would be bound to carry out jointly the measures which they decided were advisable. Had the legal staff been consulted, Anderson felt these faults would have been deleted. These two issues, he predicted, would cause much debate in the Senate and might even jeopardize the passage of the Treaty. He hoped steps might be taken to rectify these errors.

Root told Anderson that it was too late to take action. He declared that he himself had not been consulted during the final negotiations; Hughes, the only American delegate who participated in the drafting of the treaty, had been little more than a spectator. In fact, he could not do otherwise, because the United States could not properly suggest changes in the Anglo-Japanese Alliance to which it was not a party. Root told Anderson that for this reason "Mr. Hughes had let the agreement go through practically as drafted by Great Britain and Japan . . . feeling that it would be impossible to change even a word in it without jeopardizing the negotiation." [40] Hughes confirmed the exclusive nature of the negotiations by apologizing to Anderson for ignoring the legal staff. He explained that it was deemed advisable to present the treaty to the public in its finished form. Otherwise, opposition might have arisen before the delegates had an opportunity to accomplish their purpose. The need for secrecy made it imperative that the consultations be terminated before any information on the nature of the agreement became public. Consequently, there was tremendous pressure to complete the pact in the shortest possible time.[41]

In this manner the negotiations on the Four-Power Treaty were concluded hastily, and a plenary session was summoned for the next day. So quickly were these arrangements made, some of the newsmen

158

in Washington failed to learn of the meeting until after its close. Senator Lodge, for obvious reasons, was the logical choice to present the pact to the public and to the Senate. The Massachusetts Senator rose to the occasion with an eloquent address, devoting much time to an explanation of the area covered by the agreement, and of its value, but giving little time to its specific obligations and requirements. He dismissed his duty as an expositor of terms by declaring that the Treaty was too simple to be misunderstood by anyone. As to its importance, Lodge told his audience that many people would declare the area in which peace had been guaranteed precisely the part of the world in which a future war was most improbable. On the contrary, the island paradises of the Pacific were a probable scene of conflict. Said the Senator, "History unhappily has shown that there is no corner of the earth so remote or so valueless that it is not capable of giving cause for controversy or even war between the tribes and nations of mankind." Lodge described not only the threat to peace, but also the Pacific Islands themselves over which this threat hung:

There still lingers about them the charm so compelling and so fascinating which an undiscovered country has for the sons of men who are weary of main-traveled roads and the trampled highways of trade and commerce which cover the surface of the patient earth.

He turned then for assistance to Robert Browning, Robert Louis Stevenson, and, with his New England constituents in mind, Herman Melville. Some present professed astonishment at such an exhibition of erudition. Yet, no one familiar with the ways of the Senate and American politicians should have been surprised that Lodge was capable of turning to the classics, or that he was using his literary knowledge to bury the less desirable features of the Four-Power Pact under the petaled fragrance of the "lilies on lilies that overlace the sea." [42]

Lodge got his modicum of praise on this address from masters of language and oratory, but he paid for it dearly in the more numerous and less flattering references in the press and in the Senate. Elmer Davis, writing for the *New York Times,* commented that Lodge had taken the audience on a personally conducted tour of the South Sea islands and the world's best classics. The speech, Davis said, was compounded of Bartlett's *Familiar Quotations,* Brewer's *Dictionary of Literary Allusions,* and Rand McNally's latest atlas. The orator, thought Davis, deserved a vote of thanks from the National Geographic Society. Senator Reed castigated the speech and the treaty as being "unspeakable." [43] He quoted to the Senate at length from a caustic commentary by H. L. Mencken, who called the Four-Power Treaty nothing more than "amiable politeness." Mencken berated Lodge for his caution in failing to clarify its practical effects. Instead of discussing those important matters, said Mencken, the Senator had avoided the real issue and

devoted at least half of his time to a lyrical account of human happiness in the South Seas—an account obviously based upon a diligent reading of Frederick O'Brien's celebrated book, and particularly upon an examination of the illustrations thereof, with their intimate views of exquisite scenery, both geographical and anatomical. . . . Ah, to be young again and free to roam this lovely earth—

> Eating huckleberries all day long,
> And learning how to love.[44]

Even the skill of a seasoned politician like Lodge could not hide from the Senate the fact that the new Treaty carried the taint of secrecy and might be construed as an alliance. The *London Evening Standard* warned its readers that excessive optimism was not in order until the attitude of the United States Senate and the Japanese government was better known. Elsewhere in Europe the press sounded a similar note of caution and pessimism.[45] In America various newspapers attempted to determine the real attitude of the Senate by interviewing individuals and taking straw votes of the body as a whole. The *New York Tribune,* the *New York Times,* the *Philadelphia Public Ledger,* the *Washington Post,* and other papers found in the results of their polls a substantial majority of the Senate favoring the Four-Power Treaty. As additional evidence that it would approve the pact, it was noted that the administration had taken every precaution to win its support. The Treaty had won the public's approval to such a degree that the Senate would hardly care to incur the disfavor that would accompany obstruction of its passage.

Another encouraging factor was the willingness of Democrats to cooperate with the Republicans in support of the new pact. The Democrats gave their support because they regarded this Treaty as an outgrowth of the Democratic sponsored League of Nations.[46] Furthermore, the possibility of partisan obstruction was virtually can-

celed by the announcement that Senator Hitchcock, who had led the
Democratic forces in the Senate debate on the League, would join
Senator Underwood in support of the Treaty. The Republican members of the Senate, according to the press, would approve the Treaty
because it was an administration measure. In addition, the Republicans felt that Hughes and Harding had "brought about a wonderful
instrument for the peace of the world." [47]

Most senators who were interviewed made favorable but cautious
comments. Senator Walsh thought the Treaty was important because
it had abrogated the Anglo-Japanese Alliance, but he felt that it dealt
with only a small part of the work which the country was led to
believe the conference would cover. [48] Senator Jim Watson favored
the pact because it did not permit "the establishment of any super-
government or provide for the use of force to carry out its obligations." Senator Duncan U. Fletcher described the Treaty as "a fine
piece of Work." Senator Henry L. Myers was more specific, calling
the agreement a beginning toward the accomplishment of world
peace. Senator Richard P. Ernest was noncommittal in declaring that
it would accomplish the purpose for which it was intended. The irreconcilables in the Senate were not willing to be quoted immediately.
Even Borah felt that time was needed to examine the Treaty more
carefully before making a statement.

Opposition to the Treaty gathered around Senator Jim Reed, a
Democrat who had been one of the irreconcilables. Almost as soon
as the Four-Power Treaty was made public, Reed described it as
"treasonable and damnable," asserting that it contained commitments which would lead the United States into war. [49] The pact was
a Japanese victory, "a proposition to refer our rights to a tribunal of
four, in which we have but one voice," and the very type of alliance
which the United States had hitherto wisely avoided. [50] In summing
up his objection to the Treaty, Reed attacked the secrecy which had
attended the conception of the alliance. It was, he said, a gold brick
"finished one night at 11 o'clock in secret session and handed the
American people about daylight the next morning evidently with
the idea that at that time it could be sold quickly to an unsuspecting
public." [51]

It was not long before the press carried the news that "the same
group of 'irreconcilables' who led the fight against our participation

161

in the League of Nations have now rushed to arms to rescue the nation from the Four-Power Pacific Treaty." [52] Senator Borah denounced it as an armed alliance and a "war breeder." [53] Senator LaFollette characterized the pact as having "all of the iniquities of the League of Nations, with none of the virtues claimed for the document." [54] The similarity between the new Treaty and the old League was also noted by Senator A. O. Stanley, who queried, "Who would have thought it; Senator Lodge is the father of a baby League of Nations." [55] The indefatigable Borah told one member of his extensive correspondence audience that the new pact was "dynamite, a little more subtle in its structure than that of the Versailles Treaty, but no less destructive in its nature of the things which you and I believe." [56] Again he wrote, "We ought not to be asked for the mere scrapping of some battleships to become a member of a military alliance whose business it will be to dominate the Orient by military force." [57]

The administration believed that this opposition was confined to a handful of senators who could not block ratification. General opinion also subscribed to this theory. The *Providence Journal* reported that the latest canvass of the Senate revealed that Borah's fight had been lost before it began. "His battalion of death is divided," it stated. The London *Daily Chronicle* observed that the attitude of the Senate was one of "dutiful acquiescence," because Borah and Reed could not find a dozen followers. Other prognosticators estimated there would be no more than ten votes against the Treaty, and that at that time the opposition numbered only six senators. This feeling of optimism was strengthened somewhat by the announcement that ex-President Wilson, still a power in the Democratic party, had admonished his friends in the Senate to keep an open mind and wait for further developments at the conference before making a decision on the Four-Power pact. In addition, it was reported that Senator Underwood, while holding conferences with various Democratic senators, had been able to explain the Treaty to them in a very satisfactory way.

This optimism was somewhat dispelled a few days later by an unfortunate misunderstanding between the White House and the American delegates. After the announcement of the Treaty, E. I. James reported in the *New York Times* that the Four-Power pact

162

insured the Japanese homeland. Subsequently, he obtained from the State Department a confirmation of this interpretation.[58] In response to questions by newsmen, December 20, President Harding declared that the term "insular possessions" as used in the Four-Power Treaty was not intended to include the home islands of Japan.[59]

This statement caused an immediate sensation, because it was generally believed that Harding was familiar with the interpretation placed on the Treaty by the American delegation. When the question had been discussed during the negotiations of the Treaty, all the delegations had emphatically stated that the home islands of Japan were included. An undisclosed member of the American delegation in interviews with the press had insisted on this point until he had caused the newsmen to tire of it. Furthermore, the question had been debated on the floor of the Senate prior to Harding's announcement. Senator Reed had stated on this occasion that the Treaty did include the principal islands of Japan, and declared this provision to be of grave consequence to the United States.[60] Thus, the possibility that Harding was unaware of the American delegates' decision seemed remote. The only other plausible conclusion was that the President deliberately opposed the policy of his delegates.

This conflict in opinion caused "no little consternation" among those interested in the conference and produced much excitement in the Senate.[61] The American public had an ingrained aversion to and suspicion of all foreign diplomats and a deep mistrust of the Japanese, in particular. Thus, it was only natural that many persons should immediately jump to the conclusion that America had been duped by the wily diplomats of Nippon.

Harding, in a conference with Hughes, admitted that he was confused and should have kept quiet, but he answered the press because he did not want to appear "to be a dub." Finding no fundamental disagreement, Harding announced that their views were identical.[62] Enough time had elapsed, however, for numerous rumors to spread. If Harding did not wish to oppose the view of his representatives, the only alternative in judging his action was that he had been grossly stupid. However, he had his champions. One of them declared that this episode demonstrated Harding's superiority to Wilson. While the latter dominated his delegates at Paris, Harding allowed his co-workers so much independence that he did not know

163

what they were doing.[63] The President's error, according to a more skilled defense, was one of the penalties of open diplomacy. It happened only because the public had been so well informed on all developments at the conference.[64] Harding's critics were delighted with his mistake and made the most of this opportunity to detract from the popularity of the Four-Power Treaty.

Senator Reed, the most active opponent of the Treaty in the Senate, attacked the President with caustic satire. "Nearly everything that has been said by the President of the United States up to date, whether he was on a fishing expedition, sailing the turbid waters of the southern seas in a senatorial scow, or golfing on the green, has been put into the *Record.*" He suggested that Harding's most recent public address, his opinion on the Four-Power Treaty, also be included. Carrying out his suggestion, the Senator had inserted in the *Record* long excerpts from the *Washington Post,* the *New York Times,* and the Associated Press, which gave in detail the President's opinions on the status of the Japanese home islands. The Senator asserted that the President's original statement, made on the floor of the Senate, was an attempt to refute the charge that the Treaty did guarantee the home islands of Japan. The President, charged Reed, was unwilling to defend an interpretation which had aroused immediate and bitter attacks in the Senate.[65]

Two days after Harding's announcement, the *New York Times* featured the headline: "Senate Foes Want Treaty Made Clear." Senator Lodge's assertion that the Treaty was a simple and easily understood document did not seem to be justified by the facts. Furthermore, if the Treaty did not mean what it said, or did not say what it meant, then the opposition could read into its terms a vast array of objections. The *New York Herald,* two days after the disclosure of Harding's interpretation, estimated that it had ". . . exercised a tremendous effect on the Senate and, to some extent on the country generally." The irreconcilables in the Senate were joined in their opposition by a group of Wilson Democrats, led by William H. King, Carter Glass, and Claude A. Swanson. Borah stated:

I want to say this to the American people, that before the treaty gets through the Senate the American delegates will have a chance to make it plain if they want to do so. We have already drafted amendments and reservations that will leave no doubt as to the treaty's true meaning.

164

Senator Charles L. McNary seconded the latter view, stating that if the Treaty were not amended by the delegates before the conclusion of the conference, he hoped that the administration would support a Senate reservation to exclude the Japanese mainland. Senators Brandegee, Moses, and Poindexter declared their opposition to any agreement whereby the United States would guarantee the Japanese mainland.[66] Senator Hitchcock, still an important figure in the Democratic camp, expressed a hope that the Treaty would be qualified by an interpretative reservation. He felt there was no possibility of passing the Treaty in the Senate as long as the Japanese islands were included.[67]

There were various estimates as to the effect of this misunderstanding. Harding's interpretation, it was felt, had "cast the first real cloud on what have hitherto been the unqualifiedly hopeful prospects of the Conference." If the break did not actually jeopardize the treaties in the Senate, it would "prolong the debate in the Senate." [68]

One immediate result was that Senators Reed and Borah redoubled their efforts to stimulate opposition to the Treaty. Reed declared that the disarmament proposition was being burdened with "a quadruple alliance made for the protection of the interests of Great Britain and Japan in the Orient." Under its terms, he warned, the United States was being made "to underwrite in the blood of its sons the avarice and ambition of Great Britain and Japan in Pacific waters." Borah cast doubt on the future of the pact, observing that "it took six months to wake the people up to the inequities of the League, but they are already aroused against the perils and dangers of the Four-Power Alliance." The Hearst press, noting this opposition, pointed out that as a result of this confusion twenty-five Democrats could be expected to vote against the Treaty. The addition of only a dozen Republican votes to the opposition would defeat it.[69]

The public opposition of senators to the inclusion of the Japanese homeland gave Shidehara another chance to press his original demand for its exclusion. On December 19, in a conversation with Hughes on the matter, Shidehara stated that he had seen news reports of senatorial objection to the Four-Power Treaty because it included the Japanese home islands. Hughes questioned the accuracy of such reports; he doubted that the opposition raised on this score would make any difference in the ratification of the Treaty. Shidehara, nevertheless, declared his willingness to clear any obstacle from the path of the Treaty in the United States Senate and suggested that an agreement excluding the main islands of Japan might be a satisfactory solution to the problem. Hughes agreed to take the matter up with senators Lodge and Underwood.[70]

The Associated Press reported, four days later, that Japan regarded the special treatment given it under the Treaty as humiliating—placing it in the category of a weaker nation. The interpretation which had been adopted, continued the report, was as unpopular in Japan as it was in the Senate. Subsequent reports hinted that the American delegation had taken up the matter of clarifying this question, and that conversations on the problem were being held between the Japanese and American officials.[71]

Probably this was the case, for on January 14, Hughes met with Shidehara and agreed to exclude the main islands.[72] As finally accepted by the powers on February 6, 1922, the Treaty stated that the term "insular possessions and insular dominions" should, in its application to Japan, include only Karafuto (or the southern portion of the island of Sakhalin), Formosa, the Pescadores, and the islands under the mandate of Japan.[73]

Another problem which developed after the Treaty had been announced was the desire of several other nations to adhere to the agreement. Among those turned down because they did not have any insular possessions in the Pacific were Italy and Siam.[74] The Netherlands also sought to reach some understanding with the signatory powers, and here a more complex problem arose. The Netherlands did own insular possessions in the Pacific.

Jonkheer van Karnebeck first represented the case of the Netherlands to Hughes by asking, on December 9, for a formal recognition of the territorial *status quo* in the Pacific. If this were not done it would appear, he pointed out, that Holland was the only power with insular possessions in the Far East whose territorial rights found no explicit recognition at the Washington Conference.[75] This request was considered at a meeting of Kato, Hughes, and Balfour on December 12. Balfour suggested that a separate instrument might be devised by which Holland could be admitted to the Four-Power Treaty when questions affecting the Dutch islands arose. This suggestion was given carefully qualified approval by Kato and Hughes.[76]

Subsequently the possibility of including the Netherlands in the Four-Power Treaty was considered. Root, on December 28, drafted an agreement which would expand the Four-Power pact to include the Netherlands and the other nations at the Conference with the exception of China. It was to pledge their firm resolve "to respect and observe the territorial rights of each other in the regions above described." (This was the region of the Pacific Ocean.) Secretary Hughes wrote in pencil at the bottom of this draft, "Impossible for many reasons." [77] He later demonstrated why. The region of the Pacific, the area of the Root draft, was too broad. It would probably include India, and "it would certainly include Eastern Siberia where Japan has claims of an indefinite sort." Hughes did not want China included because that, too, would bring up additional problems; but, on the other hand, there was no satisfactory reason to give for excluding China while allowing that nation to sign the Nine-Power Treaty. Hughes also objected to the phrase "their interests" which he asserted had been carefully eliminated from the Four-Power Treaty. There was danger likewise in the idea of observing territorial rights, for such terms might be seized upon by Japan as recognition of the special position which she was attempting to establish in the Orient. With this analysis John MacMurray, Chief of the State Department's Division of Far Eastern Affairs, agreed. He stated that such a modification as Root proposed would include powers that had no concern with the real aims of the Four-Power pact. In addition, the widened scope of the Treaty would include the danger spots of Tibet, Siam, Korea, and Siberia. The United States could not undertake to respect territorial rights in these areas.[78] Accordingly, this plan was dropped, and no new powers were included in the agreement. The government of the Netherlands was presented, on February 3, with identical notes from the parties to the Four-Power Treaty which stated that each power was "firmly resolved to respect the rights of the Netherlands in relation to their insular possession in the region of the Pacific Ocean." [79]

With the repulse of this effort to extend the scope of the Four-Power Treaty, Hughes' work in drafting it was concluded. His general purpose had been to solidify America's opposition to Japanese expansion in the Orient. The specific implementing of this aim was the dissolution of the Anglo-Japanese Alliance, thus making Britain

167

an opponent rather than a partner of Japanese expansion. Hughes succeeded in this purpose despite the danger of offending Japan and the difficulty of framing an international agreement which would gain the approval of the Senate.

The opinion of the Senate, a source of constant concern to the press, was surveyed again at the end of the year in the wake of these developments. These studies indicated that there was more opposition to the Treaty than had been shown formerly. Charles Michelson in the *New York World* reported that the enemies of the Treaty had gathered almost enough votes to defeat it.[80] Elsewhere, it was maintained that the opposition in the Senate could not count on more than twenty-two votes; another estimate lowered the number to fourteen.

During the remainder of the conference, reports of Senate opposition to the Four-Power Treaty continued to appear in the news. Senator Borah made an address early in January in which he proposed that signatories to the pact agree to restore and protect all property and rights acquired by aggression. Unwillingness to agree would substantiate Borah's contention that the pact was a military alliance by aggressors to confirm their aggression.[81]

Other senators who joined Borah in his opposition were influential, but not numerous. One of them, Hiram Johnson, called the Pacific Treaty a joint guarantee of Japan.[82] Again he declared that in the West the man in the street was beginning to wonder if the Republican party was not throwing away the fruits of its historic victory of 1920.[83] Probably the Senate would have devoted more time to attacks on the Treaty had it not been that its interest was directed at this point to the sensational debate concerning the seating of Truman H. Newberry.[84]

The Senate and Far Eastern Policy

⬩ ⬩ ⬩ AFTER the initial enthusiasm attending the announcement of the Four-Power Treaty had subsided, it became increasingly clear that its ultimate value could be determined only in relation to the total accomplishment of the conference.

Senator Borah, recognizing this fact, told the Senate, December 12, the first day the Four-Power pact was discussed, that "the extent and vigor of my opposition to this treaty will be determined very largely by what the conference does with reference to real disarmament and by what it does with reference to China." Disarmament, Borah felt, should be carried to such a degree that submarines would be abolished and other armament reduced to token forces. In respect to China, Borah's ideal was equally utopian, for he hoped that an opportunity for the development of independence might be provided.[1]

Borah and the other members of the Senate did not have to wait long for the decision of the conference on the first of these fundamental problems. On December 15, it was announced that the powers had given their approval to the ratio of 5-5-3 suggested by Hughes.

It was also announced that this agreement had been reached by compromise. Originally, the Japanese wished the ratio to be 10-10-7. When Hughes, fearing it would be unacceptable to the public and the Senate, opposed this plan, they demanded as compensation an agreement among the powers to retain the *status quo* in the fortification of island possessions in the Pacific.[2] For a time it appeared that the negotiations on the naval ratio would end in a stalemate with the high promise of the opening day of the conference unfulfilled. Hughes was determined to achieve a limitation of naval armament. He was convinced that the adoption of the ratio of 10-10-6 was fundamental to the success of the conference, while the right to fortify Pacific islands was not vital to the United States. His col-

169

leagues from the Senate assured him that "Congress would never consent to spend the vast sums required in adequately fortifying these islands."[3] Hughes agreed to comply with the Japanese proposal. This decision he made without consulting any of his naval experts, and in disregard of the Navy's pre-conference advice that the right to fortify the Pacific islands should not be relinquished.[4]

With the first rumors of this agreement the opposition of a number of senators was aroused. Senator Poindexter, usually a stalwart advocate of administration policy, was highly incensed by the proposal.[5] Subsequently, the naval treaty itself was not discussed in Congress at length, but the matter of Pacific fortifications was much debated by the Senate during its considerations of the Four-Power Treaty.

The Senate was interested in the attempt by the conference to outlaw the submarine. This proposal was made for Great Britain by Lord Lee. The French government opposed and defeated it. France's attitude and her reluctance to accept the inferior ratio in capital ships given it under the Hughes formula resulted in a tremendous amount of unfavorable comment in the United States. The Senate took note of this reaction; Medill McCormick presented a resolution which was obviously designed to embarrass the French. It requested information as to the exact cost per year for the maintenance of land armaments by several of the European states, including France. Likewise requested was a statement of the annual deficit in the budget for each of these states. A final provision requested a comparison of this military budget with the sum of interest annually due America in settlement of war loans.[6] Although the French government was not designated by name in this resolution, the inference was clear, and a number of indignant rejoinders appeared in the French press.[7] This "effrontery" on the part of the Senate did not vitally affect the conference, although it created additional problems for the American delegates.

In regard to China, another subject of vital concern to the conference, the Senate took an active interest. This interest was the outgrowth of the traditional solicitude by the United States for the progress of China, the Senate debate on the disposition of Shantung at the close of the First World War, and the increased responsibility which had come to the United States as a result of the proposed

170

Four-Power Treaty. While the Senate professed a deep concern for the welfare of China, it showed a continuing tendency to over-simplify the solution for China's ills.

During the early stages of the conference the Chinese presented their "Bill of Rights," and the delegates adopted revisions suggested by Root and Balfour. The Senate found little opportunity at this time to express actively its interest in China. However, the application of these principles was difficult. The debate continued for weeks and grew progressively less harmonious. Senate leaders now became concerned with the matter and fearful lest no decision be made. They felt that the American public would not be satisfied with the conference and with the Republican party, unless something were done for China.[8] Specifically, the public wanted to see the independence of China fostered and the Shantung dispute settled in its favor. The Senate, therefore, considered several resolutions designed to force the conference to accomplish these purposes.

Settlement of the Shantung dispute was not on the conference agenda. The attitude of the Senate and the vital importance of the dispute in Far Eastern affairs made its solution mandatory. Accordingly, the British and American delegations persuaded Japan and China to discuss the problem in a series of meetings in which the Anglo-American delegates extended their good offices as observers.[9] These negotiations began on December 1, but no conclusion could be reached. The sessions grew so troubled that on at least two occasions they were almost discontinued. In one of these cases the Senate was instrumental in preventing disaster. The first week in January, Arthur Balfour announced that he had arranged passage home and would leave before the month was out.[10] There was no hope of concluding the discussion on Shantung and Chinese problems by that date. As a consequence Balfour's departure would amount to an admission of failure. However, he changed his plans for sailing— apparently as a result of developments at an informal gathering at the White House on January 7. There the work of the conference was discussed, with Secretary Hughes learning from several senators present that the Four-Power Treaty and the naval ratio were not likely to win the approval of the Senate unless the problems of China were solved.[11] Hughes redoubled his efforts to foster agreement on the Shantung issue. On January 10, it was announced that the con-

171

ference would continue for at least fifteen additional days, and that the British delegation would not sail, as previously announced.[12]

The Senate continued its active interest in Far Eastern problems. On January 16, Senator King introduced a resolution regarding the internal affairs of China. The traditional policy of the United States, King recalled, was to refrain from interference with the internal affairs of other nations. He, therefore, suggested that the Senate formally disapprove any policy or program that was intended to abridge the political independence, restrict the administrative or financial autonomy, or limit the national authority of China.[13] This resolution was tabled and had no apparent effect on the delegates. These men, while piously proclaiming their devotion to the independence of China, proceeded with the establishment of fiscal policies depriving it of the revenue which was the life-blood of national independence.

Shortly after the King Resolution was rejected, Senator Walsh of Montana presented a resolution requesting information as to the progress being made by the Japanese and Chinese on the solution of the Shantung controversy. Walsh in his resolution reviewed the history of the Shantung question beginning with August 15, 1914, when Japan had declared its purpose to take "the entire leased territory of Kiaochow, with a view to eventual restoration of the same to China." He asserted, and cited specific references as proof, that the American policy, from Bryan, in 1915, through Hughes, in 1921, had been non-recognition of Japanese claims to Chinese territory. The resolution recommended that the Four-Power pact, which provided for settlement of disputes in the Pacific, be invoked to solve this most outstanding of Far Eastern controversies.[14] There was a short debate on this resolution, during which Senators Underwood and Lodge declared their full sympathy with its purpose. Both of these American delegates felt that a solution of the problem would be evolved in direct negotiations between the two oriental powers. Lodge explained that the Versailles treaty guaranteed Japan its claims. Thus, the United States, which was not a party to the Versailles treaty and not directly concerned in the dispute, was already doing all that it could do properly to bring about a solution. Underwood ended the debate for the day by declaring that any effort to bring the question into plenary session and to force the hands of the negotiators "would be throwing a monkey wrench into a piece of

172

machinery which might affect the world very seriously. . . ." If the negotiations proceeded, he felt, they would result in a satisfactory solution of the problem in a short time.[15] Walsh re-introduced the resolution on January 23, and again on January 24, but failed to obtain unanimous consent to its passage.[16] Apparently, the Senate as a whole agreed with Wesley L. Jones of Washington who stated that it was "very inopportune and very unwise for the senate to pass this resolution." It would, in the long run, obstruct rather than aid the cause for which it was intended.[17]

Actually, the resolution did have some effect despite its failure to gain official adoption. After the introduction of the Walsh Resolution, few observers cared to question Walsh's statement that the Senate probably would not ratify the Four-Power Treaty if the Shantung issue and Chinese problems in general were not satisfactorily worked out. Frank Simonds, a prominent reporter, typified this opinion in declaring that without a settlement of the Chinese questions, there was little hope of getting the Four-Power Treaty approved by the Senate. This was true, said Simonds, in spite of the fact that only a month before it would have been difficult to find a half dozen votes in the Senate in opposition to the Treaty.[18] Balfour had this situation in mind too. He informed the Japanese that failure to reach "an agreement . . . on a number of these important questions" would bring serious repercussions in the United States, and might threaten the naval treaty itself.[19]

This increasing senatorial opposition impressed Secretary Hughes who exerted himself to the utmost to secure an agreement on the problems of the Far East. One means he employed was the use of pressure to gain China's consent to the Japanese terms on Shantung. Hughes to this end cabled J. G. Schurman, the American minister in China, January 25, instructing him to advise the Chinese government "that a policy of insisting obstinately upon impractical points of view may defeat the hopes of China and of China's friends."[20] Previously, Hughes had sent similar messages to his other agents in China.[21] The Chinese, evidently bowing to this pressure, agreed reluctantly to terms that fell short of their hopes. In return, they secured a new pledge to guarantee their sovereignty. This settlement was widely hailed at the time as a major triumph for the conference. However, there were those who felt the triumph was hollow; some charged Hughes with failure greater than Wilson's at Paris. The Secretary of State should have accomplished much, it was pointed out, for he had everything in his favor, yet he had squandered his assets and had salvaged nothing more than the appearance of success.[22] The criticism was made that the United States, intent on achieving success and avoiding controversy, had rushed China into an agreement which in no way solved the fundamental problems of the Far East.

Disregarding what "might have been" and the possible motives of the administration, the fact remains that a "settlement" of Chinese problems had been reached—without which the conference would have failed. In addition to this accomplishment, Hughes could point with pride to the fact that these agreements were acceptable to a majority in the Senate, and would do much to gain the approval of that body for the entire work of the conference. Furthermore, American Far Eastern policy had been reaffirmed, despite many obstacles, by the strongest sanction obtainable under international law.[23]

16 . . .

The Treaties Go to the Senate

. . . WHEN the Washington Conference was concluded and the last treaty signed, the policy of the Senate toward these pacts, long a subject for speculation, became an engrossing topic of discussion by the public and the press. Public and press opinion approved the work of the conference by a wide majority. In the Senate there was opposition from a determined clique.

The public's acceptance of the conference treaties rested on the solid basis of logic. The conference had been called to put an end to naval competition, to advance the cause of world peace, and to meet the problems of Far Eastern policy. In all of these matters, according to the public, it had made a notable achievement. The Five-Power Treaty had set a naval ratio which had ended competition between the three largest naval powers in the world. No "association of nations" had arisen to replace the rejected League of Nations, but world peace, the ultimate aim of world organization, had been substantially advanced by the conference itself and by the settlement of the armament question. The nation was on the pathway to peace. Should its progress toward this goal be threatened in the future, another conference could be called quickly and the difficulties effectively dispatched. The Far Eastern problems were not acknowledged to be of vital importance within themselves. Nevertheless, the public and the press recognized that world peace and disarmament could not become realities while tension existed in Asia. Here again the conference had done its work well. The Four-Power Treaty had abrogated the Anglo-Japanese Alliance, and the Nine-Power Treaty had secured the sanction of international law for the Open Door policy. The Yap Island controversy, the Shantung question, and Japanese intervention in Siberia had all been settled by agreements during the conference. It appeared that American Far Eastern policy was on a sound footing with the Open Door re-established and strengthened.

175

The Senate, apparently, was the only obstacle in the path of complete success. Only the Four-Power Treaty, already the subject of severe and prolonged attack, had aroused any opposition. The limitation of armament and the solution of Far Eastern problems were dependent on the abrogation of the Anglo-Japanese Alliance as provided in the Four-Power Treaty. On the fate of this treaty rested the fate of the conference.

In the weeks following the conclusion of the conference, opinion was divided on the possible defeat of the Four-Power Treaty. From the first day the pact reached the Senate the *New York Times* predicted the Treaty's eventual passage. It admitted, however, that none of the informal polls so far taken had shown a clear majority for the Treaty. In support of its prediction, the paper stated it was evident that on the Republican side all but a half dozen irreconcilables would support the Treaty, and that the Democrats would not vote against it as a unit. Thus, its success or failure would lie with those Democrats who had not declared themselves.[1]

A strong faction of the public was determined to see that the Senate did not nullify the work of a conference which had solved problems baffling western civilization for centuries. The *Literary Digest* conducted a poll to get an indication of editorial opinion on ratification. Of eight hundred and three replies from leading papers of the country, seven hundred and three were for ratification of the treaties, sixty-six opposed and fourteen noncommittal. This survey, covering forty-seven of the forty-eight states, presumably was an accurate appraisal of the attitude of the American press.[2]

President Harding voiced the sentiment of millions of his countrymen when he declared, at the last formal session of the conference, "This conference has wrought a truly great achievement. . . . The faith plighted here today, kept in national honor, will mark the beginning of a new and better epoch in human progress. . . ."[3] Likewise, few people disputed the opinion of Secretary Hughes that the naval ratio "absolutely ends the race in competition in naval armaments." Most citizens felt that the American delegation was correct in its final report to the President:

Probably no more significant treaty was ever made. Instead of discussing the desirability of diminishing the burdens of naval armament, the conference has succeeded in limiting them to an important degree. . . . No national

176

interest has been sacrificed; a wasteful production of unnecessary armament has been ended. . . .

One of the advisers to the United States delegation summed up the feeling of Americans as typified by the man in the street, when he declared that they

appear to be grateful and happy for their relief from at least a portion of their burden. They do not inquire too closely into the motives of any nations; if they are amazed, it is not that so little was done, but so much.[4]

That all this accomplishment might be discarded by an arrogant Senate was a possibility too terrible to contemplate. The public bent every effort to make certain that the débacle of the defeat of the League of Nations was not repeated. Accordingly, many factions among the populace turned once again to the procedure which they felt had been so effective before the conference was called—petitions to the Senate. Many of the organizations, which had made articulate the public's demand for a conference, took up the task of assuring ratification. One of the leaders in this movement was the National Council for the Limitation of Armament. This organization announced, January 9, that it would urge the Senate to ratify the Four-Power Treaty and, February 6, reaffirmed its purpose by listing reasons for the ratification of the agreements.[5] Other organizations continued to make their presence felt. Prominent among the voices heard were the Foreign Affairs Committee of the Chamber of Commerce of the United States, the National Student Committee for Limitation of Armament, The Gompers General Committee, and the Women's Pro-League Council. The latter wrote Senator Walsh that it was concerned over the attitude of the Senate and hoped it would be a wise deliberative body rather than ". . . a great dark cloud of obstruction on the horizon of human hopes for world peace and world unity." [6] The churches, almost as spirited in their effort to gain the ratification of the treaties as they had been to bring about the conference, presented a petition with more than sixteen thousand signatures.[7] Civic clubs in many states made concerted drives for ratification, usually expressing their opinions in telegrams to their senators. The executive committee on the League to Enforce Peace encouraged this effort. In a memorandum to the Senate Foreign Relations Committee it announced the results of an extensive and reliable

177

canvass of popular sentiment. This committee reported that the churches, civic organizations, educational institutions, women's organizations, and labor unions were unanimous in their approval of the work of the conference. On the other hand, it found "the reports of opposition . . . so negligible as to make it clear to us that the people are more significantly united on the proposals of the Conference on Limitation of Armament than they have ever been on any similar issue." [8]

It seemed that Senator Lawrence Phipps was indeed correct when he stated, "The people are in earnest about this treaty." [9] While the overwhelming opinion of the country was in favor of ratification, there was some determined opposition. In addition to the Hearst press, the principal public leaders among the opponents of the Treaty were the various chapters of the Friends of Irish Freedom—the members of the Wolf Tone Clubs, the John Boyle O'Reilly Literary Club, the Padraic Pearse Branch of the Friends of Irish Freedom, the Ancient Order of Hibernians of Terrington, *et al.* They opposed the Four-Power Treaty because they felt it was

a breeder of wars and would entangle us in European affairs which held nothing in common with us and because it involves the surrender of our policy of isolation and of many of the advantages of the great world upheaval.[10]

Another expression, typical of these groups, warned the senators "as loyal Americans to beware of the lurking schemes of foreign, particularly Anglo-Japanese, diplomacy." [11] Still other Irishmen were worried lest the Four-Power pact endanger "our traditional policy of no entangling foreign alliances, as enunciated by the immortal Washington." Again the Senate was admonished: "Stand Firm for American Independence! Keep Aloof From All Foreign Entanglements! Follow the Course Mapped Out by Washington—Jefferson—Lincoln." [12] It seemed that the Friends of Irish Freedom were anxious to protect American—rather than Irish—freedom.

As a consequence of the wave of petitions which it received, the Senate understood fully that the majority of the people wanted the work of the Washington Conference approved. Considerable debate arose on the question of a senator's obligation to accept this guidance from his constituents. Most senators were willing to acquiesce in the demands of the people. The minority, while admitting that this policy was politically advisable, felt that it might have serious consequences for the nation. The Senate ought to exercise independent judgment, because it was more completely informed than the general public and could perceive hidden dangers in a treaty which might appear harmless to the masses.

Senator Pomerene, voicing the opinion of the majority, declared that a vote against the Treaty would be "false to what I conceive to be the well-defined sentiment of the country." [13] Key Pittman, speaking for the minority, asserted:

There are Senators in this body today who are reading more intently the signs of the public sentiment of the voters in their communities than they are the conditions and the results of this treaty upon the future of this country.

He wondered how many people who petitioned the Senate that the Treaty be passed had ever read it, or having done so, understood its terms. The people, said Pittman, have a great desire for peace, and they are demanding this Treaty because they have been told that it means peace. [14]

Carter Glass elucidated this idea in a later debate when he told his colleagues:

I am getting letters from little misses in Virginia, who would not recognize this four-power pact if they should see it in the road with a red flag attached to it, urging me to support it. Somebody had deceived them into thinking that the four-power pact is a disarmament agreement. They do not know the difference, but I do.

The Virginia senator declared that upon election he had been entrusted to exercise his own best judgment. Consequently, he would refuse to vote for treaties simply because "without knowing what they are asking, misinformed persons write me to vote for them." [15]

Senator France, commenting on the number of petitions that he had received, said he had gotten "almost enough information to convince him that the treaties are desirable if I did not know something about them." Much of this agitation was mere propaganda, he said, for it was a known fact that a central committee was sending prepared speeches to women's clubs and other groups that wanted a statement on the conference and disarmament. The senator thought that the whole matter of propaganda and the amount expended in an effort to get the treaties passed should be investigated. [16] Senator

179

Williams, agreeing with France, protested against the agitation created by the Friends of Irish Freedom. This organization, which sent a daily "newsletter" to members of the Senate, called the treaties "entangling alliances," and "un-American alliances." "What they mean," said Williams, "is that it is an 'un-Irish' Alliance." [17]

Johnson and Borah, long known for independent action, decried high pressure by paid propagandists. Johnson said that he "did not care the snap of my fingers whether every editorial reference in the United States is of a certain character; I care not, sir, whether every association, civic or otherwise, directs, commands, begs, or protests in reference to the question before us." As for himself, he would vote his conscience with the hope that the Senate as a whole would do likewise.[18] Borah declared that if the advocates of the Four-Power Treaty included "every man, woman and child in the United States," he would "unhesitatingly defeat it" if possible. Again, he opined: "If I were the only man in the State of Idaho that was opposed to it, I would oppose it to the end." [19] This was the state of public and senatorial opinion when both parties met with their respective leaders, Lodge and Underwood, for an explanation of the treaties two days before the documents were formally presented to the Senate.[20]

The effort, evident throughout the conference, to ameliorate the attitude of the Senate was continued when Harding appeared before it to present the treaties and urge their adoption. His speech, as headlined in the *New York Times,* reflected the opinion of the country at large: "Ratify Quickly, Harding Urges Senate, Unless World Peace Hopes Are To Fail And America Is To Be Discredited." Harding was not so blunt in his speech as the news reports indicated, and did all that he could to reassure the Senate. "I am not unmindful, nor was the conference, of the sentiment in this Chamber against Old World entanglements." The President stated

I can bring you every assurance that nothing in any of these treaties commits the United States, or any other power, to any kind of an alliance, entanglement, or involvement. It does not require us or any power to surrender a worth-while tradition. . . . The four-power treaty contains no war commitment. . . . There is no commitment to armed force, no alliance, no written or moral obligation to join in defense, no expressed or implied commitment to arrive at any agreement except in accordance with our constitutional methods.

180

As if this was not sufficient assurance to quiet senatorial fears, the President closed his address by reminding the Senate that its "concern for freedom from entanglements, for preserved traditions, for maintained independence, was never once forgotten by the American Delegates." [21] Following this speech the treaties went to the Senate Committee on Foreign Relations. The press predicted confidently that the Committee would support the treaties which would eventually win an easy victory. [22]

The senators who professed to ignore the public demand for ratification of the Washington treaties were not moved by the President's plea. The echo of Harding's voice had hardly died away in the Senate Chamber before their attack on the Four-Power Treaty began. The greatest sensation resulting from these attacks was stirred by the charge that the Four-Power pact had been negotiated in private, and that some of its provisions had not been made public. Before the conference the Senate had expressed its hope, through the Harrison Resolution, that all the conference sessions would be open and attended by full publicity. During, and after the conference, it had been appraised by members of the press and by such prominent statesmen as Harding and Secretary Hughes as a triumph for open diplomacy, preparing the way for an era of "new diplomacy." The basis of this "new diplomacy" was to be full publicity, allowing the enlightened conscience of the public to judge the conduct of nations. Secretary of State Hughes strongly approved this new approach. The United States government had always been "candid and direct" in negotiations, and strictly accountable to the public for its decisions. The "new diplomacy," he asserted, was but a wider application of America's tradition of plain and open diplomacy, as contrasted with the European method of circumlocution and secrecy. [23] Harding agreed with Hughes and added: "If it [the conference] has developed a new-world school of diplomacy, let it be so called." [24]

Not all experts subscribed to this theory. From the beginning of the conference Senator Borah denied the administration's claim that open diplomacy was being employed. Writing a friend December 19, 1921, he stated that it had been a sad mistake to close the conference to the public. This secrecy, felt Borah, had resulted in barter, intrigue, and a betrayal of the real wishes of the people. Had the public been taken into the confidence of the leaders of the conference, a more

181

complete disarmament would have resulted.[25] The plenary sessions and the long communiques at the end of the private sessions of the Congress had been just so much window dressing, in the opinion of the Idaho senator. The vital decisions were made in private. In fact, so secret had the "open conference" of Washington become that it surpassed the clandestine conclave of Paris in the matter of back-room diplomacy.[26]

In the Senate the opposition to the treaties brought up the charge of secrecy at the beginning of the debate with the hope of awakening a real suspicion of the Four-Power Treaty. In any event, the opposition desired to rub some of the luster from the halo of open diplomacy with which the Republicans had crowned themselves.

The first charges of secret diplomacy were made by Senator Hitchcock. He called attention to the fact that the minutes of the conference, Senate Document 126, presented by Harding to the Senate, contained in its 935 pages no information as to the negotiation of the Four-Power Treaty. Because this pact was generally regarded as the key treaty of the conference, the omission of information concerning it seemed inexcusable to him. This was the Treaty about which the Senate should have had the most complete knowledge. Hitchcock asserted that additional information was needed in order to clear the confusion which had surrounded the Four-Power pact since its announcement. The prime example of this confusion was the "open and notorious disagreement between the President of the United States and his chief representative . . . Mr. Hughes, as to the meaning of the four-power treaty. . . ." Apparently in reprisal for the Republican grilling of Wilson for information about negotiations of the Treaty of Versailles, Hitchcock added that the Senate had "the best possible precedent for asking for the information." In view of these facts, he presented a resolution calling for "all drafts or forms presented to or considered by the delegates of the United States, the British Empire, Japan, or France in considering the subject of the Four-Power Treaty." The resolution requested access to all copies of proceedings, records, negotiations, arguments, debates, discussions, and conversations which occurred between the delegates of the parties to the Treaty, together with material on any supplementary notes subsequently signed.[27]

An effort was made by the Republican senators to kill this proposal by sending it to the Senate Committee on Foreign Relations. After this failed, Lodge and Underwood spoke against the resolution. They protested that it was useless since there were no memoranda, minutes, or records dealing with the Four-Power Treaty. Despite this parliamentary and oratorical opposition, the resolution was passed.[28]

The next day President Harding entered the debate by way of a press interview. He stated, as Lodge and Underwood had done, that there was no information on the negotiations of the Four-Power Treaty which could be turned over to the Senate. Four days later he made a formal reply to the resolution:

> . . . it is impossible to comply with the Senate's request. Many of the things asked for in the resolution it is literally impossible to furnish, because there were many conversations and discussions quite outside the conference, yet vital to its success. Naturally these are without record.

The President maintained that it was not compatible with the public interest or consistent with the amenities of international negotiation to reveal "informal and confidential conversations or discussions, of which no record was kept. . . ." He was able to assure the Senate that "there were no concealed understandings, and no secret exchanges of notes except the supplementary agreement which was already in the hands of the Senate." [29] The Senate, despite this testimony, was not satisfied. Secretary Hughes, some senators asserted, should be called to testify before the Foreign Relations Committee—a suggestion which was later dropped.

When the debate was resumed in the Senate, Hitchcock, returning to the theme, charged that the Four-Power Treaty was conceived in secrecy. Alluding again to Harding's unfortunate interpretation of the Treaty, Hitchcock declared that it stemmed from the fact that the President did not know what negotiations had taken place.[30]

The opposition senators, unable to gain information from the administration, turned to Senator-delegates Lodge and Underwood for information. Lodge denied that the Treaty was secret, citing the fact that the meetings between the four nations were reported in the press. However, he could offer little else to substantiate his view and evaded the issue by declaring: "No negotiations of which I have any knowledge—and I am speaking now of the conference and its work generally—were ever conducted with so little secrecy as were those held by the conference which has recently adjourned." [31]

Underwood, on the other hand, asserted that the negotiations on the Four-Power Treaty were secret, this being the only proper method of procedure in view of the fact that the Anglo-Japanese Alliance was not the direct concern of the United States. "It did not concern the American people," he declared, "until the agreement was reached that the Anglo-Japanese alliance should be canceled." Under further questioning Underwood, like Lodge, took refuge in commending the general conduct of the conference. He believed that no ". . . conference that met in the history of the world . . . was more open and more free from that criticism [secrecy] than the late conference that met in Washington." [32]

This display led Senator Reed to declare his amazement that two delegates should accept a treaty of such importance without even inquiring as to its origin.[33] Senator Robinson found it "incomprehensible" that Lodge should "be unable to answer more definitely than he has answered." In the absence of any information from those in authority the Senator now turned to imagination for an answer, asserting the Treaty was conceived by Balfour and fashioned by Prince Tokugawa.[34]

Underwood sought to clear the question by appealing to Hughes, who was acknowledged to have been the American delegate most closely associated with the Treaty. Hughes wrote him: "It seems to be implied that in some way the American delegates have been imposed upon, or that they were induced to accept some plan cunningly contrived by others and opposed to our interest." This, said Hughes, was not only a criticism of the American delegates but entirely erroneous for the "negotiations relating to the four-power treaty were conducted within limitations defined by the American Government. . . . I prepared a draft of the treaty based upon the various suggestions which had been exchanged between the delegates." This draft was first submitted to the members of the American delegation for approval; and after their agreement had been gained, it was discussed by the parties to the Treaty. In this discussion a few changes were made, but these did not affect materially the spirit of the Treaty and were approved by the other members of the American delegation. "There is," concluded Hughes, "not the slightest mystery about the treaty or basis for suspicion regarding it. It is a straightforward document which attains one of the most important

184

objects the American Government has had in view. . . ." [35] Under-wood declared, "I have laid before the Senate the unquestioned statement of the man who did make the treaty that he made and wrote it." [36] However, the die-hards refused to accept these declarations and Johnson, Borah, and Robinson continued to question the authorship of the Treaty. Robinson declared that the Hughes letter was intended to withhold rather than to furnish information and that it was of no value in answering the question.[37] Continuing to demand a better explanation of the drafting of the Treaty, he asked why the preliminary drafts of the pact were not presented to the Senate as had been the case with the Treaty of Versailles.[38]

While this questioning was proceeding, the opposition was inquiring into the possibility that the full terms of the Treaty had not been made public. Again Robinson led this phase of the debate and presented an amendment to free the Treaty of any such encumbrance. His resolution provided: "Each of the high contracting parties will refrain from entering into or being a party to any secret treaty, agreement, or understanding with any other power or powers during the life of this treaty." [39]

Robinson, in debate on the proposal, cited a *New York Times* report that Japan had made an agreement with France to exclude other countries from Siberia. Japan and Britain, according to the Senator, had a secret understanding providing for joint exploitation of China.[40] However, he was unable to stir any great concern in the Senate; his resolution was accorded little discussion and not enough votes to bring adoption.

A somewhat more successful effort to exploit secret understandings as a defect in the Treaty was carried out by Senator Borah. He stirred up a minor sensation with charges that the United States and Britain were parties to a secret understanding. As proof he cited a stenographic report of a speech delivered by Paul D. Cravath before the Council on Foreign Relations at a meeting in New York. The speaker, a prominent lawyer intimately associated with professional and business men in both England and the United States, was in a position to make an authoritative statement. What attracted the attention of Borah was the statement that the most important achievement of the conference was not contained in any of its treaties. It was "the bringing about of what seems to be a sympathetic understanding be-

185

tween the United States and Great Britain regarding the Far East and Pacific questions generally." This understanding was important in that it placed a check on the imperialism of Japan in spite of the reduction of fleets and the non-fortification of islands. There was no formal agreement between the two nations, but there did exist "a degree of understanding" which guaranteed that in case of emergency either nation could count on securing "the very closest cooperation." The Idaho senator was also impressed by Cravath's assertion that this opinion had been expressed to him by each member of the American delegation and by Balfour.[41]

Borah declared that this was proof that the two nations had secretly formed an alliance contrary to the interests of other conference powers and sufficiently strong to check Japan. He denounced this secrecy and declared it to be further proof that the Four-Power Treaty was an alliance. The Cravath speech demonstrated that the pact was indeed an alliance within an alliance.[42]

This revelation was somewhat dimmed when both Lodge and Underwood immediately disclaimed any acquaintance with Cravath, and any knowledge of the "understanding" of which he spoke. Almost in chorus they declared, ". . . there is not a word of truth in the whole statement which the Senator from Idaho has just read. . . ."[43] Lodge protested as he had done on a number of occasions that everything concerning the Treaty was already before the Senate and the country. There was nothing secret.[44]

Senator Robinson, nevertheless, was of the opinion that Cravath should be immediately called before the Senate Committee on Foreign Relations to find what source he was quoting. The possible existence of such an arrangement between the United States and Britain was another argument in favor of his amendment.[45]

The next day additional denials rang throughout the Senate chamber. Lodge read a telegram from Cravath in which the latter said ". . . this charge is unfounded. I never made such a statement nor have I ever talked with any member of the Washington Conference on the subject of the alleged statement, or on any subject remotely resembling it." Cravath sought to make his case ironclad by declaring that he did not remember making such a statement. If he had done so, it was in informal discussion "that did not accurately convey my meaning." He did not have in mind any secret agreement but

186

simply a degree of understanding which was a natural outgrowth of successful cooperation and mutual confidence.[46]

To bolster the case Lodge read a letter from Secretary Hughes affirming Cravath's position and declared: "Any such statement is absolutely false. We have no secret understandings or agreements with Great Britain in relation to the four-power treaty or any other matter. . . ." Hughes ended this note with the hope "that the American delegates will be saved further aspersions upon their veracity and honor." [47]

Also presented at this time was a "corrected" copy of the speech which Cravath asserted was more nearly representative of his thought than the first copy from which Borah had read.[48] This afterthought did not appear to Borah to alter the first statement. Norman H. Davis wrote privately that he was astonished at Cravath's denial of Borah's allegations. There were, said Davis, at least forty witnesses, and stenographic records were taken.[49]

Borah was unimpressed and remained so even in the face of subsequent denials and editions of the Cravath speech. Finally he wrote Lodge that he did not have the time or disposition to keep up with them and was satisfied with the language of the original.[50]

These efforts by the Senate to tarnish the treaties with the stigma of secrecy were largely ineffective. The public was not excited by the charges and seemed content to believe the administration's account of the case. Hitchcock and Robinson failed to discredit Republican claims that they had fostered open diplomacy in contrast to Wilson at Paris. Borah aroused the Friends of Irish Freedom, who were permanently anti-British, but was unable to start a ground-swell of opposition to the Four-Power Treaty.

Those in opposition to the Treaty during the course of the debate frequently exploited another approach. The very word *alliance* had come to have a sinister connotation for the average American. If the alliance could be described as "entangling," it was *per se* an evil which must be destroyed regardless of any other consideration. It was apparent that the Senate felt more strongly on this matter than the public at large. It was in vain that logical minds defined the vital question as the purpose rather than the name of the Four-Power Treaty.[51] Consequently, the supporters of the Treaty saw that it might be more important to the success of the Treaty to show that it was not an alliance than to make any manner of positive claims for it.

This matter was the subject of discussion before the Foreign Relations Committee. Several members of the Committee, notably Borah, Johnson, and Brandegee, were most anxious to remove from the document any possible taint of alliance. Brandegee proposed, February 18, a reservation stating that the United States assumed no legal or moral obligation to maintain the rights of other signatories. Furthermore, no adjustment or agreement made under the pact would become binding until approved by Congress.[52] Senator Lodge, acting as a liaison officer between the Committee and the White House, discussed this reservation with Harding. The President declared that the Treaty needed no reservation to make it safe, but he would not oppose a senatorial demand for one.[53]

In the midst of these negotiations, Tom Watson of Georgia sought to confound Lodge with the latter's own writings. Watson, under the guise of honoring George Washington on his birthday, read from the biography by Lodge the first President's policy on alliances. Lodge, Watson continued, had lately been engaged in saving the country from an alliance in the form of the League of Nations, but now was guiding the Four-Power Treaty, an equally dangerous alliance, through the Senate. Lodge had changed his opinion with the change of administrations. He was trying to bind the country to the very sort of alliance which, according to his writings, Washington abhorred, and Lodge himself had once denounced.[54]

Ignoring these charges of inconsistency, Lodge presented to the Committee on Foreign Relations, February 24, a reservation stating that the United States was not obligating itself to an alliance by adhering to the Four-Power Treaty. This reservation was reported to have originated with Harding. Proof of its authorship was to be found in the text which followed the exact wording of the President's speech to the Senate in presenting the treaties. This conciliatory gesture only served to stir up the stormiest meeting of the Committee since the consideration of the Versailles Treaty. Leading the opposition to the President was Senator Brandegee. Feeling became so heated that Lodge denied any responsibility for the new reservation; he declared that it was only a suggestion which did not commit the President or the Republican leader in the Senate.[55]

188

Two days later Brandegee visited the President. What the press called a "new" reservation was framed. This compromise contained none of the conditions for which Brandegee had contended, but all of the features of the so-called Harding reservation. Indeed, the compromise measure was the exact reservation which had stirred so much furor when presented two days before. This time the reservation was approved by a vote of ten to three in the Committee. Johnson and Borah supported steadfastly the original Brandegee reservation, which specifically exempted the United States from all moral as well as legal obligations under the Treaty. When their plan was defeated, they announced that they would carry the fight to the floor of the Senate. Senator France joined them, saying that he opposed all of the treaties of the conference because they repudiated the principles of Washington, Hamilton, Jefferson, and Lincoln. The treaties, despite these objections, were reported out of the Committee with the recommendation for ratification.[56]

Only one other headline incident occurred before the Treaty reached the Senate. Ambassador George Harvey had commented on the work of the Washington Conference, declaring that one of its results was a closer bond between England and the United States. This development was very desirable, Harvey felt, because the true aims of the two nations were identical. But, Senator Reed, an Anglophobe for many years and a leading opponent of the Treaty, seized upon the statement to arouse all anti-British elements in the country. The Senator demanded the recall of Harvey and his replacement by an envoy "who can put his legs under British mahogany and still keep his head." Having thus worked up his spleen, the Senator concluded by denouncing all of the works of the conference.[57]

So, when the Treaty reached the Senate, its chance for approval appeared to be uncertain, although the press predicted it would be approved. On March 5, Senator Lodge, after a conference with the President, was quoted as believing that the Treaty was in much danger. Additional reservations would be needed to get it adopted, he feared. Even with these concessions, Lodge foresaw a very close vote with stubborn opposition from those senators who had been the "bitter enders" in the debate on the League.[58]

As to the source of the opposition, there had been speculation that ex-President Wilson, on the grounds of principle, politics, and revenge, might oppose the Treaty and rally around him the faction in the Senate which was still loyal to him.[59] Such a charge was made, December 14, but was refuted, December 27, by the news that Wilson had advised Democrats to take a fair view of the Treaty. At the same time Democratic leader Underwood advised against making the conference a political issue.[60] In the middle of January the stricken ex-President was able to make a short talk to the members of the Wilson Foundation from the doorstep of his home. Once more the rumors came to life, and this speech was hailed by some Democrats as Wilson's "return from Elba." Charles Nichelson, in an article for the *New York World* at this time, stated that Wilson had declared his personal opposition to the Four-Power Treaty.[61] However, there is no evidence that Wilson influenced directly any senator's vote on the Treaty.

Rumor linked another figure in the Wilson administration, Joseph Tumulty, with the opposition to the Treaty. The press reported, December 30, that Borah, whose opposition to the Treaty was well known, had had a conference with Tumulty on a "private matter." [62] Somewhat later, at the time the Four-Power Treaty was presented to the Senate, Tumulty gave a banquet in Washington for the leaders of the Democratic party. The ostensible purpose of this affair was to afford an opportunity to discuss party strategy. Although there was no definite confirmation, it was generally felt that the presence at the meeting of all the anti-Treaty Democrats indicated that the real purpose was to develop strategy for the defeat of the work of the Washington Conference.[63]

Again, following Lodge's report, March 5, that the Treaty was facing a stiff fight, the rumors that Wilson was inciting Democratic opposition came to life. On March 8, the *New York Times* carried an article constructing, from circumstantial evidence, a case to prove that Wilson had joined hands with Borah to fight the Four-Power Treaty. It was noted that Bernard Baruch, Joseph Tumulty, and Josephus Daniels were opposed to the Treaty, and that a former Under Secretary of State, Norman Davis, had assailed it in a public speech. Furthermore, Borah was known to have conferred during the debate with all of these men except Daniels. As in previous instances, it was again denied that Wilson was taking an active part in the Treaty fight. His official position, it was said, was one of neutrality in deed, if not in thought.[64] But rumor refused to die. Two weeks later came the report that Tumulty, who was spending much time with Senator Reed, had asserted that his consuming ambition was to defeat the Treaty in the Senate. To that end he had been "pulling various wires." [65] It was not until March 16, when Wilson reiterated his neutral position, that this campaign of rumor was finally laid to rest.[66]

Whatever truth or significance may be attached to these rumors, it was apparent, throughout the debate, that strict party unity was not being maintained. Even the Democratic press felt that the issue was vital and should not be jeopardized by political considerations. Democratic senators were advised to vote for the Treaty even at the expense of the party.[67] Indeed, there was such an overwhelming demand for ratification that there seemed to be little chance for political gain by playing politics. To be sure, there were, during the course of the senate debate, frequent references to partisanship in the debate on the League of Nations. Senator Lodge, in particular, was castigated by Democrats for his inconsistency. As was to be expected, efforts were made by both parties to claim the credit for the success of the conference, but a vote on purely party lines seems never to have been a possibility. The severest critics of Republican policy were Republican irreconcilables. Actually, the problem for the majority party was to create the impression of Democratic opposition in order to enhance the glory of Republican accomplishment.

President Harding conferred with Lodge several times during the first week of the debate in the Senate. Apparently he was satisfied that the treaties would succeed, for on March 8, at the last of these conferences, he announced that he would not "lobby, trade, supplicate, or admonish to get the Four-Power Treaty passed." [68] As if to guarantee such a course, the President left immediately for Florida and the golf courses, while the Senate worked on such problems as the authorship of the Treaty.[69]

As early as March 12, the senatorial friends of the Treaty were declaring that its approval was assured with only one reservation. Three days later, after the first vote on a reservation had been taken, it was confidently predicted that the Treaty would be approved.[70] The next day the final vote on the Four-Power Treaty was set for March 24, with the press headlining the news that passage was certain. The

191

New York Times predicted the final vote would be sixty-five to twenty-six, or possibly sixty-seven to twenty-six.[71] Throughout the rest of the debate the press entertained no idea that the Treaty would be defeated.[72]

When the final vote was taken, sixty-seven to twenty-seven, it was notably lacking in the adherence to party lines which some commentators had constantly predicted it would assume. Fifty-five Republicans and twelve Democrats voted for the Treaty, while twenty-three Democrats and four Republicans voted against it. Although the vote was close and the debate had been lengthy, there was little possibility after the first week that it would fail.[73]

The other treaties of the conference were swept through with almost no debate and only minor opposition. Senator France cast the lone vote against the Treaty for the Limitation of Naval Armament.[74] Senator King, who had introduced a resolution favoring complete independence for China, voted against the Chinese Customs Tariff Treaty.[75]

Perhaps the state of mind in the Senate was best shown by the fact that the largest vote in favor of any of the treaties or amendments was ninety-one. This was the margin for the Brandegee Amendment, framed to free the Four-Power Treaty of any taint of alliance.[76] The reservations and amendments offered by the Democrats had been defeated in all cases by a strictly party vote. Therefore, the overwhelming vote for the Brandegee Amendment indicated that the Senate was almost unanimous in its support of a traditional principle.

The success of the administration in gaining the approval of the treaties was the result of skillful directing. Secretary Hughes gave much credit in this endeavor to Lodge. Writing to the Senator he said:

Permit me to extend my hearty congratulations upon your effective work in securing this result. Your action in first presenting the Four-Power Treaty was a most strategic move, and with the failure to defeat this treaty the whole opposition crumbled.[77]

Lodge's important work was recognized outside the administration. The day after the passage of the Four-Power pact he was informed that he had been awarded the Price Medal for 1922 in recognition of his achievement in securing approval of the Treaty. Around the edges of the medal were engraved the words, "Peace, Honor,

Good Will Among Nations"; the name, Henry Cabot Lodge, was in its center.[78]

Nor was Lodge himself disposed to minimize his role. During the course of the debate he had written to friends that there was considerable opposition in the Senate to the Four-Power Treaty; he had asked them to attempt to influence some of the Democratic senators who were leading the opposition.[79] At this time Lodge had despaired of aligning a solid Republican front including Borah, Johnson, and France.[80] He, subsequently, took full credit for winning enough Democratic votes to assure the passage of the treaties. Lodge boasted to George Harvey that by the time the vote was taken he could have had thirteen votes to spare on the Four-Power Treaty, although the eventual margin of victory was only five. Harvey, warm in his praise of the senator's work, thought it remarkable that a man so hated as Lodge could get a two-thirds majority on any measure.[81]

There is confirmation elsewhere that Lodge did command a greater bloc of votes than was cast for the Treaty. Deliberately he rejected some votes by Democrats that he might have secured. Thus, he enhanced the value of the conference for partisan purposes by making it appear that its success was due chiefly to the united efforts of the Republicans.[82]

The power wielded by Lodge influenced numerous votes. In general the Senate—or rather many of the individual members of the Senate—voted on the Four-Power Treaty for reasons bearing little relation to its merits. Various pressures influenced their votes. In the first place, the public favored the treaties. Senators had attacked the Four-Power pact for almost three months before it came to the Senate, yet had aroused no widespread public response. In the second place, the Senate was in disrepute for its renunciation of the Treaty of Versailles; it feared to try the patience of the public by another veto. The honor of the United States, the host to the conference, would be tarnished by disapproval of the treaties. Senator Pittman stated that the question before the Senate was not whether obstruction of the treaties would hurt the good name of the United States abroad, but whether the treaties protected the interests of the United States. However, he found little support for this view.[83] In the third place, the Senate was reminded by President Harding that it had already advised adoption of one treaty—the naval pact, which was

193

"negotiated and signed . . . in accordance with your expressed wish."
Obviously, all the treaties of the conference were necessary "to perfect the fulfillment which the Congress has in mind." [84] Harding
thus inferred that the Senate, by authorizing a conference of three
powers to consider naval armament limitation, had bound itself in
honor to sanction all the work of the Washington Conference.
Senator France, a Republican, speaking of this and other factors,
regretted that the treaties had been presented with the implication
that the Senate must vote for them. Furthermore, he said, it was
known that many members had pledged themselves to vote for them
before a single argument had been heard. The Senate was bound by
the fact that Lodge, the majority leader, and Underwood, the minority leader, as delegates had approved the work of the conference.

Lastly, it might be maintained that the approval of the treaties
was largely a result of the desire of a Republican majority to support
the Republican administration. A scholar of the time declared that
the Four-Power Treaty was much more of an entangling alliance
than the covenant of the League. Indeed, there were few objections
raised to the League covenant which would not apply with equal
force to it. Senator Pittman pointed out in debate a striking example
of convictions which changed with administrations. The reservation
on domestic affairs offered as a supplement to the Four-Power Treaty
was identical, he declared, with one of the reservations to the covenant of the League of Nations. This reservation carried a substantial
Republican majority during the debate on the League, but when reintroduced with the Washington Conference treaties, it had mustered
only four Republican votes. [85] Further evidence was the fact that most
of the reservations offered by Democrats drew their only Republican
votes from the same four irreconcilables who also voted against the
Four-Power Treaty. [86]

Hence, the vote of the Four-Power Treaty was not partisan in the
sense that party lines were strictly drawn and maintained. It was
partisan in the sense that the senators, on both sides of the chamber,
were influenced in their voting by the possibilities of political gain
far more than by a careful measurement of the intrinsic merit of the
Treaty. Much of the debate seems to have been for no purpose other
than to create the impression that the Senate was deliberating. The
Republicans maintained their advocacy without enthusiasm: the

194

Democrats and irreconcilables opposed the Treaty with a zeal tempered by the knowledge that their cause was hopeless. The debate upheld the prerogative of the Senate to pass judgment on treaties, but did little to increase confidence in its willingness to exercise this authority with wisdom.

The Debate on the Four‑Power Treaty

◦ ◦ ◦ THE debate in the Senate on the Four-Power Treaty had little influence in determining the votes of individual senators. Yet, it was not without significance. In presenting a case for and against the Treaty, the senators defined what they conceived to be the true objectives of American foreign policy and described what they believed to be the wisest methods for achieving them.

There was almost complete agreement in the Senate that the United States should support the cause of peace and should adopt in a limited way a policy of internationalism. With unanimity regarding the general objective, the debate centered on the most desirable means to employ in accomplishing this purpose. Even in this matter there was little question as to general lines of procedure. The majority agreed that no action should be taken which could not be fitted into the well-marked pattern of traditional foreign policy. The disagreements which led to debate grew out of this devotion. Did the treaties before the Senate violate or implement American ideals and traditions?

Those senators who favored the Four-Power Treaty set peace as the ultimate goal of American foreign policy. The Treaty, they insisted, was a significant step toward this goal; it was one that did not require the sacrifice of worthwhile traditions or interests.

In describing the contribution of the Treaty to the cause of peace, its advocates were unrestrained in their praise, but hardly specific in their proof. Senator Lawrence Phipps, a typical advocate, asserted that the conference "has done more toward establishing a better understanding and friendly relationships among nations than any other single event in history." [1] No less restrained in his praise was Senator Samuel Shortridge, who felt that heaven as well as earth was moved by the success of the meeting. "I love to think," he told the Senate, "that the very angels sang in joy over the work of that conference." [2]

196

Senate champions of the Four-Power Treaty constantly emphasized that it was important not only for its own provisions, but also because it was the keystone of the work of the conference. The other treaties drawn at Washington were so closely interrelated with the Four-Power pact that it would be impractical to pass them if it were defeated.[3] Senator Lodge, a spokesman for this theory, asserted:

the defeat of the four-power treaty would endanger the treaty for the limitation of naval armament, and the failure of the naval treaty would shock and startle the world and bitterly disappoint the American people. . . . The defeat of the four-power treaty would mean the failure of the conference.[4]

The consequences of this failure would be too awesome for contemplation even by those same senators who had witnessed, without flinching, the failure of the League Covenant. If the treaties were defeated, Lodge solemnly warned, the United States would "sink back into a sullen solitude, a prey to dark suspicions, a hermit nation armed to the teeth and looking forward always to wars as inseparable from the existence of mankind upon the earth."[5] Senator Irvin Lenroot, who had opposed the League of Nations, warned the Senate that the nations were already suspicious of America's intentions and would shun the United States if these treaties were defeated.[6]

With the Four-Power Treaty thus firmly identified with the cause of world peace, senators favoring its passage set about the task of demonstrating that it was consistent with American ideals in foreign affairs. Senator Oscar Underwood reminded the Senate that "Our national policy has been for peace since the beginning of our Government," and the people's "great desire is that the future peace of the world may remain unbroken." He substantiated his assertion by citing his nation's interest in arbitration, case by case, from the founding of the Republic to the current moment. This traditional love of peace was unabated, he added, for "even then [during the World War], deep in the heart, the great American heart, the call of peace remained." The people vowed that "when this Great War is over there must be peace, the peace of understanding." Therefore, concluded Underwood, "the American people approve of this treaty, because it means peace."[7] Senator Lodge, who was given responsibility for guiding the Treaty through the Senate, emphasized the importance of this new instrument for peace by painting a somber picture of the consequence of past wars:

197

The misery and the horrors of the Great War must never come again if we can do anything to stop it. . . . We who have passed through the valley of the shadow in these last years must leave nothing undone that we can do to save our children and our children's children from the awful calamity which we of this generation have been compelled to endure.

He explained that the American delegation's principal purpose had been to make a practical contribution toward world peace without jeopardizing America's cherished ideals of independence and sovereignty. Again and again he asserted that the Four-Power Treaty met these conditions. Through it, the United States could foster the cause of world peace in perfect safety, since the Treaty was "without alliances or penalties or the sanction of force lurking in the background." [8]

Despite this testimony the opposition senators wanted more specific proof of the power of the Treaty to secure these blessings without cost or sacrifice. To their demands, explanations were given, but for the most part they were exceedingly abstract. Senator Underwood quoted Prince Iyesato Tokugawa of Japan who had said: "We have arrived at a spirit of international cooperation, which is the new spirit of the new age, upon which we are launching new ships of peace." [9] Lodge and other supporters of the Treaty placed much confidence in this indefinable "new spirit," professing implicit faith in its effectiveness. One element of this "new spirit" was the development, on an international scale, of a moral power which could be employed to enforce the peace. Senator Phipps declared that the very fact that four powers had been willing to confer and had enough confidence in each other to sign treaties was evidence of the development of an effective moral force. [10] Senator Underwood added that the promise of peace in the Four-Power Treaty stemmed from "the great power, of the moral influence of four great nations." [11] Senator Lodge conceded that this agreement was no stronger than the will and honor of the powers that signed it; however, he felt that this could provide a solid basis for building a peaceful world, and he pleaded with the Senate to "make the great experiment and appeal to the men and women of the nations to help us sustain it in spirit and in truth." [12]

Other senators who favored the Treaty also attempted to demonstrate that moral force was a practical and powerful agent for enforcing peace. The most important achievement of the conference, according to Senator Fordney McCumber, was the discovery of the existence of this "world conscience." [13] Senator Arthur Capper believed that world public opinion was already developed to a point where it would be more effective in assuring justice in international affairs than armed preparedness.[14] Senator Hiram Johnson, another believer in the power of world opinion, said, "Let this public opinion operate . . . and there would be no future wars. . . . Openness, frankness, the sunlight of publicity alone are required." [15]

The advocates, moreover, maintained that the treaties had strengthened the United States in the Far East. One proof of this assertion, they claimed, was that the Four-Power Treaty had abrogated the Anglo-Japanese Alliance, which had long been regarded as a menace to the policy of America in the Orient. Furthermore, the United States had been freed of the burden of fortifying its Pacific Islands. In the opinion of many senators, such fortifications were now unnecessary, because public opinion and moral force had supplanted battleships and shore batteries as the bulwark of the nation's policy. Senators Lodge and Underwood reiterated that Congress and the people would not approve an appropriation for the fortification of United States possessions in the Pacific. These senators doubted that the military defense of the islands would be practical even if it were desirable. It had never been the policy of the United States to fortify the Philippine Islands and their approaches, or to build a navy large enough to make them secure.[16] All of these islands were small and trifling in value and population. Lodge said, "The Marshall Islands, I think, contain nothing. They are very trivial Islands." He had "been a good deal amused at the agony of apprehension which some persons have expressed in regard to Guam. . . . We have never fortified it, and nobody would vote to spend money in fortifying it." Neither would the Senate agree to fortify the Philippines, for "It would cost hundreds of millions of dollars . . . and probably take half a century to do it." [17] The moral force of the Four-Power Treaty, Lodge concluded, had rendered expensive fortifications unnecessary and guaranteed to the Philippines a security never before enjoyed.[18]

The advocates of the Treaty, having shown its advantages, also proceeded to prove that it had no disadvantages. In particular, they were anxious to clear it of any taint of alliance. The American fear of alliances was more marked, perhaps, at this time than it had ever been in history. This phobia was compounded of reverence for the precepts of George Washington and Thomas Jefferson, the desire for complete independence in the management of foreign affairs, and the fear that alliances would draw the United States into war.[19]

The sensitivity of the Senate in this respect was well known, and, before the debate had begun, the Senate had been given every possible official assurance, at each stage of development, that the Four-Power Treaty was not an alliance. This was first asserted by Senator Lodge in presenting the Treaty to the conference.[20] At the conclusion of the conference the American delegation transmitted the Treaty to the President with a definite statement to the effect that it contained no features of an alliance.[21] President Harding submitted it to the Senate with a detailed and emphatic denial of the existence of any commitment or alliance within its terms.[22] The Senate Committee on Foreign Relations recommended its ratification provided the Senate would also adopt a reservation which specifically stated that the Treaty was not an alliance.[23] Notwithstanding all of this testimony, many senators remained skeptical. Secretary of State Charles Evans Hughes assured them in a letter to Senator Underwood that the United States explicitly stated that it would not become a party to any sort of alliance before the other nations came to Washington.[24] More proof was given in an official statement by Assistant Secretary of State Fred Morris Dearing to Senator Medill McCormick.[25]

As the debate continued many senators added the weight of their opinions to that of the authorities who had previously spoken. Senator Lodge, assuming the role of historian, declared that "When Washington spoke about a 'permanent alliance' he was not referring to a treaty with another power to settle specific questions"; nor did Jefferson in his warning against entangling alliances have such treaties in mind.[26] With this opinion Senator Underwood concurred. An alliance, said the Alabama senator, bound the signatories to a definite course of action. Although this agreement provided for conferences, there was no "obligation that binds the signatory powers as to what shall be done when they meet at the conference table." [27]

This preoccupation with the exact nomenclature of the Treaty was carried so far as to become ridiculous. Senators became so engrossed in semantic studies that they carried to the debate dictionaries, encyclopedias, and treatises on international law. With the aid of these authorities they attempted, by careful definition, to prove that the term alliance was not applicable to the Four-Power Treaty. A leader in this phase of the debate was Senator Frank Willis, who concluded, after reference to the *Century Dictionary,* the *Encyclopaedia Britannica,* John Bouvier's *Law Dictionary,* Henry Campbell Black's *Law Dictionary,* and Lassa F. L. Oppenheim's work on *International Law,* that an alliance was a contract between two nations for the purpose of aggression or defense.[28] This definition cleared the Four-Power Treaty; it was not a contract, and it was not designed for aggression or defense.

Senator Selden P. Spenser complained, after this exhibition, that Willis did not seem to be able to divest his mind of the implication "that there is something in the word 'alliance' that breeds war, or that means trouble, or that has the idea of force." Also Spenser failed to see what difference it made whether one called the Four-Power Treaty an agreement to confer, or an alliance to confer.[29] In any event not all alliances were evil. "Marriage," said Spenser, "is the most familiar instance of 'an alliance.' Surely the Senator does not think that marriage is 'offensive and defensive' or is objectionable simply because it is an 'alliance.' " To this argument Willis answered with what was to the mind of a number of senators unescapable logic. He "would not vote for a treaty that took this country into an alliance. The American people decided that matter pretty fully a few months ago."[30] Willis attempted to give further proof that quibbling about the word alliance was worth while. He cited the fact that recently a senator had declared the Treaty to be, in a broad sense, an alliance. This assertion had been sufficient to cause a flood of telegrams to Willis directing him to vote against "the four-power treaty and all other such obnoxious alliances."[31] Therefore, he concluded that while actually there might not be a great deal of difference between an agreement and an alliance, to the American people there was a very definite and vital difference. To them, an alliance implied a threat to the peace and independence of the United States.[32]

The advocates of the Treaty, having "proved" that it was not an alliance in name now sought to prove that it was not one in fact. The people had demanded peace without obligation, and the Senate majority was determined to claim that virtue for the Four-Power Treaty. They maintained that the real danger in the Treaty could be measured by the degree to which it obligated America. Here the debate turned on the interpretation of Article II:

If the said rights are threatened by the aggressive action of any other Power, the High Contracting Parties shall communicate with one another fully and frankly in order to arrive at an understanding as to the most efficient measures to be taken, jointly or separately, to meet the exigencies of the particular situation.[33]

The rights referred to, they emphasized, were limited to the "insular possessions and insular dominions in the region of the Pacific Ocean," and American obligations in this area were not extensive. A typical exposition of this factor by pro-Treaty senators was Lodge's assertion that it

involves the United States in no obligation except to meet with the other signatories and consult in case of any controversy arising or in case of aggression by some outside power not a signatory. I repeat that I think the obligation to meet and consult is the only obligation existing in this treaty.[34]

Senator Willis agreed with Lodge. "As I understand this document, we are not bound to any action at all. . . . This conference is held, and the matter is talked over, and then we do whatever we please, so far as the terms of this treaty are concerned." [35] Other members of the majority party reiterated frequently that Article II contained no obligation except the obligation to communicate fully and frankly with the other signatory powers.[36] Senator Lenroot maintained that the United States would not violate the agreement by failing to put into action the decisions of a conference. Actually, this country did not agree to do anything, and consequently could not be guilty of an act of bad faith if it did nothing. Action was not implicit in the agreement.[37]

This effort to free the United States of any trace of responsibility for maintaining peace was climaxed with Senator Underwood's pragmatic analysis. He declared that in all probability there would be no obligations to discharge, because it was most unlikely that the Treaty provisions for maintaining peace would ever be called into active use. Furthermore, continued the Senator, the signatory powers were the only nations with sufficient military strength to menace the peace of the Pacific. No other nations would be able to rival, within the ten-year life of the Treaty, the might of the nations adhering to it.[38]

The Treaty was an answer to the "great heart throb of the American people, who are almost unanimous in their cry for Peace! Peace!" [39]

Thus, the case in favor of the Four-Power Treaty was completed. It would, said its advocates, be a significant stride toward the accomplishment of world peace. It would not, however, bind the United States to any obligations, moral or legal. Finally, it was the foundation on which the work of the Conference was built. The success or failure of the Washington Conference, which carried the hopes of civilization, was bound up with the passage or defeat of the Four-Power Treaty.

The senators who opposed the Four-Power Treaty, like those who advocated it, were devoted to the cause of peace, so they said, and to the preservation of American traditions in foreign policy; but the foes of the Four-Power Treaty appeared somewhat more conscious of the realities of foreign affairs than their opponents. As the debate developed, it was difficult to tell whether the opposition senators raised objections because they feared for the safety of the country, or if they raised them simply to obstruct the progress of the Treaty for partisan reasons. So great was the public's approval of the Washington Conference treaties that the press for the most part applauded any statement made on behalf of the Treaty, however weak in logic it might be, and condemned as mere obstructionism any argument in opposition, however logical it seemed.[40]

In contrast to the abstract virtues, extolled by the friends of the Treaty, its opponents revealed its tangible faults. They declared that the pro-Treaty case was based on a false premise when it held that the Washington Conference had created a moral atmosphere in which public opinion, unaided by military force, would support the Far Eastern policy of the United States and guarantee the peace of the world. In addition, they maintained that the Four-Power Treaty was an alliance which bound the nation to discharge obligations. To join such an alliance would violate the traditional policy of the United States, involve the country in quarrels which were foreign to its interests, violate its sovereignty, compromise its independence in foreign affairs, and eventually lead it into war.

The Treaty had invalidated the old standards of security and di-

203

plomacy because it had substituted friendship for enmity; it had established a "vague . . . but strong assurance."[41] The opposition conceded the vagueness of this argument but not its validity. The "new diplomacy" based on friendship and the moral force of public opinion was weak, they contended, because no real bond of friendship had been established between the powers at the Washington Conference. There was, in fact, no "new spirit" of friendship among nations.

Senator Thomas E. Watson called Japan and Britain the natural enemies of the United States. Britain would not pay her debts to the United States, said the senator from Georgia, but she could afford to dam the Nile at a tremendous cost, to irrigate three million acres of prime cotton land. The vitriolic Georgian charged that England maintained friendly relations with Japan only because it needed the soldiers of Nippon to stamp out the independence movement in India.[42] By signing a treaty with England, said Watson, "We are going into an alliance with the greatest enemy of human freedom that ever built an empire."[43]

The opposition was even more rabid in its denunciations of Japan. Senator T. H. Caraway declared that Japan was getting munitions from all parts of the world in order to attack the United States. Despite this fact, America was about to become the partner of Japan against Russia "which has been our friend always." The Japanese could not be trusted, warned Senator Johnson. To clinch this argument he quoted a speech given by Senator Lodge when the Treaty of Versailles was being debated in the Senate. Said Lodge at that time, "Does the history of the 21 Demands justify Americans now in trusting Japan, even though President Wilson says he trusts them?"[44] Returning to the present, Senator Robinson declared that

. . . the Japanese policy, which has been well recognized throughout the last twenty-five years, has been one of expansion. Japan has the viewpoint that she ought to occupy toward the Orient the relationship which the United States occupies toward the western world; that there ought to be created, recognized, and enforced a Monroe Doctrine in the East. . . .[45]

Furthermore, these aggressions by Japan were the result of economic necessities. Because this was the case, the senator thought there was

not the slightest likelihood . . . of a reversal of the policy that Japan adopted years ago of expanding and acquiring the possessions and control of territories in which are deposited . . . materials necessary for her prosperity and necessary for the maintenance of her engagements in case of war.

Robinson did not think that Japan would abandon a policy of expansion which was based on necessity simply because she had signed the Four-Power pact.[46]

In the face of these conditions it was foolish to expect that moral force alone would be sufficient to quiet the long-standing differences between America and Japan. Borah believed that treaties could have moral force only if they were built upon justice. The Washington treaties fell short in this respect because the rights and ambitions of China had been disregarded. The pacts, in Borah's judgment, were merely a recognition of the *status quo*.[47] This lack of "justice" was also observed by Senator LaFollette. He charged that the true aim of the Four-Power Treaty was to aid the big moneyed interests of the United States in the exploitation of all the natural resources of the world.[48] Senator Watson indicted Elihu Root, the lawyer "of predatory corporations," of the Belmonts, the Ryans, Boss Tweed, the Rothschilds, and J. P. Morgan and Company, as the tool at the conference for these interests.[49] Carter Glass, likewise, felt that ". . . the real purpose of this pact is not to promote peace but is to assert the supremacy of four great powers over the rest of the world in the Pacific Ocean. . . ."[50]

Borah continued the attack on the practicability of peace by moral force, asserting that all nations were still heavily armed. The Washington Conference had adjourned upon the theory that all matters must be settled by force. Until the day when all nations would reduce armaments to the bare minimum, it would be fruitless to place any faith in "justice or righteousness or the influence and power of public opinion to enforce arbitration and settlement. . . ."[51] But, said Borah, there was no prospect that armies and navies would be abolished, and consequently it was foolish to place sole dependence on the power of public opinion or moral force. If physical force was to be the last resort, then it would also be the first resort. Therefore, the Four-Power Treaty drew its effectiveness from military, not moral force.[52] Thus, these senators, along with the military heads of the country, concluded that American policy in the Far East would be only as strong as the American Navy.

These facts led the senators of the opposition to scrutinize the non-fortification agreement which had been adopted as a part of the naval ratio. Senator John K. Shields, early in the debate, pointed out that Guam was the key to American naval supremacy in the Pacific—this alone could maintain the Open Door.[53] Senator Reed added that the island of Guam was the first line of defense for the Philippines and was thereby fundamental to the development of a sound Far Eastern policy.[54] Under the non-fortification agreement, the Philippines could be taken in three days and Guam in less than twenty-four hours, according to naval officers with whom Reed had conferred.[55] In return for the "punic faith of Japan, a country which invariably attacks before it declares war," said Reed, the United States had deprived itself of fortifications, bases, coaling stations, and ships. Should Japan violate this pledge and take the Philippines and Guam, the United States could recapture them only at tremendous cost. Consequently, the United States had surrendered its positive power to protect its island possessions in return for an agreement of doubtful validity.[56]

Continuing his lecture on naval power, Reed declared, "The elementary test of one navy's power as compared with another's depends on the strength which can be brought to and kept in the main theatre of action." By this standard, it was apparent that

Japan will have gained an absolutely free hand in the Far East. . . . We will be completely unable to interfere. In agreeing not to fortify the western bases, we have, to all practical purposes, abandoned that part of the world, and we are helpless to shape any action in it.[57]

Senator Robinson, developing the same theme, noted: "The net result of this treaty, as it is written, is that Japan will dominate the Pacific Ocean and dominate the Asiatic mainland. . . ."[58] Senator Borah acknowledged that ". . . so far as the Orient is concerned, Japan has all the navy that she needs to dominate and control the entire situation."[59]

In addition to these grave faults, the opposition sought to prove that the Treaty was also an alliance. Harding, Hughes, and Lodge had denied this charge. However, other authorities disagreed. Senator Reed quoted statements by Viviani of France, Balfour of England, and Prince Iyesato Tokugawa of Japan in which they referred to the pact as an alliance. Baron Hayashi of Japan, said Reed, felt that

206

The new pact is but an enlargement and indorsement of the old friendship between Great Britain and Japan. . . . The spirit of the old alliance, which has achieved such fine work will continue, and the cooperation of the United States enables us to face the future with calm assurance.

Instead of abrogating the Anglo-Japanese Alliance the United States had joined it. "We got rid of it just like the old woman got rid of the old man, by marrying him," Reed said.[60] Senators Johnson and Robinson, among others, quoted at length statements by officials of the Japanese government revealing their belief that the Treaty was an alliance. If these quotations were representative of foreign opinion, these Senators felt, it made little difference how the United States government interpreted the Treaty. The other powers, who were parties to the pact, definitely interpreted it as such.[61]

The next phase of the debate was the opposition's attempt to demonstrate that the Treaty, regardless of what it was called, contained all the characteristics and all of the dangers of an alliance. "What the delegates from Europe brought over and gave us in the name of peace is the old hellish system whose frightful story is told upon a thousand battlefields of the Old World."[62] Senator France pointed out that whatever the pact was called—agreement, entente, alliance, or association—it was exclusive in nature. As a result, nations outside its scope would form agreements for their protection.[63] The Treaty, in effect, was an alliance and would lead to the formation of counter-alliances. Hence, if the United States was determined to depart from isolationism, the only wise policy was to join an association of all nations.[64]

Senator Borah, citing history, gave further proof that alliances inevitably produced counter-alliances. The senator's research was practically all inclusive, for it began with the alliance formed by Rameses of Egypt and the leader of the Hittites some 3,200 years earlier. Again and again, Borah asked, "Can any historian here advise the Senate of a single instance where a political group was formed that it did not give rise to a counter political group?"[65] Counter alliances would, of course, neutralize America's strength in the Far East.

The exclusive nature of the Treaty was further demonstrated by the fact that a non-signatory power was excluded from arbitration conferences, under the terms of the Four-Power Treaty, even though

207

its interest was involved. Instead of being an instrument for settling disputes, the pact actually was an alliance for winning disputes.[66] Recognizing this defect, Norman H. Davis had written to Borah, before the debate began in the Senate, urging an amendment which would include at the conference all the parties to the disputes.[67] While Borah did not offer such an amendment, several other senators did. Senator Robinson proposed that all powers interested in any controversy be invited to the conference called to settle it.[68] Variations of this proposal also were offered by Senator Walsh and Senator Pittman, but were defeated.[69]

The opposition continued its attack by asserting that this "menacing little imitation league" was in reality "a four-ply alliance, destined to involve us in distress and humiliation, if not in war."[70] Alliances had always been for the ostensible purpose of bringing about peace, said Senator Reed, and they had always ended in war. In proof of this contention he cited instances from history, beginning with the alliance between Rome and the thirty Latin cities. These early alliances had set forth peace as their aim, but had eventually resulted in war.[71] Finally, Senator Reed summed up this contention in a caustic denunciation: "In a word, the millennium is here, provided we sign this treaty, but if we do not sign this treaty two of our contemplated associates may pounce upon the United States without cause or reason." When the millennium comes, the senator prophesied, "it will be ushered in with the music of anvils beating swords into plowshares and spears into pruning hooks." It will not be ushered in by the spectacle of "the military masters of the world consorting together for a balance of military power and for the preservation, as far as they can, of the most rapid moving ships of war and the most powerful cannon."[72]

The opponents of the Treaty also denied that it was free of obligations. Senator Johnson maintained that the United States would be bound under the Treaty by moral obligations, even though no legal ones existed. The Treaty might not be an alliance under law and its terms might not specifically mention the use of force, but, said the California senator, "There is to me no distinction whatever in a treaty between what some persons are pleased to call legal and moral obligations. A treaty rests and must rest . . . upon moral obligations." The Treaty would obligate the United States, for a conference called among the four-powers, under Article II, would be called to settle a controversy. If it were agreed at this conference that the issue could only be met by force, continued Johnson, then the United States would be morally obligated to join in providing that force along with the other powers. The senator then cited various newspapers to substantiate his contention. The *New York Times* stated, "The use of force is implied as clearly in Article II as in the League of Nations." The *New York World* referred to the whole pact as an " 'Asiatic Article X' carefully phrased to meet senatorial scrutiny, yet imposing a moral obligation which a nation jealous of its honor must ever hold sacred." It was clear then, asserted Johnson, that the conference provided for by Article II would be called for the purpose of taking action, and the United States would be morally bound to honor any decision made by it. The United States should not ratify the Treaty for "we cannot and we must not pledge our faith with a mental reservation." [73] Senator Borah cited, as an example of binding moral obligation, the English government's position on the eve of World War I. While not legally bound to enter the war, it was bound in honor to come to the aid of France. [74] President Wilson, said Borah, had seen no more danger in Article X of the League Covenant in 1920, than the Republicans saw in Article II of the Four-Power Treaty in 1922. Actually, the same obligation was there. The difference lay not in the articles themselves, but in the Republican senators. While they had been able to discern the danger in Article X, presented by a Democrat, they were unable to see the danger in Article II, presented by a Republican. [75] An additional proof of the sanctity of moral obligations was presented by Senator Reed. He quoted Harding who, when a senator, had once declared ". . . if this Republic does not mean to do as it promises, it has no business to make the promise." [76]

The senators of the opposition now pictured dangers inherent in these moral obligations. America, they said, would be bound to come to the aid of any member of the pact should any of its island possessions be attacked. This possibility could not be ignored, even though the friends of the Treaty had maintained it a matter too remote to warrant consideration. Actually the menace of war was real. Japan, it was stated, was determined to continue a policy of aggression in the Orient, and in pursuance of this policy was even then attempting

209

to invest Siberia. Senator Johnson declared that it would be only a matter of time until Russia recovered its strength and would seek to drive Japan from Siberia. In such an event the United States, by the terms of the Four-Power Treaty, would be compelled to come to the aid of Japan against Russia.[77] Senator Reed felt that Russia would be able to wage war in a short time with an army of over four million men commanded by "the flower of the officers of the army of the Czar, . . . largely supplemented with German officers of high order." [78]

Summing up the Four-Power Treaty in this aspect, Reed declared that it was the "product of British diplomacy and Japanese cunning," by which the United States had been made "a pawn to be employed by Japan to sustain and protect Japan as against Russia when Russia undertakes to eject Japan from her mainland and from her island possessions." [79]

The Four-Power Treaty as a result of these obligations most certainly would involve the United States in war, according to this group of senators. "Instead of this being a treaty concerning islands in the Pacific Ocean, it is only a mere electric button which, touched there, sends the deadly current of war wherever the four powers have any possessions," said Senator Shields.[80] Once the interest of any of the powers was affected the resulting controversy would become world-wide.[81] This was a matter of grave consequence, for the traditional policy of the United States had been to work for peace. In the past, when war came, the United States had been able to take the side of honor, justice, and right, because her zealously guarded sovereignty and independence had given her perfect freedom of choice. The senators of the opposition asked if it was wise for the United States to give up this time-honored position of independence and bind itself to three other powers. From this time on, if the pact became law, the United States would be bound to go where the allies might lead even though peace, honor, and justice were sacrificed. So, said the opposition, the Four-Power Treaty would not bring peace, as its advocates contended, but a sword.

If this treaty is ratified we are . . . committed to something which will logically and inevitably lead us into war, and that war may carry us into the Pacific; and another expeditionary force will go much farther than 3,000 miles from home, and American boys will again shed their blood on foreign fields.[82]

210

It was impossible to believe that the Treaty contained no commitments, despite the assertions of its advocates.

To develop this view further, the opposition made inquiry as to how an agreement devoid of obligations could be of any possible significance. Senator Glass and others found it difficult to justify calling a conference, under Article II of the Treaty, if, as the advocates of the Treaty maintained, the decisions made there were not to be put into effect.[83] Senator Reed pictured the results of such a conference. "In the event of attack we meet, talk over the situation, and then take our hats and go home. . . . We guarantee nothing; nobody agrees to do anything; and therefore we should accept this thing because it is absolutely innocuous, to wit, absolutely worthless." It was, the Senator concluded, "a mere piece of international buncombe by which the nations agree solemnly that they will sit down and talk matters over and be bound by nothing that takes place."[84] Continuing this argument those opposed to the Treaty noted that if the United States assumed no responsibilities, then it must follow that the other members of the pact were likewise free. While the United States would not have to aid Japan, should its island possessions be threatened, neither would Japan be bound to aid the United States, should American possessions be subject to attack. The Treaty was not only useless but also dangerous. The United States decreased its military force in exchange for security which the Treaty did not actually provide. The opposition to the Treaty, insofar as logic was concerned, had confronted the friends of the Treaty with a dilemma. If the Treaty was to be a positive force, it must contain obligations; on the other hand, if it contained no obligations, it could not possibly accomplish any worthy objective.

Actually, the debate on this point revealed a more fundamental problem, for it showed that the irreconcilables in the Senate would not approve any sort of agreement or understanding with any other nation if any obligation was involved. Senator Reed, who had so scornfully decried the Treaty because it contained no obligations and would accomplish nothing, admitted that if it had included an obligation to protect the peace in the Pacific, he still would have opposed it. Thus, the irreconcilables made it impossible to frame a treaty which would accomplish any positive policy and at the same time meet their approval.[85]

211

President Wilson in 1917 in outlining the essential terms of peace declared: "Peace cannot be had without concession and sacrifice. . . . The statesmen of the world must plan for peace and nations must adjust and accommodate their policy to it as they have planned for war and made ready for pitiless contest and rivalry." [86]

The Senate in 1922 departed from this Spartan ideal. There was the cry for peace, but there was no peace, partially, at least, because the Senate did not propose to limit the independence and sovereignty of the United States in foreign affairs by accepting any obligations.

The Parchment Peace

. . . With the Senate's recommendation for ratification of the Washington treaties its role in this great episode in American foreign policy was concluded. The public approved the Senate's action yet gave it little credit for the success of the conference. To the contrary, the debate on the treaties had exasperated the entire country, proving once again the inability of the Senate to exercise its function as a constructive part of the treaty making power of the United States.[1] The *Philadelphia Public Ledger* asserted: "The treaty-killers have tried and failed."[2] Elsewhere, the Senate's work was appraised as "novel, startling and infinitely refreshing" in that it established "the welcome fact that the highest legislative body of the nation is actually capable of cooperating with executive policy and of serving civilization."[3] The Senate was charged with full responsibility for America's failure to join the League of Nations but was awarded little credit for its efforts to have a disarmament conference called. When it was reported in May 1921 that Harding was going to Florida to get away from the Senate, an editor bemoaned the fact that most people could not afford that pleasure. The Congress of this period was classified by some contemporaries as the most mediocre in the history of the nation.

Despite this low popular esteem the Senate was very influential in shaping the policy adopted by the nation in 1921-1922, largely because of the political conditions at the time.

The Republican party had come to power after the longest period of defeat it had known in its entire history. Two failures in presidential elections showed the most obstinate that only in union could be found the strength necessary to win control of government. The need for harmony had been acknowledged in the candidate and platform drawn at the Republican convention in 1920. The strong personality and large popular following of senators like Borah and

Johnson plus the desperate need for unity within the party combined to give these irreconcilables and their clique an inordinate degree of power. This was augmented by the fact that the President, nominated because he was more apt at compromising than crusading, had won election by a landslide. It was not checked by a Secretary of State who was a realist, too practical to fight a losing battle.

The reaction against Executive authority, the passing of Wilson and Wilsonism, gave the Senate a further opportunity to encroach upon the powers of the President. Attempts were made to exploit the advantage as the frequency of Senate resolutions on foreign policy in this period attests. It is reasonable to believe that Senate leaders might have succeeded in completely dominating Harding's foreign policy had it not been for the outstanding ability and tenacious resolution of his Secretary of State, Hughes.

Even so, they did dictate the larger goals of policy although nominal control of foreign affairs remained in the hands of the administration by virtue of the skill of Hughes. The Senate, or more precisely the irreconcilable wing of the Senate, shaped policy in several ways. It blocked any cooperation with the League of Nations, and thus made necessary a separate conference to deal with disarmament. The Senate did not succeed in limiting the conference to disarmament alone, a diplomatic impossibility, but it killed the idea of continued cooperation even in so nebulous a form as the Association of Nations. Thus the most vital question of the time, cooperative or unilateral policy for the United States, was decided in favor of the latter.

This was further demonstrated in what appeared to be the only defeat of the irreconcilable bloc—the passage of the Four-Power Treaty. It failed because the Treaty was carefully constructed with the prejudices of the Senate in mind and cleansed of those elements which would excite opposition. The innocuous result of these precautions was further safeguarded by an amendment. It won the support not only of irreconcilables, but of nearly all members of the Senate. In effect it was the creed of the times: "The United States understands that under the statement in the preamble or under the terms of this treaty there is no commitment to armed force, no alliance, no obligation to join in any defense." [4] It would be difficult to fashion any policy of cooperation which would meet these conditions, and these conditions were almost universally approved in the Senate.

214

This independence was based on the conviction that the United States would not need allies for defense in the foreseeable future. It was well expressed by Senator Reed who quoted Abraham Lincoln: "All the armies of Europe and Asia and Africa combined with all the resources of the earth in their military chest, with a Bonaparte for a commander, could not by force take a drink from the Ohio or make a track on the Blue Ridge in a trial of a thousand years." The Senator added that the United States was incomparably stronger than it was in 1837 when Lincoln made this assertion.[5]

Many senators asserted that this course of action did not mean isolation. It is "... the duty of the United States to exert its every proper influence to preserve peace with justice in the world," declared Senator Townsend.[6] Senator Edge stated that he had "never believed that our country should hold itself entirely aloof from all international concerns. . . . We cannot face international problems as the country faced them a hundred years ago. We live in a different world today. . . . America is more powerful and potential; the position of leadership in the world which she is destined to occupy cannot be lightly or selfishly thrust aside."[7]

The Senate professed and urged on the public the thesis that the United States while sacrificing no "worthwhile traditions" had discharged all of its international obligations.

The real keynote was sounded by Senator Shortridge of California who asserted shortly before the treaties were ratified in the Senate: "Man rejoiced because man thought, the Nation rejoiced because the Nation thought, that it was a step, a very great step, toward world peace, toward peace without sacrifice, toward peace with power unimpaired and rights guaranteed."[8] This same theme was reiterated by Senator Townsend who, when speaking of the conference, said:

No Senator can be more jealous of our country's unembarrassed sovereignty than I am, but I realize, sir, that our destiny is inextricably involved with that of the world, and that it is the duty of the United States to exert its every proper influence to preserve peace with justice in the world. . . . We have sacrificed no desirable right, we have entered into no entangling alliance, but we have substituted friendship for hatred among the nations of the world and entered into understanding with them which will reduce the causes for war and make peace more certain.[9]

Senator Walsh of Massachusetts, like Townsend, was most anxious

215

to preserve the peace of the world. He felt that this goal could only be reached if the United States took an active part in international affairs. However, he believed "that it is not necessary for America to bind herself to entangling agreements with other countries to accomplish this." On the contrary, Walsh believed that America could best serve the cause of peace by retaining unimpaired sovereignty so that it could pass "independent judgment on questions in controversy between nations."[10]

Another who subscribed to this theory was Senator Colt who asserted:

The great lesson taught by the World War is that the United States, on the ground of self-protection, can not stand aloof from the quarrels of other nations. It is manifest, therefore, that the safety of the United States is threatened in the quarrels of other nations, whether in . . . Europe or in the Fast East.

Yet Senator Colt believed that the United States could discharge its role in international affairs without accepting obligations which would prevent "the United States from exercising its own independent judgment with respect to the employment of armed forces."[11]

Probably the statement most representative of the prevailing opinion in the Senate was given by Senator France. Although as one of the original irreconcilables he voted against the Four-Power Treaty, and was the only senator to vote against the treaty for the limitation of armament, he was not opposed to international cooperation provided it could be carried out along lines he deemed safe. To this end, he drafted a plan for a "concert of nations." This title, he explained, was used because he "did not wish anything in the relationship between the nations which might be interpreted as a surrender of national sovereignty." Senator France's organization was to be a "concert of all of the nations acting together, each member acting as an independent sovereign power for the accomplishment of certain definite ends." They were to work together "for action in recognition of certain fundamental principles, which principles have been enunciated in the basic documents of our Republic, in the Declaration of Independence, and in the Constitution of the United States."[12]

These examples show clearly that the Senate's policy in foreign affairs was based on American traditions—peace, sovereignty, and independence. In meeting the difficult problem of adjusting American policy to the new role of world power, it would accept no plan that involved a sacrifice of these values. In evolving a policy which would guarantee peace and security, the Senate rejected the idea of building a super-navy. On the other hand, it had also opposed the collective security offered by the League of Nations. The super-navy would require the sacrifice of a tradition of non-militarism and as a consequence would jeopardize democracy. The League would necessitate the subordination of sovereignty and independence to the will of a super-state. The Senate professed that peace and security could be assured without resorting to either of these extremes. Its solution to the problem was international cooperation in an informal association of a few nations and a reduction of naval armament by the leading powers.

In making this decision the Senate did not forget that foreign policy derived its effectiveness from force. It acknowledged that the reduction of armament rendered Japan supreme in the Orient in the event she chose to resort to military conquest. But Japan would not resort to force, for in solemn treaties she had pledged herself to peace. The Senate, with the full approval of the public, believed that reduction of armament was practical because the conference had created a new diplomacy of trust backed by the sanction of moral force. This force would be more effective in preserving peace than fortifications and fleets. Friendship and faith had, by the work of the Washington Conference, replaced hatred and suspicion in the relations of nations.

Apparently this policy was endorsed and, indeed, dictated by the majority of voters. The only opposition came from two extremes—the military clique and the advocates of the League of Nations—both of which objected to the renunciation of military force and called it unreal. Their voices were lost in the tumult. A policy which in some respects was an acquiescence to the line of lease resistance was rationalized, by wishful thinking, into a noble ideal—the protection of democracy.

In the twentieth century this proved to be a parchment peace. It was peace conceived in the hope that pledges and public opinion unaided by international organizations and military force could meet the problems of a world power.

217

FOUR-POWER TREATY

I

The High Contracting Parties agree as between themselves to respect their rights in relation to their insular possessions and insular dominions in the region of the Pacific Ocean.

If there should develop between any of the High Contracting Parties a controversy arising out of any Pacific question and involving their said rights which is not satisfactorily settled by diplomacy and is likely to affect the harmonious accord now happily subsisting between them, they shall invite the other High Contracting Parties to a joint conference to which the whole subject will be referred for consideration and adjustment.

II

If the said rights are threatened by the aggressive action of any other Power, the High Contracting Parties shall communicate with one another fully and frankly in order to arrive at an understanding as to the most efficient measure to be taken, jointly or separately, to meet the exigencies of the particular situation.

III

This Treaty shall remain in force for ten years from the time it shall take effect, and after the expiration of said period it shall continue to be in force subject to the right of any of the High Contracting Parties to terminate it upon twelve months' notice.

IV

This Treaty shall be ratified as soon as possible in accordance with the constitutional methods of the High Contracting Parties and shall take effect on the deposit of ratifications, which shall take place at Washington, and thereupon the agreement between Great Britain and Japan, which was concluded at London on July 13, 1911, shall terminate. The Government of the United States will transmit to all the Signatory Powers a certified copy of the *proces-verbal* of the deposit of ratification.

The present Treaty, in French and in English, shall remain deposited in the Archives of the Government of the United States, and duly certified copies thereof will be transmitted by that Government to each of the Signatory Powers.

IN FAITH WHEREOF the above named Plenipotentiaries have signed the present Treaty.

DONE at the City of Washington, the thirteenth day of December, One Thousand Nine Hundred and Twenty-One.

NOTES

1. M. C. Conway, ed., *The Writings of Thomas Paine*, I, 88-89.
2. *Congressional Record,* 67 Congress, 2 session, 4016.
3. Merle Curti, *Peace or War: The American Struggle, 1636-1936,* 21.
4. Charles E. Hughes, *The Pathway of Peace,* 253.
5. David H. Miller, "American Foreign Policy, *Forum* (May, 1924), 652-656.
6. James D. Richardson, *A Compilation of the Messages and Papers of the Presidents, 1789-1908,* I, 321-324.
7. Speech by Wilson at St. Louis, Sept. 5, 1919. 66th Cong., 1 sess., Senate Doc., No. 120, pp. 42-43.
8. See especially M. H. Savelle, "Colonial Origins of American Diplomatic Principles," *Pacific Hist. Rev.,* III (1934), 334-350.
9. Richardson, *Messages,* 221-223.
10. *Cong. Rec.,* 63 Cong., 2 sess., 82-83.
11. Elihu Root Papers, Library of Congress, Box for 1919-1920.
12. *Cong. Rec.,* 67 Cong., 2 sess., 3237-3238.
13. *Ibid.,* 4075.

CHAPTER II

1. Samuel F. Bemis, *Jay's Treaty,* 211; Curti, *Peace or War,* 34: *Cong. Rec.,* 63 Cong., 1 sess., 5916.
2. William Ladd, *An Essay on a Congress of Nations for the Adjustment of International Disputes Without Resort to Arms,* Reprinted 1916, p. 98.
3. Curti, *Peace or War,* 38ff.
4. *Cong. Rec.,* 61 Cong., 2 sess., 4024.
5. *Ibid.,* 59 Cong., 1 sess., 1730.
6. Gunji Honsono, *International Disarmament,* 100-104.
7. *Cong. Rec.,* 61 Cong., 2 sess., 7244. For petition of Rhode Island Legislature and Massachusetts Legislature see 4545, 4590.
8. *Ibid.,* Petition from North Carolina Legislature, Appendix, 330-336.
9. *Ibid.,* 60 Cong., 1 sess., Index Part 1-8, H.J.R. 95, H.R. 20707; 60 Cong., 2 sess., Index Part 1-4, H.R. 27429.
10. *Ibid.,* 61 Cong., 2 sess., Index Part 1-8, H.C.R. 36; H.C.R. 45; H.J.R. 223; H.J.R. 239; H.R. 125; H.R. 23825.
11. *Ibid.,* 4017, H.R. 125; H.R. 23825.
12. *Ibid.,* 4020-21, 4027.
13. *Ibid.,* 4024, 4025, H.C.R. 36; H.C.R. 45.
14. *Ibid.,* 4310, H.J.R. 187.
15. *Ibid.,* 7432, H.J.R. 223; 8545.
16. *Ibid.,* 8546.
17. *Ibid.,* 8546.
18. *Ibid.,* 63 Cong., 2 sess., 219.
19. *Ibid.,* 217; Curti, *Peace or War,* 221, agrees with this view.
20. W. Stull Holt, *Treaties Defeated by the Senate,* 230-235.
21. *Ibid.,* 231n, quoted.
22. Harold and Margaret Sprout, *Toward a New Order of Sea Power.* 2 ed., 114.
23. *Cong. Rec.,* 63 Cong., 1 sess., 5832-5835, H.R. 298.
24. *Ibid.,* 63 Cong., 2 sess., 222.
25. *Ibid.,* 63 Cong., 1 sess., 5913-5917.
26. *Ibid.,* 63 Cong., 2 sess., 207.
27. *Ibid.,* 91.
28. *Ibid.,* 82-83.
29. *Ibid.,* 89, 91.
30. *Ibid.,* 86.
31. *Ibid.,* 386.
32. *Ibid.,* 394.
33. *Ibid.,* 410-411.
34. *Ibid.,* 81.
35. *Ibid.,* 391.
36. *Ibid.,* 479-480.
37. *Ibid.,* 386-387.
38. Decimal Files of the State Department: National Archives, 711.0013.
39. *Cong. Rec.,* 63 Cong., 2 sess., 2045-2046.
40. 711.0013/2, Wilson to Bryan, Dec. 9, 1913. Enclosed with this letter was

a copy of the resolution. Daniels was willing to cooperate but hoped a permanent plan would be adopted, 711.0013/1.

41. 711.0013/5, Norman H. Davis to Josephus Daniels, Jan. 7, 1921.

42. Harley Notter, *The Origins of the Foreign Policy of Woodrow Wilson,* 300-302; Charles Seymour, *The Intimate Papers of Colonel House,* I, 234-243.

43. *Cong. Rec.,* 63 Cong., 3 sess., Index 1-5, S.J.R. 233; S.J.R. 219; H.J.R. 401; H.J.R. 405; H.J.R. 59; H.J.R. 396.

44. *Ibid.,* 64 Cong., 1 sess., Index 1-13, S. 2710 same as S.J.R. 233; S.J.R. 11 same as S.J.R. 219 and H.J.R. 401; H.J.R. 75 same as H.J.R. 405; H.J.R. 32 same as H.J.R. 396.

45. *Ibid.,* 9142.

46. C. Leonard Hoag, *Preface to Preparedness,* 17.

47. *Cong. Rec.,* 64 Cong., 1 sess., 8813.

48. Navy Department, *Annual Reports,* 1920, 3. It will be noted in a comparison of the final text with the original proposal that the first plan called for a meeting to "suggest" methods, while the second called for a meeting to "formulate" a plan. The first plan called for disarmament and the establishment of an international organization at the same time, while the second, and final plan, provided that an effective world organization be founded before any step was taken toward disarmament.

49. *Cong. Rec.,* 64 Cong., 1 sess., 9140-9141.

50. *Ibid.,* 9144.

51. *Ibid.,* 9143.

CHAPTER III

1. Hughes, *The Pathway of Peace,* 3.

2. See Tyler Dennett, "How Old is American Policy in the Far East," *Pacific Rev.* (Dec., 1921), 468-469; G. M. Stratton, "American Mind in the Orient," *Atlantic Monthly* (April, 1922), 562; George H. Blakeslee, *The Recent Foreign Policy of the United States,* 244; Foster R. Dulles, *Forty-Years of American-Japanese Relations,* 104.

3. Notter, *Foreign Policy of Woodrow Wilson,* 233-234, 241-243, 385-386, 410-411.

4. United States, *Foreign Relations,* 1914, Supp., 164-170; Charles N. Spinks, *The Anglo-Japanese Alliance* (Stanford, 1936), unpublished doctoral dissertation, 630-34; A. Whitney Griswold, *The Far Eastern Policy of the United States,* 179.

5. *For. Rel.,* 1915, 105-111.

6. *Ibid.,* 146.

7. Treat, "The Shantung Question," *Pacific Rev.* (Sept., 1921), 298-308.

8. Charles E. Hughes Papers, Library of Congress, Box 170, MacMurray to Hughes, April 20, 1922.

9. Lansing said we would agree to recognize "special interests" in the non-political, geographical sense if Japan would agree not to infringe on the independence or territorial integrity of China or contravene the Open Door. Griswold, *Far Eastern Policy,* 214-15. Ishii said, "We do not seek to assail the integrity or the sovereignty of China, but we will eventually be prepared to defend and maintain the same integrity and independence of China against any aggressor." M. J. Bau, *The Foreign Relations of China.* Lansing told the Chinese Ambassador that he "must be aware that the American Government recognized that Japan had special interests in Manchuria." No declaration to that effect had been made by the United States, yet this government had repeatedly shown a practical recognition of the fact and did not desire to do anything to interfere with Japan's interests. *For. Rel.,* 1917, pp. 117-118. Ishii in his memoirs declared that Japanese "interests" existed in the basic nature of Oriental affairs and would continue to exist whether the United States wished to recognize it or not. . . Kikujro Ishii, *Diplomatic Commentaries,* ed. and trans. by W. R. Langdon.

10. Bemis, "Yap Island Controversy,"

Pacific Rev. (Sept., 1921), 315; *For. Rel.,* 1917, p. 264 gives the text.

11. Griswold, *Far Eastern Policy,* 223.

12. Thomas A. Bailey, *Woodrow Wilson and the Lost Peace,* 279-281.

13. Griswold, *Far Eastern Policy,* 226-239. See also Hughes Papers, Box 171, Advisory Committee Reports.

14. Notter, *Foreign Policy of Woodrow Wilson,* 538-541.

15. Seymour, *Colonel House,* II, 316-317.

16. *Ibid.,* IV, 65-71. Wilson felt very strongly on this point. He wrote Secretary of the Navy Josephus Daniels later on: "As you and I agreed upon the other day, the British Admiralty had done absolutely nothing constructive in the use of their navy and I think it is time we were making and insisting upon plans of our own." Josephus Daniels Papers, Library of Congress, Box 13, Wilson to Daniels, July 2, 1917. Plans for joint action were discussed until the end of the war. See *Ibid.,* Box 15, Franklin D. Roosevelt to Daniels, July 27, 1918 and Oct. 1, 1918.

17. Arnold J. Toynbee, "What was Done," *Treaty of Versailles and After,* 56-57.

18. Seymour, *Colonel House,* IV, 185.

19. *Ibid.,* 418-420.

20. Ray Standard Baker, "Woodrow Wilson and World Peace," *New York Times,* Jan. 22, 1922.

21. Seymour, *Colonel House,* IV, 496-499.

22. C. N. Spinks, "The Termination of the Anglo-Japanese Alliance," *Pacific Hist. Rev.,* VI (1937), 326.

23. Papers of the American Delegation, Senator Underwood, Box 305. Recommendations of the General Board of the Navy, 21; *Cong. Rec.,* 66 Cong., 1 sess., 4682.

24. 741.9411/3, states that this suggestion was made in note 711.41/2, Feb. 7, 1911. This foreshadowed the Four-Power Treaty of the Washington Conference.

25. 741.9411/7; 741/9411/10, states that the renewed alliance relieves the United States of fear that Britain would support Japan in a war on the United States, and consequently strengthens the British position in halting Japanese aggression by maintaining the balance of power.

26. Woodrow Wilson Papers, Library of Congress, Series II, Balfour to House, July 8, 1917, in reply to earlier suggestion. It was sent by House to Wilson.

27. 741.9411/19B, American Legation in China from State Department, July 23, 1918.

28. 741.9411/13;/20;/21.

29. Lansing Papers, Memorandum by Major Siqueland, May 8, 1919.

30. 741.9411/23A and /23B, Gilbert to London Embassy and Tokyo Embassy, Oct. 2, 1920.

31. *For. Rel.,* 1920, II, 680.

32. 741.9411/26, Memo by Martin, April 28, 1920; 741.9411/33, Polk to Embassy, May 24, 1920.

33. *For. Rel.,* 1920, II, 680-681.

34. 741.9411/34, Davis to Secretary of State, June 7, 1920.

35. 741.9411/58, Davis to Secretary of State, Dec. 24, 1920. See Hughes Papers, Box 171, Beerits Memo, Four-Power Treaty.

36. Underwood, Box 305, Report of the General Board.

37. 500A 41a/32, Army War College Report, Box 5264.

38. 500A 41a/58, Davis to Secretary of State, Dec. 24, 1920.

CHAPTER IV

1. Wilson Papers, Wilson to John Sharpe Williams, Jan. 13, 1919.

2. Josephus Daniels felt it to be good politics and a moral responsibility for Wilson to come out strongly for disarmament. Wilson felt such a course would not be consistent with his naval program and preferred to speak for "organized peace." Daniels Papers, Box 13, Daniels to Wilson, Aug. 2, 1916; Wilson to Daniels, Aug. 16, 1916.

3. Notter, *Foreign Policy of Woodrow Wilson,* 596, 596n.

4. *For. Rel.,* I, 1917, Supp., 24-29.

5. Notter, *Foreign Policy of Woodrow Wilson,* 596n. Lansing was responsible for the rumor that Wilson

planned to establish the League by executive action without consulting the Senate. It was emphatically denied by many prominent men, including Democratic Senator Hoke Smith.

6. *For. Rel.,* I, 1917, Supp., 24-29.
7. *Cong. Rec.,* 65 Cong., 2 sess., 680-681.
8. Baker, "Woodrow Wilson and World Peace."
9. This had long been the view of Congress as is shown by the resolutions on disarmament in 1910, 1913, and 1916.
10. 66 Cong., 1 sess., Sen. Doc., No. 106, p. 499.
11. *Cong. Rec.,* 66 Cong., 2 sess., 3800. See also Holt, *Treaties Defeated by the Senate,* 298.
12. *Cong. Rec.,* 66 Cong., 2 sess., 3955.
13. *Ibid.,* 3958.
14. Holt, *Treaties Defeated by the United States Senate,* 305. This authority is inclined to doubt the sincerity of the Senate's concern for prerogatives, pointing out that this anxiety was limited to the Republican members of the body.
15. *Cong. Rec.,* 63 Cong., 2 sess., 13896, H.R. 595. This was a resolution "authorizing the Secretary of State to communicate with the Japanese Government that the United States views with concern the issuance of its ultimatum to Germany."
16. Bailey, *Woodrow Wilson and the Lost Peace,* 282-285.
17. R. E. Hosack, "The Shantung Question in the Senate," *South Atlantic Quarterly,* XLIII (1944), 181-193.
18. Sprout, *Toward a New Order of Sea Power,* 75.
19. *New York Times,* March 7, 1920.
20. *Cong. Rec.,* 65 Cong., 3 sess., 2771, 3085, 3086.
21. *Ibid.,* 2717.
22. Dulles, *Forty Years of Japanese-American Relations,* 131-132.
23. *Cong. Rec.,* 66 Cong., 2 sess., 4660.
24. Henry L. Stoddard, *Presidential Sweepstakes,* F. W. Leary, ed., 70.
25. Quoted in Karl Schriftgiesser, *This Was Normalcy,* 4.
26. Quoted in Thomas A. Bailey, *Woodrow Wilson and the Great Betrayal,* 299.
27. William Allen White, *Autobiography of William Allen White,* 582.
28. Bailey, *Woodrow Wilson and the Great Betrayal,* 301-302.
29. Elihu Root Papers, Misc. Letters, 1919-1920, Root to Lodge, May 13, 1920.
30. *Ibid.,* Lodge to Root, May 17, 1920.
31. Bailey, *Woodrow Wilson and the Great Betrayal,* 300.
32. White, *Autobiography,* 585.
33. James E. Watson, *As I Knew Them,* 215-216.
34. Fleming, *The United States in World Organization,* 33.
35. White, *Autobiography,* 585.
36. Schriftgiesser, *This Was Normalcy,* 10.
37. Stoddard, *Presidential Sweepstakes,* 70.
38. *Ibid.,* 66-69; Samuel H. Adams, *The Incredible Era,* 145-146.
39. George Harvey quoted in Alan Cranston, *The Killing of the Peace,* 266.
40. Wilfred E. Binkley, *President and Congress,* 216-217.
41. Schriftgiesser, *This Was Normalcy,* 45.
42. Quoted in Mark Sullivan, *Our Times,* IV, 124.
43. Schriftgiesser, *This Was Normalcy,* 131.
44. Robert Lansing Papers, Desk Diaries, Jan. 1-Dec. 31, 1920, Nov. 3, 1920.
45. *Ibid.,* Vol. 54, 1920, Lansing to John W. Davis, Nov. 5, 1920.
46. *Cong. Rec.,* 67 Cong., 2 sess., 4238.

CHAPTER V

1. *For. Rel.,* 1921, I, 510, 499.
2. *Ibid.,* 315. For a complete discussion of the problem of China and the suggestions of American diplomats for solving the difficulties, see 313-355.
3. William S. Graves, *Current History* (May, 1921), 239.
4. For Hughes' part in these negotiations see Hughes Papers, Box 176, Japan. Some of this material is pub-

lished in *For. Rel.,* 1921, II, 263-267; 273-307.

5. Quoted in *New York Times,* March 10, 1921.

6. Blakeslee, *Recent Foreign Policy of the United States,* 247-250.

7. G. M. Walker, "Can We Escape War With Japan?" *Forum* (April, 1921), 398-410.

8. Quoted in Dulles, *Forty Years of American-Japanese Relations,* 152.

9. William E. Borah Papers, Library of Congress, Box 629, Clyde Hanson to Borah, Oct. 29, 1921.

10. *Cong. Rec.,* 66 Cong., 3 sess., 742.

11. Walter Lippmann, *U. S. Foreign Policy: Shield of the Republic,* 54.

12. Borah Papers, Box 620 (3).

13. *Literary Digest* (Nov. 12, 1921), 16-17.

14. *New York Times,* Dec. 11, 1920.

15. *Nation* (April 10, 1920), 453.

16. *Round Table* (Dec., 1920), 87-97.

17. *New York Times,* Nov. 24, 21, 1920.

18. *Ibid.,* Dec. 16, 12, 1920.

19. Sprout, *Toward a New Order of Sea Power,* 80.

20. *Cong. Rec.,* 66 Cong., 3 sess., 204.

21. *Ibid.,* 205-206.

22. *New York Times,* Dec. 14, 1920.

23. *Ibid.,* Dec. 11, 1920.

24. *Cong. Rec.,* 66 Cong., 3 sess., 150.

25. *Ibid.,* 205; *New York Times,* Dec. 12, 1920.

26. *Ibid.,* 310, S.J.R. 225.

27. *New York Times,* Dec. 15, 1920.

28. Borah Papers, Box 630 (I), Borah to William Lemon, Dec. 15, 1920.

29. *Ibid.,* Borah to L. R. Thomas, Dec. 22, 1920.

30. *Ibid., New York World* to Borah, Dec. 21, 1920.

31. *Ibid.,* Swope to Michelson, Dec. 29, 1920. Senator Walsh took issue with the *World* for overlooking his resolution in favor of Borah's. Walsh maintained that his proposal met the real issue while Borah's dealt with only one phase of the problem of disarmament. He challenged the state- ment that a reduction in naval build- ing, such as Borah proposed, would result in any great saving. Only a small part of naval cost went to building. Furthermore, he asserted that to stop building would aid Great Britain to maintain supremacy since the United States was actually build- ing at a much faster rate than Brit- ain. Thomas J. Walsh Papers, Li- brary of Congress, Box 268, Walsh to *New York World,* Jan. 12, 1921.

32. One example of the close cooperation between the senator and this paper during the campaign for the confer- ence was the correspondence on a proposed mass meeting in New York which was to be addressed by Borah. Swope surveyed public opinion in New York and advised the senator that such a meeting would not fur- ther the cause of disarmament. Borah accordingly canceled the speech. *Ibid.,* Swope to Borah, Dec., 1920.

33. *New York World,* Dec. 18, 1920; Jan. 13, 1921.

34. *New York Times,* Dec. 30, 1920.

35. *Ibid.,* Dec. 26, 1920.

36. *Ibid.,* Dec. 27, 1920.

37. *Ibid.,* Dec. 28, 1920.

38. *Philadelphia Public Ledger,* Jan. 3, 1921.

39. *New York World.* This paper found that thirty-four governors and the mayors of twenty-five leading cities were in favor of disarmament.

40. *New York Times,* Dec. 14, 1920.

41. *Ibid.,* Dec. 15 and Dec. 28, 1920; Jan. 4, 1921. Daniels declared that Pershing and Bliss, prominent in the disarmament movement at this time, were advocates of world disarmament rather than the three power proposal of Borah.

42. *Ibid.,* Dec. 5, 1920.

43. Borah Papers, Box 630 (1), Borah to Fredrick L. Allen, Dec. 31, 1920.

44. *Literary Digest* (Jan. 15, 1921), 7-8.

45. *Ibid.,* 9, 12.

46. *Ibid.,* 7, 8.

CHAPTER VI

1. *New York Times,* Jan. 23, 1921; *Hearings on Disarmament; Its Rela- tion to the Naval Policy and Naval* *Building Program of the United States,* (1920-1921), 66 Cong., 3 sess., 588.

2. *Hearings on Disarmament,* 552.
3. This was the Brooks Resolution, H.J.R. 424, which had been introduced before the House on December 21, 1920, and again on January 15, 1921. *Cong. Rec.,* 66 Cong., 3 sess., 616.
4. *New York Times,* Jan. 23, 1921.
5. *Cong. Rec.,* 66 Cong., 3 sess., 3154.
6. See pages 17-18.
7. *Cong. Rec.,* 66 Cong., 3 sess., 3155-3156.
8. *Ibid.,* 3156.
9. *Ibid.,* 3161.
10. Hoag, *Preface to Preparedness,* 65. Quoting the *Marion Star,* Dec. 31, 1920.
11. *Cong. Rec.,* 66 Cong., 3 sess., 1796.
12. *Ibid.,* 2983.
13. *Literary Digest* (Feb. 19, 1921), 14. Fortunately for Daniels, he was not on the bridge of the *Ostfiedland* a few months later when Army bombers using two thousand pound bombs sank her in twenty-five minutes. Many persons agreed with the verdict of the *New York American:* "To build $40,000,000 battleships is a stupid waste of money done only to please ship-builders."
14. *Cong. Rec.,* 66 Cong., 3 sess., 2825-2828.

15. *Ibid.,* 4273. Quoting *Scientific American* (Feb. 12, 1921).
16. *Ibid.,* 4273-4280.
17. See page 39.
18. In 1913 a law had been passed by Congress specifically stating that the President could not call an international conference without the authorization of Congress. The validity of this statute, however, was never demonstrated.
19. *Cong. Rec.,* 66 Cong., 3 sess., 4114-4115.
20. *Ibid.,* 3320-3321.
21. *Ibid.,* 3319-3320.
22. *Ibid.,* 4141.
23. *Ibid.,* 3754.
24. *Ibid.,* 4141-4145. Borah said of the Edge amendment as compared to his own amendment: "There is really no difference except in the question of adding governments of France and Italy." However, in final form France and Italy were omitted from the Edge Resolution.
25. *Ibid.,* 4172. The debate covers pages 4141-4172.
26. *Literary Digest* (March 12, 1921), 10.
27. *Ibid.,* 11.

CHAPTER VII

1. Sullivan, *Our Times,* IV, 121-122.
2. *New York Times,* Oct. 8, 1920.
3. One poll taker, when sampling opinion among Republicans all over the country, found that four-fifths of the Republican voters believed that in voting for Harding they were voting for entry into the League. Denna F. Fleming, *The United States and World Organization,* 37n.
4. *New York Times,* Dec. 15, 1920.
5. *Ibid.,* Dec. 16, 1920.
6. Nicholas Murray Butler, *Across the Busy Years,* I, 393.
7. Hughes, *The Pathway of Peace,* 296. Hughes quoted this statement in his memorial address at the funeral of Harding, and asserted that it represented the President's policy, later fulfilled at the Washington Conference.

8. Hoag, *Preface to Preparedness,* 64-65.
9. *New York Times,* Dec. 15, 1920. Daniels, no admirer of Republicanism, continued to work for a big navy. He wrote a series of five articles on this subject for the *Saturday Evening Post,* March 19, 26, April 9, 23, and May 21, 1921. See also Daniels Papers, Scrapbook, Box 697.
10. *Ibid.,* Jan. 12, 1921.
11. *Ibid.,* Jan. 15, 1921.
12. *Ibid.,* Jan. 24, 1921.
13. 711.0013/14.
14. *New Republic* (Feb. 23, 1921), 354.
15. J. B. Scott, "The Foreign Policy of the United States," *Am. Jour. of Int. Law,* XV (April, 1921), 233.
16. *New York Times,* March 5, 1921.
17. *Literary Digest* (March 19, 1921), 14.
18. *New York Times,* Feb. 20, 1921.

Harding's first choice was Senator Albert B. Fall, who was eventually given the post of Secretary of the Interior. Other men prominently mentioned for the position of Secretary of State were Senator Philander C. Knox, Elihu Root, and David J. Hill. "Enter Hughes," *The Independent and Weekly Review* (March 5, 1921), 235.

19. *New York Times,* Feb. 20, 1921. A contrary opinion was expressed in the Associated Press account which reported that the selection of Hughes was a concession to Borah and John-son. Associated Press releases, Jan. 6, 1921.

20. H. W. Horwill, "Charles Evans Hughes," *Contemporary Review* (Nov. 1921), 593-599.

21. Bailey, *Woodrow Wilson and the Great Betrayal,* 352.

22. Associated Press releases, April 13, 1921.

23. J. B. Scott, "President Harding's Foreign Policy," *Am. Jour. of Int. Law,* XV (July, 1921), 409-411.

24. *Literary Digest* (April 23, 1921), 6-8.

CHAPTER VIII

1. *Literary Digest* (Feb. 12, 1921), 30.
2. Hoag, *Preface to Preparedness,* 100-101.
3. Borah Papers, Box 630 (1).
4. *Ibid.*
5. *Ibid.,* John L. Monroe to Borah, March 4, 1921.
6. *Ibid.,* Borah to Roger William Riis, June 6, 1921.
7. *Literary Digest* (June 11, 1921), 8.
8. Borah Papers, Box 630 (1).
9. *Ibid.,* Borah specifically suggested that letters be written to President Harding and to Patrick H. Kelley, House Manager of the naval bill. Borah to Herbert J. Friedman, March 19; Dan-iel G. Chalan, June 25; Rev. J. Bradford Pengelley, June 15, 1921.
10. *Ibid.,* Borah to Nanette Silbert, April 1, 1921.
11. *Literary Digest* (Nov. 26, 1921), 50.
12. Hoag, *Preface to Preparedness,* 93.
13. *Literary Digest* (Nov. 26, 1921), 51.
14. *New York Times,* April 19, 1921.
15. *Ibid.,* April 22, 23, 1921.
16. Hoag, *Preface to Preparedness,* 103.
17. *Ibid.,* 93.
18. *Literary Digest* (June 4, 1921), 34.
19. *New York Times,* June 23, 1921.
20. *Cong. Rec.,* 67 Cong., 1 sess., 5096.
21. White, *Autobiography,* 602.

CHAPTER IX

1. *Cong. Rec.,* 67 Cong., 1 sess., 99, H.J.R. 5, Rep. Ed. E. Browne; 357, H.J.R. 53, Rep. John J. Rogers; 357, H.J.R. 54, Rep. P. B. Johnson; 630, H.J.R., Rep. W. Bourke Cockran.

Browne's resolution provided for a meeting of all nations for disarmament. Rogers recommended that the United States maintain a navy second to none until such a time as a disarmament conference was arranged. It provided that when the conference was called it should include Britain, France, Italy, Japan and any other nations which the President thought proper to invite. Johnson suggested that naval expenditures be decreased for a period of five years. Cockran's plan required naval supremacy by the United States as a prerequisite to the discussion of disarmament.

2. *Ibid.,* 618.
3. *Ibid.,* 680,682. These resolutions were ruled out of order on technical grounds.
4. *Ibid.,* 757.
5. *Ibid.,* 761.
6. *Ibid.,* 766.
7. Hoag, *Preface to Preparedness,* 66.
8. *New York Times,* May 4, 1921.
9. *Cong. Rec.,* 67 Cong., 1 sess., 1672.
10. *Ibid.,* 1416, 1418. King, and not Borah, was correct in his information on British policy, since that country resumed naval building in March, 1921.
11. *Ibid.,* 1408.
12. *Ibid.,* 1676, 1630.
13. *Ibid.,* 1734-1749.

14. *Ibid.,* 1418.
15. *Ibid.,* 1418, 1419.
16. Associated Press releases, May 18, 1921.
17. *Ibid.,* May 26, 1921.
18. *Cong. Rec.,* 67 Cong., 1 sess., 3225.
19. *Literary Digest* (Aug. 6, 1921), 12. Later in the year after the conference had been called, Harding was called the real leader of the party. "Hardly anybody in Washington nowadays doubts that President Harding is the actual leader of the Republican majority in both House and Senate. . . ."
20. *Cong. Rec.,* 67 Cong., 1 sess., 5095. In spite of this denial, the thesis presented by Senator Harrison was apparently corroborated from other sources. Senator Borah, in an interview some years later, stated that Harding opposed the resolution for the reasons given by his adherents in the Senate: a usurpation of executive leadership was involved; and the time was not ripe for a conference. This opposition collapsed, Borah explained, because public opinion became so strong that the administration senators refused to continue the

unpopular fight without the open support of the President. The President was unwilling to meet this demand and agreed to let the resolution pass. Bailey, *The Diplomatic History of the American People,* 688n, April 21, 1937.
21. *Literary Digest* (June 11, 1921), 7.
22. *Cong. Rec.,* 67 Cong., 1 sess., 5096.
23. *Literary Digest* (June 11, 1921), 9.
24. *Cong. Rec.,* 67 Cong., 1 sess., 1846.
25. *Ibid.,* 3225.
26. Borah Papers, Box 630 (1), Cobb to Borah, June 1, 1921.
27. *Cong. Rec.,* 67 Cong., 1 sess., 2173, H.J.R. 143.
28. *Ibid.,* 2091.
29. *Ibid.,* 2203.
30. *Ibid.,* 2200-2205.
31. *Ibid.*
32. *Ibid.,* 3225.
33. *Ibid.,* 3223-3224.
34. *Ibid.,* 3226. Rep. Ben Fairchild declared "that the President, long before the Borah Amendment was offered in the Senate, had already opened negotiations with other nations looking toward general disarmament."
35. *Ibid.,* 3225-3226.

CHAPTER X

1. Secretary of State Hughes wrote later that he suggested a conference to Harding shortly after taking office. Harding approved and Hughes then waited until international conditions were right to call it. Hughes Papers, Box 169, Beerits Memo, Calling of the Conference.
2. Willis F. Johnson, *George Harvey,* 333.
3. *For. Rel.,* 1921, I, 374-397.
4. *Ibid.,* 578-579.
5. *Ibid.,* 596, 584.
6. 711.0013/3. Bell to Secretary of State, Jan. 8, 1921.
7. 711.0013/10. Bell to Secretary of State, Jan. 18, 1921.
8. 711.0013/12. Bell to Secretary of State, Feb. 11, 1921.
9. 711/0013/13. Naval Intelligence to State Department, no date.
10. *Literary Digest* (May 7, 1921), 18.
11. The author has examined these files,

as well as the files of confidential dispatches, without finding any evidence of negotiations.
12. *For. Rel.,* 1921, I, 22.
13. Sprout, *Toward a New Order of Sea Power,* 129n. Charles E. Hughes, letter to Sprout, Aug. 5, 1940.
14. *New York Times,* Jan. 18, 1921; Associated Press releases, Jan. 16, 1921.
15. *Ibid.,* Feb. 9, 10, 1921.
16. *Cong. Rec.,* 66 Cong., 3 sess., 3161.
17. *New York Times,* Feb. 13, 1921.
18. *Ibid.,* March 17, 1921.
19. "Britain for Small Navies," *Independent* (April 2, 1921), 343-344.
20. *New York Times,* March 29, 1921.
21. E. J. Young, *Powerful America,* 49-50. Ochs sent the message by Ernest Marshall, a reporter.
22. *Literary Digest* (April 2, 1921), 16.
23. *New York Times,* June 1, 1921. These conversations do not appear in

the Decimal Files of the State Department.

24. "Present Problems of the Commonwealth of British Nations," *International Conciliation,* No. 167 (Oct., 1921), 364-365.

25. *Ibid.,* 379-380.

26. See page 30.

27. 741.9411/33. Polk to American Embassy in London, May 24, 1920.

28. 741.9411/136A. Hughes to Harvey, July 6, 1921.

29. 741.9411/132. M. A. Oudin, General Electric Co., to Fletcher, July 5, 1921.

30. Spinks, *The Anglo-Japanese Alliance,* 706, 718, 719. Spinks says, "We have yet no positive evidence that the Japanese Government desired to renew the Alliance at this time, although Baron Hayashi, the Japanese Ambassador in London, personally advocated such a policy." C. N. Spinks, "The Termination of the Anglo-Japanese Alliance." 339.

31. 500A.4A/160.

32. Hughes Papers, Box 176, Japan.

33. 741.9411/39. Smith to Hughes, June 23, 1920.

34. 741.9411/96. Sir Arthur Willert, conversation, Under-Secretary of State, May 31, 1921.

35. 741.9411/103. American Consulate, Australia, to Hughes, June 8, 1921.

36. *Literary Digest* (July 2, 1921), 11.

37. "Present Problems of the Commonwealth of British Nations," 364.

38. *Ibid.,* 378. Prime Minister Hughes suggested that the British take the lead in a conference for naval limitation.

39. *Ibid.,* 371.

40. Hughes Papers, Box 169, Beerits Memo, Calling of the Conference.

41. 741.9411/140½. Hughes and Geddes, June 23, 1921.

42. *For. Rel.,* 1921, II, 314-316.

43. 741.9411/136A. Hughes to Harvey, July 6, 1921. There had not been a great deal of comment in the Senate on the Anglo-Japanese Alliance. However, Senator Reed had made headlines by his charge, early in January, that the Anglo-Japanese Alli-

ance had a secret agreement appended to it which was dangerous to American interests, 711.9411/59. Senator Borah in answer to a query declared that he felt that the Alliance was extremely unfortunate, and that if it were renewed, it would be difficult to reach any conclusion other than that it was intended to operate against America. Borah Papers, Box 630 (2).

44. *For. Rel.,* 1921, II, 314-316.

45. 741/9411/140½. Memorandum of interview with British Ambassador, June 23, 1921. This part of the conversation is not included in *For. Rel.,* 1921, II, 314-316.

46. Hughes Papers, Box 175, Great Britain.

47. Hughes Papers, Box 169.

48. *For. Rel.,* 1921, I, 18.

49. Brebner, "Canada and the Anglo-Japanese Alliance," *Pol. Sci. Quarterly,* L (1935), 55.

50. *Parliamentary Debates,* July 11, Vol. 144, 914-918.

51. Hughes Papers, Box 169; 741.9411/-140.

52. 741.9411/136A. Hughes to Harvey, July 6, 1921. Hughes got this information from Ambassador Geddes and reprimanded Harvey in a dispatch, July 7, 1921.

53. *For. Rel.,* 1921, I, 19-20.

54. Hughes Papers, Box 169.

55. *Ibid.*

56. *Ibid.*

57. *For. Rel.,* 1921, I, 18.

58. *Ibid.,* 20.

59. *Ibid.,* 22-23. See *Parliamentary Debates,* July 11, 1921, pp. 915-919.

60. *Ibid.,* 23. The British proposal provided also for the limitation of armament.

61. *Ibid.,* 24.

62. *Ibid.,* 25-26.

63. *Ibid.,* 24.

64. Lloyd George told Lord Riddell that the idea of the Washington conference had originated at the Imperial Conference, and that on behalf of the Imperial Conference he had dispatched letters to the United States, China, and Japan asking their views.

However, it was important that President Harding have the honor of acting as originator of the Washington conference. Lord Riddell, *Intimate Diary of the Peace Conference and After, 1918-1923*, 305-306. Lloyd George, in addressing Commons July 11, stressed the leadership of England. He referred to Harding's invitation as a satisfactory answer to the previously issued British invitation.

The only initiative credited to Harding was the suggestion of a preliminary Far Eastern Conference which the American President did not suggest, and which America steadfastly and successfully opposed. *Parliamentary Debates*, July 11, 1921, pp. 915-919.

65. Hughes Papers, Box 169.
66. *Ibid.*, Box 176, Japan.
67. *Literary Digest* (July 23, 1921), 5.

CHAPTER XI

1. Senator Underwood, Papers of the American Delegation, Box 304.
2. *For. Rel.*, 1921, I, 18.
3. *Literary Digest* (July 30, 1921), 12.
4. Senator Walsh took great satisfaction in the fact that the final invitation seemed to include reduction of all types of armament as he had proposed in his resolution rather than limiting disarmament to the navy as suggested in the Borah Resolution. Walsh Papers, Box 268, Walsh to E. S. Hall, Aug. 2, 1921.
5. *Ibid.*, Box 630 (1), Borah to Raymond Robins, July 22, 1921.
6. Borah Papers, Box 629, Borah to Henry Powell, November 28, 1921.
7. *Literary Digest* (July 30, 1921), 12.
8. Root Papers, Misc. Letters, 1899-1929, Charles D. Hilles to Harding, Aug. 17, 1921.
9. Borah Papers, Box 629, Borah to Frank Borah, Aug. 23, 1921.
10. *Ibid.*, Borah to Chas. P. McCarthy, Aug. 23, 1921.
11. Lodge Papers, Massachusetts Historical Society, Lodge to Henry White, Aug. 31, 1921.
12. *For. Rel.*, 1921, I, 65.
13. *Ibid.*, 65.
14. *Literary Digest* (Sept. 24, 1921), 8-9. Taft in congratulating Root wrote: "I am not enthusiastic about Lodge in any way but for this purpose he was indispensable." Root Papers, Box 284, Taft to Root, Sept. 14, 1921.
15. *Cong. Rec.*, 67 Cong., 2 sess., 4190.
16. *Ibid.*, 4242-4244; Fleming, *The United States and World Organization*, 88n.
17. *For. Rel.*, 1921, I, 28-29. The British maintained that Ambassador Harvey had given assurance of American participation in a preliminary conference at the time he extended the invitation to a general conference. Hughes Papers, Box 175, July 30, 1921, Memo, Hughes and the British Ambassador.
18. *Ibid.*, 37-39.
19. *Ibid.*, 45-47. British Foreign Office to British Ambassador (Geddes). The Japanese were also invited by Britain.
20. *Ibid.*, 47-49.
21. *Literary Digest* (Dec. 17, 1921), 17.
22. *Ibid.* (Sept. 3, 1921), 9.
23. *Ibid.* This editor was mistaken in his belief that Hughes had no intention of permitting the United States to join the Alliance. However, in its estimate of public opinion the *Transcript* was correct. One of Hughes' major problems prior to the conference was to counteract the idea that the British were coming to Washington to win America's consent to becoming a party to an alliance. The greatest tribute to Hughes' ability to manage public opinion was the open acceptance which the public, if not the Senate, accorded the Four-Power pact in December. Inasmuch as the pact finally drawn up at the conference was fundamentally the same as Lloyd George's suggestion of August, the change in public attitude is little short of miraculous. Certainly the transformation in public opinion which occurred justified Hughes' adamant opposition to a preliminary conference.

228

24. Borah Papers, Box 629, Bender to Borah, Aug. 6, 1921.
25. *Ibid.*, Box 627 (1), Borah to William Kent, Dec. 20, 1921.
26. *Ibid.*, Box 629, Theo H. Lunde to Borah, Nov. 13.
27. *Ibid.*, C. A. Ritchie to Borah, October 29, 1921.
28. *Cong. Rec.*, 67 Cong., 1 sess., 5094.
29. *Ibid.*, 5711-5712.
30. *Ibid.*, 6787-6788.
31. *Ibid.*, 7534, 7537.
32. *Ibid.*, 7536-7537.
33. *Ibid.*, 7538; *New York Times,* Nov. 9, 1921.

> Whereas the Senate of the United States wishes every success for the conference on limitation of armaments called by President Harding to meet in the city of Washington on the 11th day of November, 1921; and
> Whereas the Senate of the United States believes that the greatest publicity to which, in reason, consideration of the questions for which the conference is called will admit will tend toward the success of the conference: Therefore be it
> Resolved, That the Senate of the United States respectfully requests the representatives of the Government of the United States at the conference to use their influence to have the conference admit representatives of the press to the meetings of the full conference where the questions for which the conference was called are considered.
> Resolved further, That the Senate of the United States respectfully requests the representatives of the Government of the United States at the conference to use their influence to have the conference maintain and preserve a record containing the proceedings of the conference when the matters for which the conference was called are considered and acted upon.
> Resolved further, That the Senate of the United States respectfully requests the representatives of the Government of the United States at the conference to use their influence against any form of censorship upon the part of the conference that will prevent the public from being informed through the press of the correct attitude of delegations and nations touching the questions considered in the conference.
> The last clause was omitted from the resolution which the Senate adopted.

34. *Ibid.*, 6877-6890, from *Collier's Weekly* (Oct. 15, 1921).
35. Hughes Papers, Box 172, Beerits Memo, Separate Peace With Germany. . . .
36. Associated Press releases, April 13, 1921.
37. *Cong. Rec.*, 67 Cong., 1 sess., 3299.
38. Hughes Papers, Box 172, Beerits Memo, Separate Peace With Germany. . . .
39. *Cong. Rec.*, 67 Cong., 1 sess., 5777-5778.
40. *Ibid.*, 5769.

CHAPTER XII

1. Hoag, *Preface to Preparedness,* 127-130. During the conference this committee compiled more than fifty news summaries and fifty-five editorial summaries, utilizing for this purpose all newspapers available in Washington, in addition to one hundred and eighty-five papers which had correspondents in Washington.
2. 500.A 4081/353. Barbara Dillon to Hughes.
3. Sen. Com. on For. Rel., Packet 67, A-J 22-23, 158.
4. Hoag, *Preface to Preparedness,* 75.
5. *Literary Digest* (Dec. 3, 1921), 14. Despite this statement, steel dropped one to four points on the market the first business day after Secretary Hughes proposed the scrapping of ships.
6. Hoag, *Preface to Preparedness,* 113-114.
7. *New York Times,* Oct. 27, 1921.
8. *Literary Digest* (Dec. 3, 1921), 28.
9. *Cong. Rec.*, 67 Cong., 1 sess., 7159, H.J.H. 215.

10. *Ibid.*, 7199, S.C.R. 14. *New York Times*, Nov. 3, 5, 6, 1921.
11. *New York Times*, Nov. 6, 1921.
12. Recording of Harding's speech in the National Archives; Associated Press releases, Nov. 12, 1921.
13. *Cong. Rec.*, 67 Cong., 2 sess., 4008.
14. *New York Times*, Nov. 13, 1921.
15. White, *Autobiography*, 598.
16. 67 Cong., 2nd sess., Sen. Doc. Vol. 10, *Conference on Limitation of Armament*, 39.
17. *Ibid.*, 41-47; Mark Sullivan, *The Great Adventure at Washington*, 35-41.
18. Marlo Pusey, *Charles Evans Hughes*, II, 464-465. Pusey obtained this information in an interview with

Hughes, Nov. 26, 1946. Lord Lee in an address May 9, 1922, stated that the speech was not revealed to the British before it was delivered. Hughes Papers, Box 172, comments on the conference.
19. *New York Times*, Oct. 26, Nov. 4, 1921.
20. Sullivan, *The Great Adventure at Washington*, 35-41.
21. *Independent* (Jan. 24, 1925), 85.
22. Sullivan, *The Great Adventure at Washington*, 41-46.
23. *Round Table* (March, 1921), 279.
24. *Literary Digest* (Dec. 3, 1921), 12. The replies of many other governors are also printed in this issue.
25. *Ibid.* (Dec. 24, 1921), 28.

CHAPTER XIII

1. Com. on Gen. Info. Special Bulletin, No. 5.
2. Butler, *Across the Busy Years*, 393.
3. Root Papers, Misc. Letters, Hilles to Harding, Aug. 17, 1921.
4. Anderson Papers, Box 47, Anderson to Hughes, Sept. 15, 1921.
5. *Ibid.*, Box 5, Diary Notes, V, Hughes to Anderson, Oct. 28, 1921.
6. *Literary Digest* (Oct. 1, 1921), 7.
7. *New York Times*, Oct. 20, 1921.
8. Hoag, *Preface to Preparedness*, 129.
9. *Literary Digest* (Dec. 10, 1921), 5.
10. *New York Times*, Nov. 26, 1921.
11. Associated Press releases, Nov. 26, 1921.
12. *Ibid.*, Nov. 27, 1921; *New York Times*, Nov. 27, 1921.
13. *Ibid.*, Nov. 27, 1921.
14. *New York Times*, Nov. 27, 1921.
15. *Ibid.*, Nov. 28, 1921; *Literary Digest* (Dec. 10, 1921), 5, 6.
16. Borah Papers, 629, Borah to John D. Moore, Nov. 29, 1921.
17. Fleming, *The United States and World Organization*, 238.
18. Senator Lodge, Am. Del., Box 298, Report from State Department—Current Information.
19. Associated Press releases, Dec. 3, 1921.
20. *New York Times*, Dec. 3, 1921.
21. *Literary Digest* (Dec. 10, 1921), 5-6.

22. Senator Lodge, Am. Del., 298. Report, State Dept.—Current Info.
23. Norman H. Davis and others, "American Foreign Policy," *Foreign Affairs* (Sept. 15, 1924), 25. Hughes states that shortly after the beginning of the Harding administration the irreconcilable bloc made clear its opposition to ". . . participation in the League on any terms." It threatened to wreck the administration if its wishes were ignored in this matter. Hughes Papers, Box 172, Beerits Memo, Separate Peace with Germany, the League of Nations. . . .
24. Hughes Papers, Box 171, Misc. Memo, (W.R.C. Jr.) Nov. 23, 1921; "Armed Truce Conference," *New York Times*, Dec. 11, 1921.
25. *New York Times*, Jan. 9, 1922. Hughes cited the difficulty of establishing a rival league in later correspondence, Hughes Papers, Box 31, Hughes to A. L. Lowell, July 20, 1922.
26. *Ibid.*, Feb. 7, 1922.
27. *Ibid.*, March 15, 1922.
28. Hughes Papers, Box 172, Beerits Memo.
29. *Ibid.*, Box 31, A. Lawrence Lowell to Hughes, March 17, 1922; Hughes to Lowell, July 20, 1922.
30. *For. Rel.*, 1922, I, 302.
31. *Literary Digest* (April 8, 1922), 13.

CHAPTER XIV

1. *Cong. Rec.,* 67 Cong., 1 sess., 7642.
2. Borah Papers, Box 629, Borah to Adm. P. Hayes, Attorney, Nov. 22, 1921.
3. *Literary Digest* (July 23, 1921), 7.
4. *Macon Daily Telegraph,* Nov. 12, 1921; *New York Times,* Nov. 2, 1921.
5. *Literary Digest* (Nov. 26, 1921), 8.
6. *New York Times,* Oct. 19, 1921.
7. Com. on Gen. Info., Dec. 3, 1921; *New York Times,* Dec. 3, 1921.
8. *Ibid.,* Dec. 5, 1921.
9. *Ibid.,* Dec. 7, 1921.
10. *New York Times,* Dec. 8, 9, 10, 1921.
11. *Ibid.,* Dec. 10, 1921.
12. Hughes Papers, Box 175, Great Britain, Hughes and British Ambassador, Memo, Sept. 20, 1921.
13. Anderson Papers, Diary, V, Box 5, Hughes to Anderson, March 10, 1922. In this letter Hughes states that there were no negotiations between the United States and Britain on the Alliance after Hughes' conversation with Geddes in late June.
14. 500.A 4A/160; Hughes Papers, Box 169, Four Power Treaty.
15. *For. Rel.,* 1922, I, 3. As late as Nov. 26, it was reported that Harding was willing to have the results of the conference drawn up in the form of gentlemen's agreements rather than formal treaties. However, by early December it had been decided that formal treaties would have to be used. (Associated Press releases, Nov. 26, 1921; Dec. 10, 1921).
16. Anderson, Papers, Diary, V, Box 5, Mar. 10, 1922.
17. Root-Takahira Agreement, *For. Rel.,* 1908, pp. 511-512. As subsequently interpreted by the State Department, the Root-Takahira notes were "simply a joint declaration of policy rather than a convention establishing a legal status which either party might invoke against the other"; *Ibid.,* 1914, Supp., 186-189.
18. See Thomas A. Bailey, "Root-Takahira Agreement of 1908," *Pacific Hist. Rev.,* IX (1940), 28-36. The term "special position" was never clearly defined. Secretary of State Elihu Root declared, "My arrangements—negatived the special interests of Japan in China"; Jessup, *Root,* II, 40. On the other hand, Theodore Roosevelt, President at the time, wrote Taft in 1910, "Our interest is not to take steps that will make Japan think we are hostile to their interest"; Roosevelt to Taft, Dec. 22, 1910, quoted in Griswold, *Far Eastern Policy of the United States,* 131.
19. *For. Rel.,* 1922, I, 1-2; The longhand original memo of this conversation is in Hughes Papers, Box 169, Four Power Treaty.
20. 500. A 4A/160.
21. Since Balfour used the older Alliance as a basis his draft was similar to the American version. Anderson thought this was the first draft. Anderson Papers, Diary, V, Box 5, Dec. 10, 1921.
22. *Ibid.,* Nov. 20, 1921.
23. *Ibid.,* Box 47, Nov. 22, 1921.
24. *Ibid.,* Diary, V, Box 5, Nov. 22, 1921.
25. 500. A4A/160.
26. Anderson says that he heard nothing after he wrote Lodge a letter concerning the arrangement on November 26. Nielsen, Scott, and Wilson, the other legal advisers, likewise had not been consulted. *Ibid.,* Dec. 10, 1921. Root said the drafts were not submitted by Hughes to the legal advisers or to the other American delegates.
27. 500. A4B/½.
28. *For. Rel.,* 1922, I, 4.
29. 500. A4A/160.
30. *Ibid.*
31. *Ibid.* See also *For. Rel.,* 1922, I, 5-7.
32. *Ibid.* See also *For. Rel.,* 1922, I, 7-8. This draft was not in the same form as the Anderson draft. The provision guarding against a separate arrangement with other powers was dropped, but articles I and II were similar to Anderson's articles I and II.
33. *For. Rel.,* 1922, I, 4ff. Earlier drafts

had defined the area as follows: Balfour—"the regions of Eastern Asia . . . the islands of the Pacific"; Shidehara—"Regions of the Pacific Ocean and of the Far East"; Hughes—"Insular possessions and dominions in the Pacific Ocean." Lodge, it will be remembered, had limited the territory covered in the original Anderson draft to "insular possessions."

34. 500. A4A/160.
35. *Ibid.*
36. 500. A4A/162.
37. 500. A4A/160.
38. *For. Rel.,* 1922, I, 13-23.
39. *Ibid.,* 23.
40. Anderson Papers, Diary, V, Box 5, Dec. 27, 1921.
41. *Ibid.;* Box 47, Dec. 16, 1921.
42. *Conference on the Limitation of Armament,* 159-166. See *New York Times,* Dec. 25, 1921, for a discussion on the use of poetry in the Senate.
43. *New York Times,* Dec. 11, 1921.
44. Reed quoting, *Cong. Rec.,* 67 Cong., 2 sess., 438.
45. *Literary Digest* (Dec. 24, 1921), 16.
46. Hughes Papers, Box 171, Misc. Memo, interview of Hitchcock by (W. R. C. Jr.), Dec. 23, 1921.
47. Com. on Gen. Info., Dec. 12, 1921.
48. Walsh Papers, Box 268, Walsh to John T. Flynn, Dec. 13, 1921.
49. Com. on Gen. Info., Dec. 12, 1921.
50. *New York Times,* Dec. 17, 1921; *Cong. Rec.,* 67 Cong., 2 sess., 534-547.
51. *Cong. Rec.,* 67 Cong., 2 sess., 436.
52. *Literary Digest* (Dec. 24, 1921), 5.
53. Com. on Gen. Info., Dec. 13, 1921.
54. *Literary Digest* (Dec. 24, 1921), 5.
55. Com. on Gen. Info., Dec. 12, 1921.
56. Borah Papers, 627 (1), Borah to Arthur H. Vandenberg, Dec. 19, 1921.
57. *Ibid.,* Borah to Mrs. U. S. Vincent, Dec. 16, 1921.
58. Com. on Gen. Info., Dec. 13, 14, 16, 1921; *New York Times,* Dec. 16, 1921.
59. 500. A4A/160.
60. *Cong. Rec.,* 67 Cong., 2 sess., 442; *New York Times,* Dec. 20, 1921.
61. Com. on Gen. Info., Dec. 20, 1921.

62. Hughes Papers, Box 169, Beerits Memo, Four-Power Treaty.
63. Abbott, E., "The Red Herring at Washington," *Outlook* (Jan. 4, 1922), 15.
64. Com. on Gen. Info., Dec. 21, 1921.
65. *Cong. Rec.,* 67 Cong., 2 sess., 629.
66. Com. on Gen. Info., Dec. 21, 23, 26, 29, 1921.
67. Hughes Papers, Box 171, Misc. Memo, interview of Hitchcock by (W. R. C. Jr.).
68. *Literary Digest* (Jan. 7, 1922), 20.
69. *Ibid.,* 10. Actually 23 Democrats did vote against the Treaty, but only 4 Republicans joined them.
70. *For. Rel.,* 1922, I, 37-38; Hughes Papers, Box 169, Beerits Memo, Four-Power Treaty.
71. Com. on Gen. Info., Dec. 23, 24, 27, 29, 1921; Jan. 3, 1922; *New York Times,* Dec. 28, 29, 1921.
72. Hughes Papers, Box 169, Beerits Memo, Four-Power Treaty.
73. 500. A4A/160; 500. A4A/162. This supplementary agreement took effect upon the ratification of the main Treaty.
74. *For. Rel.,* 1922, I, 39-42, 45, 47-48.
75. *Ibid.,* 29-30.
76. *Ibid.,* 98-99.
77. 500. A4A/162/15b. Root drafted a proposed treaty including the Netherlands which he says was to cover a request by that nation.
78. *Ibid.*
79. *For. Rel.,* 1922, I, 45.
80. Com. on Gen. Info., Dec. 30, 31, 1921.
81. *New York Times,* Jan. 2, 1922. The idea that the delegates dealt in stolen goods had been given a more sensational, if less official, treatment sometime before Borah made this speech. Urban Ledoux had spent much of December picketing the building in which the conference sessions were being held. He paraded back and forth, with his heart shaped umbrella in hand, demanding warrants for the arrest of all the delegates to the conference on the ground that the lands which they held were stolen goods. *New York Times,* Dec. 18, 1922.

82. Com. on Gen. Info., Jan. 5, 1922.
83. *New York Times,* Jan. 14, 1922.
84. Newberry had defeated Henry Ford for senator in Michigan in 1918. Subsequently, the charge of corruption and excessive campaign expenditures was brought against Newberry.

The case was in the courts in 1919-1921. A Senate investigation came in 1921. Finally on January 12, 1922, the Senate adopted a resolution seating Newberry, but condemning the methods used to gain his election. *Ibid.,* Jan. 13, 1922.

CHAPTER XV

1. *Cong. Rec.,* 67 Cong., 2 sess., 231; Borah Papers, Box 629, Borah to Hon. John Sparge, Nov. 16, 1921; Hughes Papers, Box 171, Misc. Memo. (W. R. C. Jr.) to Hughes, Nov. 4, 1921.
2. *For. Rel.,* 1922. I, 91. The Japanese wished to retain the *Mutsu,* their newest ship, although this retention unbalanced the number of tons granted each nation under the Hughes formula.
3. Sprout, *Toward a New Order of Sea Power,* 171. Hughes in a letter to Sprout, Aug. 5, 1940. The senators, Lodge and Underwood, reiterated this view in the Senate debate on the Four-Power Treaty.
4. *Ibid.,* 172. The drafts of this treaty are in Hughes Papers, Box 171, Fortifications in Pacific.
5. *New York Times,* Dec. 10, 1921.
6. *Cong. Rec.,* 67 Cong., 2 sess., 1181.
7. Com. on Gen. Info., Jan. 18, 1921.
8. Political leaders noted this trend early in the Conference, Hughes Papers, Box 171, Misc. Memo., (W. R. C. Jr.) to Hughes, Nov. 23, 1921.
9. Hughes discussed this matter with the Japanese Ambassador on a num-ber of occasions between the time the Conference was called and the time it opened. Hughes Papers, Box 176, Japan. See also 500. A 4002/79a.
10. *New York Times,* Jan. 10, 1922.
11. Latané, *From Isolation to Leadership,* 281; Buell, *The Washington Conference,* 261. Many of the foreign delegates felt the United States would sacrifice Far Eastern issues in the interest of disarmament and general harmony. Hughes Papers, Box 171, Misc. Memo., (W. R. C. Jr.) to Hughes, Nov. 23, 1921.
12. *New York Times,* Jan. 10, 1922.
13. *Cong. Rec.,* 67 Cong., 2 sess., 1182.
14. *Ibid.,* 1432.
15. *Ibid.,* 1434; *New York Times,* Jan. 21, 1922.
16. *Ibid.,* 1558-1559, 1618.
17. *Ibid.,* 1619.
18. Com. on Gen. Info., Jan. 20, 1921.
19. Sprout, *Toward a New Order of Sea Power,* 253.
20. *For. Rel.,* 1922, I, 945.
21. *Ibid.,* 274-275.
22. *New York Times,* Dec. 25, 1921.
23. Griswold, *The Far Eastern Policy of the United States,* 331.

CHAPTER XVI

1. *New York Times,* Feb. 5, 1921.
2. *Literary Digest* (April 8, 1922), 12.
3. *Conference on the Limitation of Armament,* 400.
4. Hoag, *Preface to Preparedness,* 143.
5. *New York Times,* Jan. 9, Feb. 6, 1922.
6. Walsh Papers, Box 268, Woman's Pro-League Council to Walsh, Dec. 6, 1921.
7. Hoag, *Preface to Preparedness,* 147.
8. *Literary Digest* (April 8, 1922), 12; Senate Petitions, Bundle I and 67-A-K.
9. *Cong. Rec.,* 67 Cong., 2 sess., 4322.
10. Senate Petitions, 67-A-K-2.
11. Borah Papers, Box 629 (1), Christine Donohue to Borah, Oct. 23, 1921.
12. Senate Petitions, 67-A-K-2.
13. *Cong. Rec.,* 67 Cong., 2 sess., 4250.
14. *Ibid.,* 3894.
15. *Ibid.,* 4326, 4327.
16. *Ibid.,* 4005.

17. *Ibid.*, 3907-3908.
18. *Ibid.*, 4190.
19. Borah Papers, Box 627, Borah to Mrs. F. M. Simpson, Jan. 19, 1922; Borah to White, Jan. 4, 1921.
20. *New York Times,* Feb. 8, 1922.
21. *For. Rel.,* 1922, I, 301-302.
22. *New York Times,* Feb. 12, 1922.
23. Charles E. Hughes, "Some Observations of the Conduct of Foreign Relations," *Am. Jour. of Int. Law.,* XVI (1922), 365-369.
24. *Sen. Doc.* No. 9, 67 Cong., 2 sess., *Conference on the Limitation of Armament,* p. vi.
25. Borah Papers, Box 627 (1), Borah to Marcus Day, Dec. 19, 1921.
26. O. G. Villard, "Publicity and the Conference," *Nation* (Jan. 18, 1922), 65-66.
27. *Cong. Rec.,* 67 Cong., 2 sess., 2587; *New York Times,* Feb. 16, 17, 18, 1922.
28. *Ibid.,* 2640; *New York Times,* Feb. 17, 1922.
29. *Ibid.,* 2771; *New York Times,* Feb. 17, 1922.
30. *Ibid.,* 3233.
31. *Ibid.,* 3547.
32. *Ibid.,* 3715.
33. *Ibid.,* 3608-3609.
34. *Ibid.,* 3609.
35. *Ibid.,* 3712. Hughes did not state that Balfour and Kato prepared drafts of the Treaty, but otherwise reported the true course of the negotiations.
36. *Ibid.,* 3715.
37. *Ibid.,* 4124.
38. *Ibid.,* 3857.
39. *Ibid.,* 3906.
40. *Ibid.,* 4068.
41. *Ibid.,* 4119.
42. *Ibid.,* 4120. Borah's copy of this speech is to be found in Box 630 (3) of his papers.
43. *Ibid.,* 4120.
44. *Ibid.,* 4123.
45. *Ibid.,* 4124.
46. *Ibid.,* 4157-4158.
47. *Ibid.,* 4158.
48. *Ibid.*
49. Borah Papers, Box 627 (1), Norman H. Davis to Joe T. Robinson, March 21, 1922. Cravath wrote Hughes that he regretted ". . . the misuse that has been made of a garbled report of informal remarks that I made at what I supposed to be a private dinner." Hughes Papers, Box 17, Cravath to Hughes, March 22, 1922.
50. *Ibid.,* Box 620 (3), Borah to Lodge, April 5, 1922.
51. *Cong. Rec.,* 67 Cong., 2 sess., 3560.
52. *New York Times,* Feb. 18, 1922.
53. *Literary Digest* (March 11, 1922), 12.
54. *Cong. Rec.,* 67 Cong., 2 sess., 2940-2942.
55. *New York Times,* Feb. 24, 1922.
56. *Ibid.,* Feb. 26, 1922.
57. *Ibid.,* Feb. 25, 1922.
58. *Ibid.,* March 5, 1922.
59. *Ibid.,* Dec. 14, 1921.
60. *Ibid.,* Dec. 27, 1921.
61. Com. on Gen. Info., Jan. 17, 18, 1922.
62. *Ibid.,* Dec. 30, 1921.
63. *Ibid.,* March 2, 8, 1922.
64. *Ibid.,* March 8, 1922.
65. Borah Papers, Box 627 (1), Helen H. Hill to Borah, March 14, 1922.
66. *New York Times,* March 17, 1922. In a letter to William T. Quarterly in January 1922, Wilson stated, ". . . you need not fear that I will place any partisan obstacles in the way of the success of the Washington Conference." On February 13, 1922, he wrote W. P. Merrill that he did not feel able to comment on the Washington Conference treaties, for he had not had an opportunity to study them. March 10, 1922, he told Rowland T. Beers not to believe anything he saw in the papers. "As a matter of fact," continued Wilson, "I am diligently minding my own business. . . ." Wilson Papers, Index series IX.
67. *Cong. Rec.,* 57 Cong., 2 sess., 4188.
68. *New York Times,* March 8, 1922.
69. *Ibid.,* March 10, 1922.
70. *Ibid.,* March 12, 15, 1922. Vote on the Robinson amendment. The final vote was 67 to 27.

71. *Ibid.,* March 16, 1922.
72. *Ibid.,* March 23, 24, 1922. The last prediction was 65 to 28, showing an estimated loss of two votes for the Treaty in the last week of debate.
73. *Ibid.,* March 25, 1922.
74. *Cong. Rec.,* 67 Cong., 2 sess., 4719.
75. *Ibid.,* 4791.
76. *Ibid.,* 4496.
77. Lodge Papers, Hughes to Lodge, April 1, 1922.
78. *Ibid.,* William Price to Lodge, March 25, 1922.
79. *Ibid.,* Lodge to W. W. Vaughn, Esq., March, 1922.
80. *Ibid.,* Lodge to Dr. James L. Barton, March 10, 1922.
81. Johnson, *Harvey,* 333-334.
82. Cranston, *The Killing of the Peace,* 280; Howland, *Survey of American Foreign Relations,* 221; Schriftgiesser, *This Was Normalcy,* 138.
83. *Cong. Rec.,* 67 Cong., 2 sess., 3899.
84. *For. Rel.,* 1922, I, 299.
85. *Cong. Rec.,* 67 Cong., 2 sess., 4541.
86. *Ibid.,* 4543.

CHAPTER XVII

1. *Cong. Rec.,* 67 Cong., 2 sess., 4321.
2. *Ibid.,* 4238.
3. *Ibid.,* 3552.
4. *Ibid.,* 3552; Secretary of State Hughes wrote to Underwood that the failure of the Treaty would be nothing short of a national calamity. Hughes to Underwood, March 11, 1922. *For. Rel.,* 1922, I, 48-50.
5. *Ibid.,* 3552.
6. *Ibid.,* 3847; 4251.
7. *Ibid.,* 3710-3713.
8. *Ibid.,* 3552.
9. *Ibid.,* 3720.
10. *Ibid.,* 4321, 3722.
11. *Ibid.,* 4612.
12. *For. Rel.,* 1922, I, 166.
13. *Cong. Rec.,* 67 Cong., 2 sess., 3837.
14. *Ibid.,* 4087. Capper also quoted Harding: " 'I once believed . . . in armed preparedness. I advocate it. But I have come now to believe there is better preparedness in a public mind and a world opinion made ready to grant justice precisely as it exacts it. And justice is better served in a conference of peace than in a conflict at arms.' "
15. *Ibid.,* 3775.
16. *Ibid.,* 3711.
17. *Ibid.,* 4682-4683.
18. Colonel Theodore Roosevelt, Jr., Assistant Secretary of the Navy, confirmed this opinion, declaring that America had gained in the agreement. The United States had given up the right of fortification which it never would have exercised. In return, the Japanese had to suspend the building of defenses which they would have completed. Sprout, *Toward a New Order of Sea Power,* 274.
19. This feeling was reflected in the results of a poll taken by the *Literary Digest* on the policy which the United States should adopt toward France. Editors of 228 magazines, from a total of 273, favored military and financial aid to France in case of unprovoked outside aggression. Yet, only 66 editors favored guaranteeing such aid to France by alliance. Apparently, a word meant more to these American editors than a policy. *Literary Digest* (Dec. 31, 1921), 5-9.
20. "There is no provision for the use of force to carry out any of the terms of the agreement, and no military or naval sanctions lurks anywhere in the background or under cover of these plain and direct clauses." *For. Rel.,* 1922, I, 30-31; *Conference on the Limitation of Armament,* 162.
21. In addition to quoting Senator Lodge's statement, given above, the delegation declared: "When controversies arise of the character stated in the Article, the Powers merely agree to confer together concerning them. No Power binds itself to anything further; and any consents or agreements must be reached in accordance with its constitutional methods." *For. Rel.,* 1922, I, 337.
22. Harding stated: "I am not unmindful, nor was the conference, of the sentiment in the Chamber against Old World entanglements. Those who made the treaties have left no doubt

about their true import." Later in his address, he declared: "I can bring you every assurance that nothing in any of these treaties commits the United States, or any other power, to any kind of an alliance, entanglement, or involvement. It does not require us or any power to surrender a worthwhile tradition."

"The four-power treaty contains no war commitment. . . . There is no commitment to armed force, no alliance, no written or moral obligation to join in defence, no expressed or implied commitment to arrive at any agreement except in accordance with our constitutional methods." In concluding, he reminded his listeners again: "The Senate's concern for freedom from entanglements, for preserved traditions, for maintained independence, was never once forgotten by the American Delegates." *Ibid.*, 301-302, 305.

23. The Four Power Treaty was understood to contain "no commitment to armed force, no alliance, no obligation to join in any defense." *Cong. Rec.*, 67 Cong., 2 sess., 4496.

24. *For. Rel.*, 1922, I, 49.

25. *Ibid.*, 51.

26. *Cong. Rec.*, 3551.

27. *Ibid.*, 3714.

28. *Ibid.*, 4005-4006.

29. *Ibid.*, 4009; 4013.

30. *Ibid.*, 3910.

31. *Ibid.*, 4004.

32. *Ibid.*, 4006.

33. *For. Rel.*, 1922, II, 25.

34. *Cong. Rec.*, 67 Cong., 2 sess., 3551-3552.

35. *Ibid.*, 4007; 4321.

36. *Ibid.*, 4321.

37. *Ibid.*, 3616.

38. *Ibid.*, 3711; 3412; 3719; 3412.

39. *Ibid.*, 1678.

40. "Not Allies But Friends," *Outlook* (April 5, 1922), 536-537.

41. *Ibid.;* "A Conference of Friends, Not a Mass Meeting," *Independent* (March 25, 1922), 302; "Diplomacy of Trust," *Outlook* (Dec. 21, 1921), 640.

42. *Cong. Rec.*, 67 Cong., 2 sess., 4348.

43. *Ibid.*, 4341.

44. *Ibid.*, 4346.

45. *Ibid.*, 4068.

46. *Ibid.*

47. *Ibid.*, 3613.

48. *Ibid.*, 4233.

49. *Ibid.*, 4013-4016.

50. *Ibid.*, 4325.

51. *Ibid.*, 236.

52. *Ibid.*, 3235.

53. *Ibid.*, 3618-3619, quoting article by W. H. Gardner in *World's Work*. Gardner was associated with the Navy League which advocated naval supremacy.

54. *Ibid.*, 3614.

55. *Ibid.*, 3945; 3554-3555.

56. *Ibid.*, 3611.

57. *Ibid.*, 3955.

58. *Ibid.*, 4324.

59. *Ibid.*, 4704.

60. *Ibid.*, 3946-3947.

61. *Ibid.*, 4241.

62. *Ibid.*, 3787, 3789.

63. *Ibid.*, 4009.

64. *Ibid.*, 4010.

65. *Ibid.*, 3787-3788.

66. The *New York World* said that this was the only real defect in the Treaty disclosed by the debate in the Senate. *Literary Digest* (April 8, 1922), 12.

67. Borah Papers, Box 627, Davis to Borah, Feb. 26, 1922.

68. *Cong. Rec.*, 67 Cong., 2 sess., 3606.

69. *Ibid.*, 3849, 3893.

70. *Ibid.*, 4325.

71. *Ibid.*, 440.

72. *Ibid.*, 3722.

73. *Ibid.*, 3778, 3779.

74. *Ibid.*, 3613.

75. *Ibid.*, 4318.

76. *Ibid.*, 4343.

77. *Ibid.*, 3782.

78. *Ibid.*, 3719, 3717.

79. *Ibid.*, 3614.

80. *Ibid.*, 3615.

81. *Ibid.*, 231-232.

82. *Ibid.*, 3851.

83. *Ibid.*

84. *Ibid.*, 3558-3563.

85. *Ibid.*, 3554-3555.

86. *For. Rel.*, 1917, I, 24-29.

CHAPTER XVIII

1. *New York Times,* March 25, 1922.
2. *Literary Digest* (April 8, 1922), 12.
3. *Ibid.,* 12; see also *Outlook* (March 22, 1922), 453-454.
4. *Cong. Rec.,* 67 Cong., 2 sess., 2391-2392.
5. *Ibid.,* 435.
6. *Ibid.,* 4252.
7. *Ibid.,* 4159.
8. *Ibid.,* 4238.
9. *Ibid.,* 4252.
10. *Ibid.,* 4253-4254.
11. *Ibid.,* 4308.
12. *Ibid.,* 4011.

SELECTED BIBLIOGRAPHY

I. MANUSCRIPT SOURCES: OFFICIAL AND PRIVATE PAPERS

A. Official

Department of State Archives, 1920-1922.

 The decimal files contain the official records of the State Department in the period of the Washington Conference. All of this material is now open for research and presumably the complete record is available. There is very little material relating to the movement for the limitation of armament. The Anglo-Japanese Alliance, on the other hand, was the subject of a vast number of dispatches. A representative selection of this material is presented in the official publication of the State Department, *Foreign Relations*. No effort was made to include all of the material, and in several important instances significant material has been deleted in the printed version.

Papers of the American Delegation to the Washington Conference: Collection in the National Archives.

 These files contain the material supplied by the government to each of its delegates for their information on the various subjects to be taken up by the conference. Also included are a few petitions which were addressed to individual members of the delegation. There is no indication as to whether these files are complete. They are practically devoid of letters, notes, or dispatches of a personal or confidential nature, and most of what they contain can be located elsewhere.

Petitions to the United States Senate: National Archives.

 These contain petitions sent to the Senate before, during, and after the Washington Conference. They give an excellent idea of the interest and aims of the American people in the Washington Conference. They are mute testimony to the diligence with which citizens worked to impress their desires upon the Senate.

B. Private

Anderson, Chandler P.: Collection in Division of Manuscripts, Library of Congress.

 This collection contains a number of letters from Anderson, a member of the legal staff of the American delegation, to prominent Republicans such as Root, Lodge, and Hughes. The most important item for this work was the diary which tells in detail of the preliminary work on the Four-Power Treaty and confirms the secret nature of the negotiations leading to the drafting of the pact.

238

SELECTED BIBLIOGRAPHY

Beveridge, Albert J.: Collection in Division of Manuscripts, Library of Congress.

There are many letters between Beveridge and his friends in the Senate, Lodge, Knox, Borah, Brandegee, and others during the debate on the League of Nations and also concerning the Republican Convention of 1920. However, there is little correspondence relative to the Washington Conference itself.

Borah, William E.: Collection in Division of Manuscripts, Library of Congress.

This collection is composed of letters to Borah by average citizens throughout the United States and his answers to these letters. They indicate Borah's attitude and influence during the period of the conference. There are very few letters from him to prominent officials in the government and very little information on his behind-the-scenes work for the conference or against the Four-Power Treaty.

Daniels, Josephus: Collection in Division of Manuscripts, Library of Congress.

The correspondence covers a variety of subjects dealing with the navy department from 1913 to 1921. Most of the material is political and routine and little of it deals with naval policy, disarmament, or the Washington Conference. There are a number of Wilson and Franklin D. Roosevelt letters in this collection.

Hughes, Charles Evans: Collection in Division of Manuscripts, Library of Congress.

A great deal of the material dealing with the Washington Conference is in the form of official transcripts of conversations and negotiations. These have been extensively published in the *Foreign Relations*. The chief items of interest are full memos of important events written for Hughes by his secretary, Henry C. Beerits; the complete memos of the meetings with the ambassadors of England, France, China, and Japan; and the personal correspondence. In the latter category it is regrettable, at least from the historian's view, that there are no letters for the period of the conference to such men as Harding, Lodge, and Root and only a few, relative to the death of his mother, to Underwood.

Knox, Philander C.: Collection in Division of Manuscripts, Library of Congress.

There are a few letters relating to the separate peace with Germany and to political strategy in relation to the League of Nations debate and the election of 1920.

Lansing, Robert: Collection in Division of Manuscripts, Library of Congress.

The desk diaries, which are very complete, give a good account of Lansing's reaction to the defeat of the Democrats in 1920 and his opinion

239

as to the future course of American foreign policy. Also of value are letters and dispatches relative to Japan's action at the Paris conference.

Lodge, Henry Cabot: Collection of the Massachusetts Historical Society.

The Lodge papers are disappointing in that they contain almost no information on the confidential work of the conference and the backroom negotiations relative to the passage of the Four-Power Treaty. As a delegate to the conference, Chairman of the Senate Committee on Foreign Relations, and a leader of the Republicans in the Senate, Lodge probably knew more about the political aspects of the conference and the treaties than any man of his time. The fact that there is so little left in his papers to record his role appears to be more than mere coincidence.

McNary, Charles P.: Collection in Division of Manuscripts, Library of Congress.

McNary's chief interest was agriculture and the few letters dealing with foreign affairs are of no great value.

Root, Elihu: Collection in Division of Manuscripts, Library of Congress.

This collection, like the Lodge papers, contains almost nothing on the Washington Conference, although Root was a delegate and the father-adviser to the Republican party. There are many letters from Root to Republican senators during the debate on the League of Nations, but, unfortunately, no such material is included in the Senate debates on the Four-Power Treaty.

Walsh, Thomas J.: Collection in Division of Manuscripts, Library of Congress.

There are a number of letters in which Walsh comments on the League of Nations, his resolution for cooperation with the League in bringing about disarmament, and the Washington Conference.

Williams, John Sharp: Collection in Division of Manuscripts, Library of Congress.

Senator Williams' papers include very little information relative to the Washington Conference and the debates on the treaties. Most of the material in this period is made up of letters to friends in which politics is mentioned only in passing.

Wilson, Woodrow: Collection in Division of Manuscripts, Library of Congress.

There is much information relative to the period of presidency. The collection shows Wilson did not exert any important influence on the Democratic senators during the Washington Conference.

II. PRINTED SOURCES: OFFICIAL DOCUMENTS, ETC.

Great Britain: Parliamentary Debates, *House of Commons,* 1920-1922.

The volumes 1920-1921 throw little light on British policy, since Parliament was not informed as to the negotiations on the Anglo-Japanese Alliance or the preliminaries leading to the Washington Conference.

The *Congressional Record:* Proceedings and debates of:
61st Cong., 2nd sess.
63rd Cong., 1st sess.
63rd Cong., 2nd sess.
64th Cong., 1st sess.
66th Cong., 3rd sess.
67th Cong., 1st sess.
67th Cong., 2nd sess.

The earlier volumes are important in tracing the growth of the sentiment for disarmament in Congress. For the Washington Conference, the Sixty-sixth Congress includes the introduction of and early debate on the Borah Resolution. The Sixty-seventh Congress includes the passage of the Borah Resolution, the work of the Senate during the conference, and the debate (which is more than two hundred pages), on the Four-Power Treaty.

71st Cong., 2nd sess., Senate Naval Committee, *Hearings on the London Naval Treaty of 1930.*

This report gives the opinion and criticism of the Washington Conference by the Navy high command.

Senate Documents:
66th Cong., 3rd sess., *Hearings on Disarmament: Its Relation to the Naval Policy and the Naval Building Program of the United States.*

This is the record of the hearings on disarmament held by the House in January and February, 1921. It is important because it represents the opinions on disarmament of the most prominent leaders of public opinion in the United States.

67th Cong., 2nd sess., No. 126. *Conference on the Limitation of Armaments.*

This report gives the formal record of the Washington Conference, including the proceedings of the plenary sessions, the Minutes of the Committee on Limitation of Armament, and the Minutes of the Committee on Pacific and Far Eastern questions. It also contains the President's address in presenting the treaties to the Senate in addition to other information. It is of special importance, since it was made available to the Senate, and indicates what a diligent senator might have learned about the work of the conference.

Department of State:
Conference on the Limitation of Armament.

This is the complete record of the formal proceedings of the Washington Conference with the exception of the minutes of the subcommittees.

241

Conference on the Limitation of Armament, Subcommittees.

This is simply an extension of the work just cited and deals in the same manner with the proceedings of the numerous subcommittees.

Papers Relating to the Foreign Relations of the United States, 1913-1925.

Volume I, 1921, and Volume I, 1922, are valuable to the study of the Washington Conference. The first volume, insofar as anyone has been able to discover, is a complete record of the official steps taken by the government of the United States to invoke the conference. The second volume is a source for the record of the unofficial or informal gatherings in which the real work of the conference was conducted. Other volumes are indispensable for the study of the problems which the conference sought to solve. The record seems to be complete and well edited.

The London Naval Treaty, 1930. Conference Series No. 2, Washington, 1930.

This document contains the testimony by naval experts on the advisability of limiting armament at the Washington Conference.

III. NEWSPAPERS AND PERIODICALS.

Associated Press releases.

These releases are important because they were drawn up independently and reflect opinions at variance with other standard news services, such as the *New York Times,* on a number of occasions.

Committee on General Information.

This Committee surveyed press reaction all over the United States and abroad to every phase of the work of the conference and in regular reports made these findings known to the American Delegation. The Committee also conducted a number of surveys of public opinion on important topics.

Current Information—State Department.

The State Department maintained its own staff to gather and analyze opinion on all questions before the conference. These findings were turned over to all members of the American Delegation.

Periodicals.

The *Literary Digest* was of especial value for its weekly survey of press opinion over the country. *Foreign Affairs* and the *American Journal of International Law* contained a number of interpretations of current foreign policy by national authorities. The *Outlook, Review of Reviews, The Independent, The Spectator, The Living Age, Round Table, Current Opinion,* and *World's Work* contained many articles on the conference giving an accurate reflection of editorial opinion on the conference in the United States and Great Britain.

242

IV. LETTERS, DIARIES, MEMOIRS, ADDRESSES, ETC.

Butler, Nicholas Murray, *Across the Busy Years.* New York: Charles Scribner's Sons, 1940.

Daniels, Josephus, *The Wilson Era Years of War and After, 1917-1923.* Chapel Hill: The University of North Carolina Press, 1946.

Dugdale, Blanche E. C., *Arthur James Balfour.* New York: G. P. Putnam's Sons, 1937.

Ishii, Kikujiro, *Diplomatic Commentaries* (Edited and translated by W. R. Langdon). Baltimore: The Johns Hopkins Press, 1936.

Lansing, Robert, *War Memoirs.* New York: The Bobbs-Merrill Co., 1935.

Lodge, Henry Cabot, *The Senate and the League of Nations.* New York: Charles Scribner's Sons, 1925.

Powell, John B., *My Twenty-Five Years in China.* New York: The Macmillan Company, 1945.

Riddell, G. A., *Lord Riddell's Intimate Diary of the Peace Conference and After, 1918-1923.* New York: Reynal and Hitchcock, 1934.

Seymour, Charles, *The Intimate Papers of Colonel House.* Chicago: Houghton Mifflin Co., 1928, IV.

Underwood, Oscar W., *Drifting Sands of Party Politics.* New York: The Century Company, 1928.

White, William Allen, *The Autobiography of William Allen White.* New York: The Macmillan Company, 1946.

V. SPECIAL STUDIES

a. The Washington Conference:

Bailey, Thomas A., *A Diplomatic History of the American People.* New York: F. S. Crofts Co., 1948.

Brebner, J. B., "Canada, the Anglo-Japanese Alliance and the Washington Conference," *Political Science Quarterly,* 50 (March, 1935), 45-48.

Buell, Raymond Leslie, *The Washington Conference.* New York: D. Appleton and Company, 1922.

Chang, Chung-Fu, *The Anglo-Japanese Alliance.* Baltimore: The Johns Hopkins Press, 1931.

Clyde, Paul H., *The Far East: A History of the Impact of the West on Eastern Asia.* New York: Prentice-Hall, Inc., 1948.

Dennis, Alfred L. P., *The Anglo-Japanese Alliance.* Berkeley: University of California Press, 1923.

Hoag, C. Leonard, *Preface to Preparedness: The Washington Disarmament Conference and Public Opinion.* Washington: American Council on Public Affairs, 1941.

Hosono, Gunji, *International Disarmament.* Société D'Imprimere, D'Ambilly-Annemasse, 1926.

Ichihashi, Yamato, *The Washington Conference and After.* Stanford: Stanford University Press, 1928.

Latané, John Holladay, *From Isolation to Leadership.* New York: Doubleday, Page and Company, 1922.

Latimer, Hugh, *Naval Disarmament: A Brief Record From the Washington Conference to Date.* London: Royal Institute of International Affairs, 1930.

Lippmann, Walter, *United States Foreign Policy: Shield of the Republic.* Boston: Little, Brown and Company, 1943.

"Present Problems of the Commonwealth of British Nations," *International Conciliation,* No. 167 (Oct., 1921), 339-419.

Simonds, Frank H., *American Foreign Policy in the Post-War Years.* Baltimore: The Johns Hopkins Press, 1935.

Spinks, Charles Nelson, *The Anglo-Japanese Alliance.* Stanford: Unpublished Doctoral Dissertation, 1936.

Sprout, Harold and Margaret, *Toward a New Order of Sea Power.* Princeton: Princeton University Press, 1940.

Sullivan, Mark, *The Great Adventure at Washington.* New York: Doubleday, Page and Company, 1922.

Wright, Quincy, editor, *Interpretations of American Foreign Policy.* Chicago: University of Chicago Press, 1930.

Young, Eugene J., *Powerful America.* New York: Frederick A. Stokes Company, 1936.

b. Studies on the Far East:

Bau, Mingchien Joshua, *The Open Door Doctrine.* New York: The Macmillan Company, 1923.

⸺, *The Foreign Relations of China: A History and a Survey.* New York: Fleming H. Revell Company, 1921.

Blakeslee, George H., *The Recent Foreign Policy of the United States.* New York: The Abingdon Press, 1925.

Clyde, Paul Hibbert, *A History of the Modern and Contemporary Far East.* New York: Prentice-Hall, Inc., 1937.

⸺, *International Rivalries in Manchuria 1689-1922.* Columbus: The Ohio State University Press. 1926.

Dulles, Foster Rhea, *Americans in the Pacific: A Century of Expansion.* Boston: Houghton Mifflin Company, 1932.

⸺, *China and America.* Princeton: Princeton University Press, 1946.

⸺, *Forty Years of American-Japanese Relations.* New York: D. Appleton-Century, 1937.

Griswold, Whitney A., *The Far Eastern Policy of the United States.* New York: Harcourt, Brace and Company, 1938.

Hornbeck, Stanley K., *The United States and the Far East.* Boston: World Peace Foundation, 1942.

Hsia, Ching-Lin, *Studies in Chinese Diplomatic History.* Shanghai: The Commercial Press, Limited, 1925.

La Fargue, Thomas Edward, *China and the World War.* Hoover War Library Publications, No. 12. Stanford University Press, 1937.

Morse, H. B. and H. F. MacNair, *Far Eastern International Relations.* New York: Houghton Mifflin Co., 1931.

Pollard, Robert T., *China's Foreign Relations, 1917-1931.* New York: The Macmillan Company, 1933.

Soyeshima, Michimasa and P. W. Kuo, *Oriental Interpretations of the Far Eastern Problem.* Chicago: The University of Chicago Press, 1925.

Treat, Payson J., *The Far East.* New York: Harper and Brothers, 1928.

Willoughby, Westel W., *Japan's Case Examined.* Baltimore: The Johns Hopkins Press, 1940.

Wood, Ge-zay, *The Shantung Question. A Study in Diplomacy and World Politics.* New York: Fleming H. Revell Company, 1922.

Woodhead, H. G. W., Julean Arnold, and Henry Ketridge Norton, *Occidental Interpretations of the Far Eastern Problem.* Chicago: University of Chicago Press, 1926.

Wong, Ching-Wai, *La Chine et les Nations* (C. Heywood, translator). Paris: Libraire Gallimard, 1928.

c. Studies on the United States:

Allen, Frederick Lewis, *Only Yesterday.* New York: Blue Ribbon Books, Inc., 1931.

Bailey, Thomas A., *Woodrow Wilson and the Lost Peace.* New York: The Macmillan Company, 1944.

--------------, *Woodrow Wilson and the Great Betrayal.* New York: The Macmillan Company, 1945.

Cranston, Alan, *The Killing of the Peace.* New York: The Viking Press, 1945.

Fleming, Denna Frank, *The United States and the League of Nations.* New York: G. P. Putnam's Sons, 1932.

--------------, *The United States and World Organization, 1920-1923.* New York: Columbia University Press, 1938.

Schriftgiesser, Karl, *This Was Normalcy.* Boston: Little, Brown and Company, 1948.

Sullivan, Mark, *Our Times, 1900-1925.* New York: Charles Scribner's Sons, 1935, VI.

d. The Secretary of State:

Hughes, Charles E., *The Pathway of Peace: Representative Addresses Delivered During His Term as Secretary of State.* New York: Harper and Brothers, 1925.

Hulen, Bertram D., *Inside the Department of State.* New York: Whittlesey House, 1939.

Hyde, Charles Cheney, *Charles Evans Hughes. (The American Secretaries of State and Their Diplomacy,* X, S. F. Bemis, editor). New York: Alfred A. Knopf, 1929.

Pusey, Marlo, *Charles Evans Hughes.* New York: The Macmillan Company, 1951, II.

245

Ransom, William Lynn, *Charles E. Hughes, The Statesman as Shown in the Opinions of the Jurist.* New York: E. P. Dutton and Company, 1916.

Stone, Irving, *They Also Ran.* New York: Doubleday, Doran and Company, Inc., 1943.

Umbreit, Kenneth Bernard, *Our Eleven Chief Justices.* New York: Harper and Brothers, 1938.

e. *The Presidents:*

Adams, Samuel Hopkins, *Incredible Era: The Life and Times of Warren Gamaliel Harding.* Boston: Houghton Mifflin Company, 1939.

Chapple, Joe Mitchell, *The Life and Times of Warren G. Harding: Our After-War President.* Boston: Chapple Publishing Company, Limited, 1924.

Coolidge, Calvin, *Autobiography.* New York: Cosmopolitan Book Corporation, 1929.

Fuess, Claude M., *Calvin Coolidge: The Man from Vermont.* Boston: Little, Brown, and Company, 1940.

Johnson, Willis Fletcher, *The Life of Warren G. Harding.* Published by the author, 1923.

f. *The Senate:*

Binkley, Wilfred E., *The President and Congress.* New York: Alfred A. Knopf, 1947.

Bryce, James, *The American Commonwealth.* New York: The Macmillan Company, 1899.

Colegrove, Kenneth, *The American Senate and World Peace.* New York: The Vanguard Press, 1944.

Dangerfield, Royden J., *In Defense of the Senate: A Study of Treaty Making.* Norman: University of Oklahoma Press, 1933.

——————, "The Senatorial Diplomats," *American Mercury,* XXXVII (March, 1936), 359-362.

Dennison, Eleanor E., *The Senate Foreign Relations Committee.* Stanford: Stanford University Press, 1942.

Fleming, Denna Frank, *The Treaty Veto of the American Senate.* New York: G. P. Putnam's Sons, 1930.

——————, *The United States and World Organization.* Garden City, N. Y.: Doubleday, Doran and Company, 1945.

Haynes, G. H., *The Senate of the United States.* Boston: Houghton Mifflin Company, 1938.

Holt, W. Stull, *Treaties Defeated by the Senate.* Baltimore: The Johns Hopkins Press, 1933.

Larned, H. B., "The Attitude of the United States Towards the Versailles Treaty: 1918-1920," H. V. V. Temperley, editor, *A History of the Peace Conference of Paris* (5 vols. London, 1924), VI, ch. V.

Laski, Harold J., *The American Presidency: An Interpretation.* New York and London: Harper & Brothers, 1940.

246

Mathews, J. M., *American Foreign Relations*. New York: The Century Company, 1928.

Rogers, Lindsay, *The American Senate*. New York: Alfred A. Knopf, 1926.

Watson, J. E., *As I Knew Them: Memoirs of James E. Watson*. Indianapolis: Bobbs-Merrill Co., 1936.

Wright, Quincy, *The Control of American Foreign Relations*. New York: The Macmillan Company, 1922.

g. Public Opinion:

Bruner, J. S., *Mandate from the People*. New York: Duell, Sloan and Pearce, 1944.

Dean, Vera Micheles, "U. S. Foreign Policy and the Voter," *Foreign Policy Reports*, XIX, 15 (Oct. 15, 1943).

Lippmann, Walter, *Public Opinion*. New York: The Macmillan Company, 1922.

Smith, Charles William, *Public Opinion in a Democracy*. New York: Prentice-Hall, Inc., 1939.

Tupper, Eleanor and George McReynolds, *Japan in American Public Opinion*. New York: The Macmillan Company, 1937.

h. Leaders:

Jessup, Philip C., *Elihu Root*. New York: Dodd, Mead and Company, 1938, II.

Johnson, Claudius O., *Borah of Idaho*. New York: Longmans, Green and Company, 1936.

Johnson, Willis Fletcher, *George Harvey: A Passionate Patriot*. Boston: Houghton Mifflin Co., 1929.

Schriftgiesser, Karl, *The Gentleman From Massachusetts*. Boston: Little, Brown and Company, 1944.

i. Miscellaneous:

Bartlett, Ruhl J., editor. *The Record of American Diplomacy*. New York: Alfred A. Knopf, 1948.

Bemis, Samuel Flagg, *Jay's Treaty: A Study in Commerce and Diplomacy*. New York: The Macmillan Company, 1923.

Conway, M. D., editor, *The Writings of Thomas Paine*. New York: G. P. Putnam's Sons, 1894-1896, 4 vols.

Curti, Merle, *Peace or War: The American Struggle, 1636-1936*. New York: W. W. Norton Company, 1936.

Richardson, James D., editor. *A Compilation of the Messages and Papers of the Presidents*. Washington: Government Printing Office, XI.

Yardley, Herbert O., *The American Black Chamber*. Indianapolis: The Bobbs-Merrill Company, 1931.

INDEX

armament, 95; Democrats attack explanation, 95-96; comments on Geddes's conference with U. S. officials, 103; issues invitation to conference in Washington, 112-113; policy on calling a conference, 114; and invitations to the Conference, 116; and selection of delegates to the Conference, 119; works to obtain open diplomacy, 124-127; on peace with Germany, 128; proclaims November 11 a national holiday, 134; dedicates tomb of unknown soldier, 135; speech opening Conference, 136; and Hughes' speech, 138; and "association of nations," 140, 141-142, 143*ff*; and Four-Power Treaty, 151-152; interpretation of Treaty, 163-165, 182; on accomplishments of the Conference, 176-177; assures Senate that Conference treaties conform to American traditions, 180; approves open diplomacy, 181; letter to Senate refusing additional information on Treaty, 183; and Brandegee Amendment, 188-189; does not work for passage of Treaty, 191; implies Senate committed to approve treaties of Conference, 193-194; asserts Treaty not an alliance, 200, 206, 235-236 (22n); quoted by Reed, 209; selection of Secretary of State, 225 (18n); described as leader of his party, 226 (19n); role in calling Conference, 226 (20n), 228 (64n); on possibility of not putting Conference agreements in treaty form, 231 (15n); views on peace by moral force, 235 (14n)

Harding administration, 1, 4, 6, 40, 59, 115; opposition to Borah Resolution, 92-93; and disarmament, 99-105; and Anglo-Japanese Alliance, 105; influence on calling of Conference, 114; and "association of nations," 140; and Four-Power Treaty, 162

Harris, William J., 132

Harrison, Pat, 90-91

Harrison Resolution, 124; debated, 124-127; passed, 127; text of, 229 (33n)

Harvey, George, 69, 98, 104; states Alliance no concern of U. S., 111; urges U. S. to gain initiative in calling a conference, 112; and preliminary conference, 120; comments on Anglo-American friendship, 189; Lodge writes relative to Four-Power Treaty, 193;

and preliminary conference, 228 (17n)

Hayashi, Gonsuké, 100, 227 (30n); favors renewal of alliance, 105; quoted by Reed, 206

Hayden, James L., 17

Hearst press, 52; opposes Four-Power Treaty, 165, 178

Heflin, Thomas, 14

Hensley, Walter, 13, 15, 17, 19

Hensley Resolution, 13; debate on, 14-15; passed by House, 15; of 1916, 17-18, 19

Hill, David J., mentioned for Secretary of State under Harding, 225 (18n)

Hilles, Charles D., advises on selection of the Conference delegation, 117-118; suggests "association of nations" for conference agenda, 141

Hitchcock, Gilbert M., for Four-Power Treaty, 161; seeks reservation to Treaty, 165; calls for additional information on Treaty, 182-183; charges of secret diplomacy ignored, 187

Hobson, Richmond P., 13, 14; presents resolution on armament and arbitration, 10, 11

House, E. M., 25, 26; mission to Europe in 1914, 15-16

House Naval Affairs Committee, 10, 36, 61, 73; investigation of steel companies, 1894, 88

House of Commons, 111; and disarmament, 8

House of Representatives, 136, 137; and disarmament, 13; hearings on disarmament, 58, 59-60; favors naval supremacy, 62; debates disarmament, 85-86; defeats all resolutions for disarmament, 86; debates Naval Appropriation Bill, 85, 86; passes Naval Appropriation Bill, 86; Bill reintroduced, 92; debates disarmament, 92-96; passes Borah Resolution, 96

Hughes, Charles Evans, 21, 32, 39, 102, 123, 129, 136, 183, 224 (7n); on peace as aim of State Department, 3; discusses international affairs with Harding, 70; selected as Secretary of State, 75; views on League of Nations, 75, 76; and disorder in China, 98-99; and Chinese Eastern Railway, 99; confers with Geddes on Alliance, 108; and U. S. objections to Alliance, 108-109; approves tripartite pact as substitute to Alliance, 109-110; demands considera-

258